ENGAGING IN NARRATIVE INQUIRIES WITH CHILDREN AND YOUTH

Renowned scholar, and founder of the practice of narrative inquiry, D. Jean Clandinin and her coauthors provide researchers with the theoretical underpinnings and processes for conducting narrative inquiry with children and youth. Exploring the unique ability of narratives to elucidate the worldview of research subjects, the authors highlight the unique steps and issues of working with these special populations. This book:

- addresses key ethical issues of anonymity and confidentiality, the relational issues of co-composing field and research texts with subjects, and working within the familial contexts of children and youth;
- includes numerous examples from the authors' studies and others – many from indigenous communities – to show narrative inquiry in action;
- should be invaluable to researchers in education, family relations, child development, and children's health and services.

DEVELOPING QUALITATIVE INQUIRY

ENGAGING IN NARRATIVE INQUIRIES WITH CHILDREN AND YOUTH

D. Jean Clandinin, Vera Caine,
Sean Lessard, and Janice Huber

Routledge
Taylor & Francis Group

NEW YORK AND LONDON

First published 2016
by Routledge
711 Third Avenue, New York, NY 10017

and by Routledge
2 Park Square, Milton Park, Abingdon, Oxon, OX14 4RN

Routledge is an imprint of the Taylor & Francis Group, an informa business

© 2016 Taylor & Francis

The right of D. Jean Clandinin, Vera Caine, Sean Lessard, and Janice Huber to be identified as authors of this work has been asserted by them in accordance with sections 77 and 78 of the Copyright, Designs and Patents Act 1988.

Library of Congress Cataloging-in-Publication Data

Names: Clandinin, D. Jean, author.
Title: Engaging in narrative inquiries with children and youth / D. Jean Clandinin, Vera Caine, Sean Lessard, and Janice Huber.
Description: Walnut Creek, CA : Left Coast Press, Inc., [2016] | Series: Developing qualitative inquiry ; volume 16 | Includes bibliographical references and index.
Identifiers: LCCN 2015041837 | ISBN 9781629582184 (hardback : alk. paper) | ISBN 9781629582191 (pbk. : alk. paper)
Subjects: LCSH: Children—Research—Methodology. | Youth—Research—Methodology. | Narrative inquiry (Research method) | Education—Research—Methodology.
Classification: LCC HQ767.85 .C53 2016 | DDC 305.235072—dc23
LC record available at http://lccn.loc.gov/2015041837

ISBN: 978-1-62958-218-4 (hbk)
ISBN: 978-1-62958-219-1 (pbk)
ISBN: 978-1-315-54537-0 (ebk)

Typeset in Sabon
by Straight Creek Bookmakers

Contents

Acknowledgments   9

Chapter 1.   Narrative Inquiry: A Relational Research Methodology   11

    Understanding Experience as a Narrative
      Phenomenon: Only Part of Narrative Inquiry   13
    Coming to Terms: What Do We Mean by Narrative
      Inquiry?   14
    Narrative Inquiry: Shaped by Particular Ontological
      and Epistemological Commitments   17

Chapter 2.   Elements of Design in Narrative Inquiry   21

    1. Four Key Terms in Narrative Inquiry: Shaping
      Design Considerations   22
    2. The Three-Dimensional Space of Narrative
      Inquiry: Shaping Design Considerations   23
    3. Imagining a Narrative Inquiry from Field to
      Field Texts to Research Texts: Shaping Design
      Considerations   24
    4. Writing Ourselves into Narrative Inquiries:
      Shaping Design Considerations   25
    5. Framing Research Puzzles: Shaping Design
      Considerations   26
    6. Positioning an Inquiry Within the Scholarly
      Literature: Shaping Design Considerations   28
    7. Justifying Our Work: Shaping Design
      Considerations   29
    8. Finding Participants and Co-composing an Inquiry
      Field: Shaping Design Considerations   30
    9. Moving from Field to Field Texts: Shaping Design
      Considerations   31
    10. Response Communities: Shaping Design
      Considerations   31
    11. Moving from Field Texts to Interim and
      Final Research Texts: Shaping Design
      Considerations   32
    12. Relational Ethics: Shaping Design
      Considerations   33

Chapter 3.   Narrative Beginnings in Work with Children and Youth   35

Necessarily Troubling: Layers of Complexity   38
What We Know About the Why of Autobiographical
   Narrative Inquiry   55

Chapter 4.   Living Within the Layered Landscapes of Narrative
             Inquiry   59

Muskwacicy   61
Moving Slowly into Unfamiliar Layered
   Landscapes   63
Slowing Down, Attending to Landscapes and Who
   We Are and Are Becoming as Researchers   65
Attending to Multiple Layered Landscapes as We
   Engage in Narrative Inquiry   69

Chapter 5.   Finding Participants Within and Outside Institutional
             Contexts   71

A Starting Point: Research Ethics Boards   71
Finding Participants: A Process of Ongoing
   Negotiations   73
Staying Wakeful: Tensions of the Shaping Influences
   on Research Designs   82
Negotiating Entry with Children and Youth in
   Narrative Inquiries   83

Chapter 6.   Negotiating Entry with Children and Youth   85

Negotiating Entry with Participants   86
Negotiating Entry: Revisiting Vera's Negotiation of
   Entry at Ravine Elementary School   87
Negotiating Entry: Revisiting Entering Lives in the
   Midst Alongside Youth and Families of Aboriginal
   Heritage   91
Negotiating Entry: Revisiting the Early
   School Leavers Study Attentive to the Ways
   That Researchers Are Only Part of the
   Negotiations   93
Negotiation of Entry as an Ongoing Process   95

Chapter 7.   Ongoing Wakefulness to Multiple Stories to Live By:
             Ripples into Lives   97

Ongoing Wakefulness Through Narrative Inquiry at
   Ravine School   98
Inquiring into the Need for Ongoing
   Wakefulness   99
Ripples into Lives: Being Attentive to Our
   Participation Alongside Children and Youth   104

Ongoing Wakefulness: Learning to "World"-Travel
as Part of Narrative Inquiry 106

Chapter 8.   Coming Alongside Children and Youth in the Field
Within Familial Contexts   109

Understanding Living Alongside 109
Tammy and Vera: Living Alongside in the Field
Within Nested Familial Contexts 110
Attending to Places Within the Nested Familial
Contexts of Children and Youth's Lives 113
Attending to the Intergenerational Within Nested
Familial Contexts of Children and Youth's
Lives 114
Attending to Mutual Visibility Within Nested Familial
Contexts of Children and Youth's Lives 116
Attending to Bumping Places as We Try to Come
Alongside Within the Nested Familial Contexts of
Children and Youth 117
Gathering Threads on Coming Alongside Children
and Youth in Familial Contexts 118

Chapter 9.   Co-composing Field Texts with Children and Youth   119

Co-composing Field Texts Alongside Aboriginal
Youth and Families 120
Co-composing the Art Club: Connections Between
Place and Co-composing Field Texts 121
Co-composing Different Kinds of Field Texts Within
the Narrative Inquiry with the Youth 124
Co-composing Field Texts Alongside the Youth Who
Left School Early 129
Field Notes and Other Kinds of Field Texts 131
Ongoing Tensions in Co-composing Field Texts 132

Chapter 10.   Moving to Interim Research Texts with Children and
Youth   133

Calling Forth Past Experiences 133
Returning to Research Puzzles and
Justifications 136
Returning to Understandings of Negotiations 137
Co-composing and Negotiating Narrative Accounts
with Matson and Tiny Tim 137
Looking Across Our Experiences 141

Chapter 11.   Meeting Donovan: A Narrative Account   143

Grade 7-8 Beaver Hills House School 143
Learning to Listen to What I Could Not Hear 144

Awakening Time   148
Donovan and Lane: Co-Composing: Finding Their
    Songs Within   150
Learning to Listen to Each Other, to Hear Our
    Stories   152
Kookum Muriel: "She Was an Elder to
    Everyone"   160
Remembering School   162
In Response to Stories   166
Thinking with the Narrative Account   167

Chapter 12. Representations in Final Research Texts: Moral and
    Ethical Considerations   169

Contemplating Vulnerability   3171
Living Alongside: Considerations for What Does and
    Can Become Visible   172
Silences in the Living and in the Research Texts   173
From Interim Research Texts to Final Research
    Texts   175
Returning Again to Research Puzzles   177
Significance of Narrative Inquiries: So What?   178
Further Issues in Representation   179
Returning to the Three-Dimensional Narrative
    Inquiry Space   182

Chapter 13. Issues of Quality: Touchstones of Narrative Inquiry
    with Children and Youth   185
Touchstones of Narrative Inquiry   187

Chapter 14. The Relational Ethics of Narrative Inquiry   199
Relational Ethical Commitments at the Heart of
    Narrative Inquiries   199
Lingering in Relational Responsibilities   201
Grounding Our Relational Work Within Ethical
    Theories   203
Practicing Wakefulness   207
Lingering in the Relational Tensions   209
Telling Different Stories: Considering the Impacts of
    Narrative Inquiries   210

References   215
Appendix 1. Examples of Consent and Assent Forms   219
Index   231
About the Authors   237

Acknowledgments

A book like this is not possible without relationships. We are grateful to the children, youth, families, and teachers who worked alongside us in their and our life making, sometimes over months and years. We are grateful for the support of principals and school district personnel that enabled our narrative inquiries in classrooms and schools. Along the way they offered us guidance as we navigated institutional landscapes. We are also grateful for the guidance of Elders and community agencies who came alongside us and child and youth participants; always, they gently shaped spaces for understanding.

We used pseudonyms for all participants, schools, other institutions, and geographic places. Where pseudonyms are not used, we discuss these negotiations in the book.

With gratitude we also acknowledge the funding agencies who supported the narrative inquiries we draw on in the book, including the Social Sciences and Humanities Research Council of Canada; the Alberta Centre for Child, Family, and Community Research; Alberta Education; Homeward Trust; the Alberta Homelessness Consortium; the Urban Aboriginal Network; and the Canadian Institute of Health Research. These funding agencies provided consistent support over many years for multiple studies. Without their financial support it would not have been possible to engage in the studies we draw from in this book.

As we stayed at the hard work of narrative inquiry, we are grateful for the response community at the Centre for Research for Teacher Education and Development at the University of Alberta, where our ideas have been nurtured. The Centre provides an important academic home place for us, and it is through our participation in the Centre that we have been able to develop these ideas.

Chapter 11 is taken from Sean's dissertation, *Red Worn Runners: A Narrative Inquiry into the Stories of Aboriginal Youth and Families in Urban Settings*.

To our families we also express our love and gratitude. Living alongside Felix, Ellee, Kamaya, Sedona, Kael, Peter, and Katie as parents and as a grandparent has continually kept us awake to who we are and are becoming as narrative inquirers. We have felt the support of our families over the long days of writing this book. To them we are grateful.

DJC
VC
SL
JH

CHAPTER 1

Narrative Inquiry: A Relational Research Methodology

It has been six months since I last saw Tara. Summer, autumn start-up, and a big move on top of my already too busy autumn schedule kept me from seeing her. We had sent messages back and forth on Facebook, and I knew she was settling into her secondary school. Finally in December I sent a note via Facebook, apologized for the long time lag, and asked whether I could pick her up after school, have a snack, and drive her home. Yes, she happily agreed, and we chose the date. The day before our meeting she sent another note and asked whether I could come to her secondary school to help get ready for the Christmas feast that the Aboriginal student group was organizing for the day of our meeting. I agreed, happily, glad Tara felt she could ask, that she could let me know her plans and how I might fit into them.

It was a bitterly cold day, bone chilling, with snow falling and wind blowing, one of those days when people should stay home, one of those days when exposed skin freezes in minutes. I drove slowly to her new high school, carefully maneuvering around cars sliding through traffic lights and stop signs. I was late, but there she was, standing on the front sidewalk in her school clothes, no parka. As I hurried toward her, she ran toward me. Arms wrapped around each other as we smiled, like friends who had not seen each other for a while. (Clandinin Interim research text, December 18, 2013)

We, as coauthors of this book, begin with this story fragment as a way to think about what it means to engage in narrative inquiry and what it means to understand experience as a storied phenomenon that can be best studied through attending closely to the stories we live and tell. These ideas of experience as stories lived and told are not new ones. Human beings have lived stories and told stories about that living since the earliest historical records. "The truth about stories is that that's all we are," writes King (2003, p. 153). He is not the first to write this, as writers have made similar statements over many years and from within different disciplines, different cultures, different perspectives. We live stories and we tell stories of our living. Stories are ways of telling about the experiences people have. Experience is a storied phenomenon (Clandinin & Connelly, 2000).

We draw on the work of psychologists (Bruner, 1986; Kerby, 1991), philosophers (Carr, 1986; Dewey, 1938), anthropologists (Bateson, 1994), religious scholars (Crites, 1971), physicians (Coles, 1989), and others to help us ground our narrative understandings of experience as storied. Clandinin and Connelly (2000) and Clandinin and Rosiek (2007) worked carefully through the writings of these authors to build a case for understanding experience as a narrative phenomenon. In what follows we draw on their work and touch on some of these important ideas.

Bateson (1994) writes, "Our species thinks in metaphors and learns through stories" (p. 11). Clandinin and Connelly (2000) pick up on what Bateson intends in her work and write, "She means much more than do those who simply say that we communicate with one another through stories, that our experiences are recorded and transmitted in story form. To Bateson, it is clear that anthropologists, all of us, lead storied lives on storied landscapes" (p. 8). Clandinin and Connelly draw attention to Bateson's writings to show that she sees experience, her own and that of students, teachers, artists, and others with whom she engages, as having a narrative quality. Coles (1989) also shows that experience is a narrative construction as he draws on William Carlos Williams and writes, "We have to pay the closest attention to what we say. What patients say tells us to think about what hurts them; and what we say tells us what is happening to us—what we are thinking and what may be wrong with us. . . . Their story, yours, mine—it's what we all carry with us on this trip we take, and we owe it to each other to respect our stories and learn from them" (p. 30).

As with Bateson, we learn more from what Coles shows in his accounts of teaching and learning about the nature of human experience than from what he says directly. Clandinin and Connelly (2000), in a brief analysis of his work, show that for Coles, "narrative is life, learning and fiction" (p 14). Crites also draws attention to the storied quality of experience, noting that the "formal quality of experience though time is inherently narrative" (Crites, 1971, p. 291). Okri (1997) shows an understanding of experience as narrative composition as he writes, "In a fractured age, when cynicism is god, here is a possible heresy: we live by stories, we also live in them. One way or another we are living the stories planted in us early or along the way, or we are also living the stories we planted—knowingly or unknowingly—in ourselves. We live stories that either give our lives meaning or negate it with meaninglessness. If we change the stories we live by, quite possibly we change our lives" (p. 46).

Bruner focused the attention of the discipline of psychology on narrative when he posited that there are two modes of thought or cognitive functioning: the traditional logical scientific (paradigmatic) and the narrative. The narrative mode of thought "looks for particular conditions and is centered around the broader and more inclusive question of the meaning of experience" (Bruner, 1986, p. 13).

While we draw on many of these ideas to help us ground our conceptual understandings of experience as narrative composition, it is Dewey's conception of experience that underlies narrative inquiry. We work from Dewey's conception, a conception of "a changing stream that is characterized by continuous interaction of human thought with our personal, social, and material environment" (Clandinin & Rosiek, 2007, p. 39).

Understanding Experience as a Narrative Phenomenon: Only Part of Narrative Inquiry

Although having an understanding of experience as a narrative phenomenon and carefully constructing an argument to show that experience is part of our work as narrative inquirers, it is not enough. As researchers, our interest is both in the phenomenon we are studying and in the ways we inquire into the phenomenon. All researchers, despite different ontological and epistemological assumptions, share a view of research as searching again, a search for deeper understandings of particular phenomenon.

As narrative inquirers, we know that our work is to research, to try to understand, to systematically inquire into the phenomenon of experience—that is, the storied experiences of people. Our work is to inquire into experience, to inquire into the stories that we live and tell, that we listen and respond to, that we watch being lived around us, that we live out in our own experiences. Thus, although we see that we need an argument for understanding experience as the storied phenomenon of living and telling stories, as narrative inquirers, we need also to understand that our task is an inquiry task, a research task. As Clandinin and Rosiek (2007) ended their chapter in the *Handbook of Narrative Inquiry,* they wrote, "What Charon draws our attention to is that stories matter and that, increasingly, we are interested in knowing the stories that all people live and tell. As we, and other narrative inquirers now know, inquiry, narrative inquiry, into those stories that people live and tell, also matters" (p. 71). This idea that we need to attend to both the storied nature of experience as phenomenon under study and to the inquiry into the storied experiences is central to the ideas we lay out in this book. Thinking again about the opening story fragment, we see that it tells something of Jean's experience with a young woman called Tara, but that the story itself is not enough. Although as narrative inquirers, we attend to lived and told stories, which are experience, we also inquire into the lived and told stories. There is much more that we need to come to know about this moment represented in the brief fragment. The story fragment is, in our way of thinking, a moment that allows us to narratively inquire into the experience. We hope to show something of narrative inquiry throughout the first two chapters of this book. As we move through these chapters we tell more stories of Jean's experiences alongside Tara.

> Drifting backward in time, I think about how it has been almost four years now since I met Tara. I first met her when she came to the arts club at the start of her grade seven school year. She came with her sister and participated on a somewhat irregular basis, as she was often busy with other afterschool commitments, and travel to and from her home on the nearby reserve, one of the communities established for peoples of First Nation heritage in treaty negotiations, sometimes made it difficult for her to attend the afterschool club. Those early days of the art club were important ones as we met in that empty classroom in the junior high school that we, as a research team, filled with food and art supplies each Wednesday for two years. In those first days Tara and a few other girls joined four or five researchers, and together we spent ninety minutes getting to know each other and trying out possibilities with each other and with the art supplies. (Clandinin Interim research text, December 18, 2013)

As we hear stories of Jean's experiences with Tara, we see they have known each other for four years, a long time in the life of a girl. They have known each other in different places within school but perhaps not outside school places. As we begin to narratively inquire into these fragments, a sense of the inquiry into experience starts to emerge, to take shape.

Coming to Terms: What Do We Mean by Narrative Inquiry?

We use the following definitions of narrative inquiry that have been developed since 1990 (Connelly & Clandinin, 1990). As researchers have continued to work with narrative inquiry as a methodology, the definition and terms have been refined and further developed.

> People shape their daily lives by stories of who they and others are and as they interpret their past in terms of these stories. Story, in the current idiom, is a portal through which a person enters the world and by which their experience of the world is interpreted and made personally meaningful. Narrative inquiry, the study of experience as story, then, is first and foremost a way of thinking about experience. Narrative inquiry as a methodology entails a view of the phenomenon. To use narrative inquiry methodology is to adopt a particular view of experience as phenomenon under study. (Connelly & Clandinin, 2006, p. 375)

The 2006 definition picks up on ideas from an earlier definition.

> Narrative inquiry is a way of understanding experience. It is a collabora-
> tion between researcher and participants over time, in a place or series
> of places, and in social interaction with milieus. An inquirer enters this
> matrix in the midst and progresses in the same spirit, concluding the
> inquiry still in the midst of living and telling, reliving and retelling, the
> stories of the experiences that made up people's lives, both individual and
> social. (Clandinin & Connelly, 2000, p. 20)

Simply put, narrative inquiry is the study of experience understood narratively. As we attend closely to the words in the definitions, we can begin to unravel the layers of complexity carried in those words. Through engaging in and reading narrative inquiries for many years now, we see that although those words show much, there is much that lives implicitly behind those words. Narrative inquiry, the study of experience understood narratively, means much more than telling stories, more than living stories.

Although in previous sections we outlined some theoretical resources that help us argue for a narrative view of experience, it is Dewey's (1938) work that mostly inspires our understanding of experience. It is Dewey's work that inspires the ways we bring experience alive in our narrative conception of experience. Dewey's theory of experience (1938), often cited as the philosophical underpinning of narrative inquiry (Clandinin & Connelly, 2000), is central to our understandings of narrative inquiry. We see, for example, Deweyan foundations in the metaphorical three-dimensional narrative inquiry space, with its dimensions of temporality, place, and sociality. Dewey's two criteria of experience—interaction and continuity enacted in situations—ground a narrative conception of experience. Clandinin and Connelly linked Dewey's criterion of interaction—that is, that a person is always in interaction with his/her physical world—to the dimension of sociality. The criterion of interaction is understood narratively as the dimension of sociality. Narrative inquirers attend both to personal conditions and, simultaneously, to social conditions. By personal conditions, "we mean the feelings, hopes, desires, aesthetic reactions and moral dispositions" (Connelly & Clandinin, 2006, p. 480) of the inquirer and participants. Social conditions refer outward, to the milieu, the conditions within which people's experiences and events are unfolding.

Dewey's criteria of interaction is closely linked with his concept of situation. As Dewey writes,

> The statement that individuals live in a world means, in the concrete, that
> they live in a series of situations. And when it is said that they live in these

situations . . . . it means, once more that interaction is going on between an individual and objects and other persons. The conceptions of situation and of interaction are inseparable from each other. An experience is always what it is because of a transaction taking place between an individual and what, at the time, constituted his environment. (Dewey, 1938, p. 43)

As Clandinin and Connelly worked with Dewey's theory of experience, they initially did not work with a third dimension, leaving interaction and situation linked as Dewey had linked them. However, as they continued to engage in narrative inquiry, particularly with people attentive to place (Basso, 1996; Marmon Silko, 1996), they began to attend more closely to place, linking it to Dewey's concept of situation. Within the three-dimensional narrative inquiry space, place is "the specific concrete, physical, and topological boundaries of place or sequences of places where the inquiry and events take place" (Connelly & Clandinin, 2006, p. 481). Dewey's notion of situation allows us to draw attention to the place or places where events occur.

Clandinin and Connelly linked Dewey's second criterion of experience, continuity—that is, how a person's experience both takes up and moves forward from past experiences to present and future experiences with their narrative inquiry dimension of temporality. As Connelly and Clandinin (2006) noted, "Events under study are in temporal transition" (p. 479). The dimension of temporality draws attention to ways in which the past, present, and future of people, places, things, and events are interrelated—that is, always in temporal transition, always on the way, in the making.

Working with a narrative conception of experience, Clandinin and Rosiek (2007) pointed out that

> Framed within this view of experience, the focus of narrative inquiry is not only on individuals' experience but also on the social, cultural, and institutional narratives within which individuals' experiences are constituted, shaped, expressed, and enacted. Narrative inquirers study the individual's experience in the world, an experience that is storied both in the living and telling and that can be studied by listening, observing, living alongside one another and writing and interpreting texts. (pp. 42–43)

What we hope is becoming clear is that inquiry is an essential part of narrative inquiry. Although holding a particular narrative view of experience is important as is attending to experience through the living and telling of stories, it is also essential that we learn how to inquire into experiences, into the living and telling of stories, into stories as lived and told.

I think we liked each other, at least I liked her and admired her shifting experimental sense of who she was and who she was becoming. During

her grade eight year I went to watch her at a cheer competition in the local
mall, a school activity. Later that year we walked to the local fast food
place for lunch the day before she was going to be given her Cree name in
a naming ceremony. She sought me out in the art club when she lost her
auntie and then her grandfather. We walked and talked and hugged each
other as she mourned their loss. She and I were close in a way. (Clandinin
Interim research text, December 18, 2013)

What starts to unfold in the telling of these fragments is that Jean
came to know Tara over time, in a place or series of places and in multiple and diverse situations. But to say this is not yet to narratively inquire
into the stories. In order to inquire narratively into their experience we
need to see how particular places shaped their unfolding experiences. We
need also to see time in both of their lives and in the complex intergenerational times that shaped both of them at the same time as we attend
closely to the emotions, moral judgments, and cultural understandings
that shaped their experiences.

NARRATIVE INQUIRY: SHAPED BY PARTICULAR
ONTOLOGICAL AND EPISTEMOLOGICAL COMMITMENTS

One defining feature of narrative inquiry, as we have so far presented it,
is that it is the study of experience as it is lived and told. We laid out our
argument for a Deweyan-inspired view of experience and linked it to the
development of the three-dimensional narrative inquiry space, with its
dimensions of sociality, temporality, and place. What we have not yet
highlighted is the ontological commitments of narrative inquiry. Working
from a Deweyan conception of experience, Clandinin and Rosiek (2007)
showed that Dewey's ontology is transactional. They write,

> The epistemological implications of this view ... implies that the regulative
> ideal for inquiry is not to generate an exclusively faithful representation of
> a reality independent of the knower. The regulative ideal for inquiry is to
> generate a new relation between a human being and her environment—her
> life, community, world—-one that 'makes possible a new way of dealing
> with them, and thus eventually creates a new kind of experienced objects,
> not more real than those which preceded but more significant, and less
> overwhelming and oppressive' (Dewey, 1981, p. 175). In this pragmatic
> view of knowledge, our representations arise from experience and must
> return to that experience for their validation. (p. 39)

Clandinin and Rosiek (2007) highlight several features of this
ontology of experience that make it particularly well suited for framing narrative inquiry. First, the temporality of knowledge generation is
emphasized. As they write, "narratives are the form of representation

that describes human experience as it unfolds through time" (p. 40). Second, a pragmatic ontology of experience emphasizes continuity as not only perceptual but also as ontological: "Experiences do not simply appear to be connected through time; they are continuous" (p. 40). Thirdly, the social/personal dimensions of understandings are emphasized. The stories people live and tell are the result of "a confluence of social influences on a person's inner life, social influences on their environment, and their unique personal history" (p. 41).

Part of the social dimension of this view of experience is the relational aspect of narrative inquiry—that is, that it is not the person under study alone but both researcher's and participant's experiences under study. It is not a study about the other but a study of the experience of researcher and participant as they engage with each other that is under study. Morris's (2002) distinction between thinking *about* stories and thinking *with* stories helps sharpen this ontological commitment. Morris writes, "The concept of thinking with stories is meant to oppose and modify (not replace) the institutionalized Western practice of thinking about stories. Thinking about stories conceives of narrative as an object. Thinking with stories is a process in which we as thinkers do not so much work on narrative as of allowing narrative to work on us" (Morris, 2002, p. 196). And the stories that are under study are the experiences of both researcher and participants. These ontological commitments shape how we engage in narrative inquiry.

In July 2013 it was summer vacation in our northerly community. Tara had just graduated from grade nine. I had wanted to be with her for that celebration and for one last visit while she was in junior high. That didn't happen as schedules collided, hers and mine. I knew how important that time between junior high and high school was in my stories, and I wanted to know how she was experiencing that time. I messaged her on Facebook and asked whether we could meet up, go for an early evening movie, have a snack together. She agreed gladly, and we made plans to meet at a movie theater. I arrived early, nervous about seeing her again, happy she had so willingly agreed to meet.

When I arrived at the mall I called her to confirm I was there. She answered the phone, distraught. It would not work. Her mom could not drive her. I asked whether I could pick her up at her home. Hanging up, she said she would ask. Moments later she called back with directions to her house and her mother's approval.

I drove out of the city on a main road and into the reserve, which was just off the main highway, slowly checking houses until I found one that matched her description of hers. She met me at the front door. She was home with her older sister. Before they left, her parents had told her she needed to mow the lawn before she went to the movies. As I sat on the front step of the semirural house, she got out the mower and tried to start it. I watched her struggle with the motor as I sat on the step and felt the warm summer air

surround me. I was taken back to memories of my childhood on the small
farm where grass mowing was a responsibility shared with my siblings.
Reluctantly, finally, the motor started, and she mowed for a while until
she ran the mower over something laying in the grass. Whatever the object
was, it snarled the rotors and the mower stopped. Impatiently she turned
it over and tried to fix it, without success. "Oh well," she announced and
asked me into the house. There she showed me her latest traditional danc-
ing moves that she had been practicing in a summer art program. (Interim
research text, December 18, 2013)

What starts to become apparent as we inquire into the story fragment above is the relational sense of the unfolding experiences of Jean and Tara. Their lives intersect infrequently, but when they do, it becomes evident that they both embody stories of their experiences together. The experiences they shared together make it possible for a Facebook message to bring them together in a place and time outside of school. Jean shares her experience of the long-ago move from her junior high to high school and is interested in knowing something of Tara's experience of her move from junior high and her imagined stories of high school. There is continuity evident in Jean's own temporal shifting across her life from a junior high school student moving to high school and to her interest in Tara's stories of her experience of that shift in her life. There is another way in which we see the temporal unfolding of their lives, as they have known each other since Tara's entrance into junior high and now as she leaves junior high schooling for secondary schooling. We also see temporal unfolding as Jean moves from urban mall to reservation to Tara's home. These larger intergenerational narratives of Aboriginal peoples in Canada are evident as we move from city to reserve, reserves that were established as part of the treaties that shaped the colonial settlement of Canada. As Tara moves from struggling with the motor of a lawn mower, she moves into sharing her latest traditional dance steps, steps learned as part of who she is becoming as a young woman of her Cree First Nations ancestry. Jean sits on the front step of the house and draws forward memories of when she grew up on a farm where grass mowing was one of the responsibilities she held, particularly when large family gatherings were planned for the long summer days. The smell of cut grass called forward the past into the present and reminds us that, in narrative inquiry, both researcher and participant experiences, and their experiences, co-composed in the living, are under study.

Narrative inquiry, working from a particular ontological and epistemological stance, is a way of understanding and inquiring into experience. It is nothing more and nothing less. Narrative inquiry is always with and within stories—the stories of participants, the stories of inquirers, the social, cultural, institutional, familial, linguistic narratives within which all stories are lived, told, and inquired into.

> Beginning with a respect for ordinary lived experience, the focus of nar-
> rative inquiry is not only a valorizing of individuals' experiences but also
> an exploration of the social, cultural, and institutional narratives within
> which individuals' experiences were constituted, shaped, expressed, and
> enacted—but in a way that begins and ends that inquiry in the storied lives
> of the people involved. Narrative inquirers study an individual's experi-
> ence in the world, and through the study, seek ways of enriching and trans-
> forming that experience for themselves and others. (Clandinin & Rosiek,
> 2007, p. 42)

As narrative inquirers, we do not try to get outside of stories. We
linger in the complex layers of the intertwined and interwoven stories.
It is within the stories, within experience, where we can engage in the
inquiries that will help us understand the lives of people and the worlds
they and we live within.

Stories are lived and told, not separated from each person's living and
telling in time, place, and relationships, not seen as text to be separated
from the living and telling and analyzed and dissected. Narrative inquiry
is situated in relationships and in community and attends to each person's knowledge in relational and participatory ways. Narrative inquiry
is relational research including the relation between researcher and participant. These relational elements mark the distinctive relational ontology of narrative inquiry as distinct from many other forms of research.
Although narrative inquiry is often used to designate any research that
involves narrative or story, we work from a precise definition of narrative inquiry.

We explore what these ideas mean for engaging in narrative inquiries
in subsequent chapters of this book. Whereas this opening chapter provides a more philosophical grounding of narrative inquiry, in Chapter
2 we move to considerations of how we design particular narrative
inquiries.

CHAPTER 2

Elements of Design in Narrative Inquiry

Tara and I headed out to the car, and she carefully guided me on a different route back into the city. I got our tickets for the movie, and Tara let me know what snacks to purchase. We laughed our way through the movie Despicable Me 2. *She told me her mother had already seen it and loved it. I felt a bit of rush of relief because there were moments in the movie when I felt a little uncomfortable with the dialogue. Would her mother approve of the movie, I wondered. After the movie we walked slowly and comfortably back to the car, enjoying the warm summer air, talking about the arts summer program she was in, the people she was working with, the performances she was engaged in. Something began to shift as we got in the car and drove through the still light dusk, through the reserve rather than on the main road, with Tara pointing out areas, homes, and an unfinished apartment complex, all the while guiding me to her house.*

When we drove up to her house in that still-light summer evening, her stepfather was out front. From within the car I asked her whether I could meet him, and she agreed easily. I wondered as I opened the car door if my presence would make the half-mowed lawn less of an issue. We walked up the driveway together and she said, "This is Jean. I know her from school." Her stepfather greeted me, shook my hand, and said, "Thanks for helping Tara out." Tara and I hugged, and somehow I felt that there, in the dusk of a long Alberta summer night, I had been allowed into Tara's world a little bit more. (Clandinin Interim Research Text, December 18, 2013)

This interim research text represents a moment temporally well more than three years into a narrative inquiry. We see Jean, a narrative inquirer, and Tara, a participant, still in the midst of composing a narrative inquiry. The inquiry place shifts from car to movie theater to car to driveway in front of Tara's house. They travel from urban mall to reserve, with its distinct features that Tara draws Jean's attention to as they travel. Jean begins to understand complex social and institutional narratives in which the buildings, roads, and infrastructure are embedded as Tara shows her what to notice in the places they drive through. Jean is introduced to another family member, someone she has not met. As becomes evident in Jean's words, she sees that this is another movement into Tara's multiple worlds, worlds to which she is slowly introducing Jean.

We start with this story fragment from a narrative inquiry in the midst. And from this temporal time and place in the midst we see that while much is unfolding, the beginnings of the inquiry enfold and shape what is now occurring. Elsewhere (Connelly & Clandinin, 2000; Clandinin, 2013) we have described design elements. We bring these forward here in order to both remind readers of methodological work already done but also to shape the starting points for how some design elements offer different possibilities and concerns when we engage in narrative inquiry with children and youth.

1. FOUR KEY TERMS IN NARRATIVE INQUIRY: SHAPING DESIGN CONSIDERATIONS

In Chapter 1 we outlined a narrative conception of experience, one in which experience is the stories people live and tell. As part of a narrative conceptualization of experience, we say that people live and tell stories; that is, we understand people live out stories and tell stories of that living. Although we can make this sound like a linear process of living and then telling, the nature of experience is less clear, as tellings shape livings and livings shape tellings in iterative ways.

In narrative inquiry, alongside participants, we engage in a process of retelling stories—that is, of inquiring into stories. There are other complexities at work here, but for now we want to show that the terms **telling** and **living** are key to narrative inquiry. So, too, are the terms **retelling** and **reliving**. These terms have special meanings for narrative inquirers and frame important research design considerations.

In narrative inquiry, retelling points toward the inquiry as participants and researchers inquire into the lived and told stories through the three-dimensional narrative inquiry space of temporality, place, and sociality. We retell the stories with attentiveness to the inquiry space. As researchers and participants inquire into the storied experiences, new possibilities for ways to live and tell stories emerge. Sometimes these retold stories shape the future reliving of stories; that is, stories are lived in new and previously unimagined ways. We recognize that this set of terms is frequently difficult for researchers to grasp as it makes visible the ongoingness of lives, that stories are not fixed and frozen, and that engaging in narrative inquiry changes the lived and told stories of participants and researchers. The ways narrative inquirers take up these key terms shape their inquiries.

Connelly and Clandinin (2006) write of two possible starting points for narrative inquiries: beginning with telling stories or beginning with living stories. When we start with telling stories our narrative inquiries take the shape of having participants tell us stories of their living.

Usually as we engage with participants in narrative inquiries that begin with telling stories, we are alongside participants over a period of time, so we also hear stories of unfolding lives.

In the narrative inquiry from which the fragments of the narrative account with Tara are taken, the study was designed with a starting point of living stories—that is, of living alongside. A group of researchers (Caine et al, 2010a, 2010b) designed an art club within a school as a way to come alongside youth of Aboriginal heritage who could become possible research participants in a narrative inquiry. As Caine and her colleagues imagined the study, they wanted to first attend to the youths' experiences as they were lived within the art club and then to begin to understand their lives outside of school as the youth invited them to their homes and other places outside of school.

They designed the study within the time of an afterschool club and in a school classroom. Within this design they were attentive to the three-dimensional narrative inquiry space. As they imagined activities and material resources like art-making supplies and snack food, they continued to attend to the three-dimensional narrative inquiry space. As they invited youth from the school to the art club, they thought carefully about time, place, and sociality. However, as they began to live alongside the youth and each other in the art club, they continued to attend to the three-dimensional space as they began to co-compose field texts, interim texts, and research texts with youth and their families.

What becomes important to recognize is that all of these elements of a narrative inquiry need to be considered in the imaginative design processes prior to beginning a study. Without careful attentiveness to these design elements in this imaginative planning of each study, it is difficult to ensure that a narrative inquiry can occur in ways that allow the study of experience.

2. THE THREE-DIMENSIONAL SPACE OF NARRATIVE INQUIRY: SHAPING DESIGN CONSIDERATIONS

In Chapter 1 we described the metaphoric three-dimensional narrative inquiry space with dimensions of temporality, sociality, and place. It is important to understand that working within this metaphoric space shapes the design of a narrative inquiry from the framing of research puzzles through the moves from field to field texts and interim and final research texts. Temporality draws our attention to temporal transitions. Events, places, and people always have a past, present, and future. Sociality draws our attention to personal conditions and, at the same time, to social conditions. By personal conditions we mean the feelings, hopes, desires, aesthetic reactions, and moral dispositions of both inquirer and participants. By social conditions we draw attention to the existential conditions, the environment, surrounding factors and forces, people and otherwise, that form each person's context. Place, the third dimension, draws our attention to the specific concrete, physical, and topological boundaries of place or sequence of places where the inquiry and events take place.

In the narrative inquiry in which Tara was a participant the three-dimensional narrative inquiry space was a constant consideration from the design of the narrative inquiry through to the preparation of research texts. As a team of researchers, we were mindful of always working within the space with each youth and his/her family members.

3. IMAGINING A NARRATIVE INQUIRY FROM FIELD TO FIELD TEXTS TO RESEARCH TEXTS: SHAPING DESIGN CONSIDERATIONS

As we design a narrative inquiry, we need to consider the reflexive, itera-tive processes of moving from being in the field, to field texts, to research texts. As narrative inquirers, we first co-compose a field of experience with participants and then begin to engage in processes of co-composing field texts (what is often called data). As we begin to retell these field texts—that is, as we begin the narrative turn from telling to retelling—we begin to compose interim research texts such as narrative accounts and final research texts such as articles, books and dissertations. This is not a straightforward linear process.

Importantly we need to consider how we can design a narrative inquiry that allows us to always hold this metaphoric unfolding three-dimensional narrative inquiry space within our imaginations. The research design requires at the outset an exercise in imagination, trying to imagine the unfolding inquiry even as we realize that we cannot fully imagine a study without the participants whose experiences will shape the study. We realize what we are proposing is a paradox—that is, an impossible task because we cannot imagine the study without partici-pants and yet we need to imagine the study. In order to work within the paradox we are helped by continually returning to narrative understand-ings of experience. As we design a narrative inquiry, the process involves engaging in imaginative thinking about the research puzzle along with possible participants as existing in an ever-shifting life space and figur-ing out and describing the kind of field texts needed. What this suggests is the importance of imagining the space as open enough, filled with possible ways to engage with participants and to be open enough to go where our lives take us. Part of the imaginative processes of designing the inquiry involves considerations of the moves from field to field texts to research texts.

When we began the inquiry within which the study with Tara is included, Jean could not imagine the ways in which her experiences would be interwoven with Tara's throughout the study and beyond. At the imaginative design phase Jean did not imagine the drive from urban mall to reserve, watching a movie, visiting Tara at her high school, and so on. Jean could not imagine what experiences of her childhood would be evoked and opened for inquiry. The particularities were not imagined. It was only in the ongoing negotiation of the relational experiences that such possibilities could be lived. What made the imaginative design work possible and that enabled the inquiry to unfold in these ways was the grounding in narrative understandings of experience.

4. WRITING OURSELVES INTO NARRATIVE INQUIRIES: SHAPING DESIGN CONSIDERATIONS

Beginning with autobiographical narrative inquiries, or what we call narrative beginnings, is part of the process of writing ourselves into the research. The importance of this autobiographical work emerges in part from understanding that narrative inquiry is the study of experience when experience is understood as a narrative phenomenon. Most importantly, we need to remember that it is not the experience of the other that we are studying; rather, we are studying our experience as inquirers in relation with the experiences of participants.

> Narrative inquiry is the study of experience, and experience, as John Dewey taught, is a matter of people in relation contextually and temporally. Participants are in relation, and we as researchers are in relation to participants. Narrative inquiry is an experience of the experience. It is people in relation studying with people in relation. (Clandinin & Connelly, 2000, p. 189)

Our lived and told stories are always in relation to or with those of participants and with their and our landscapes. As we tell our stories and listen to participants tell their stories in the inquiry, we as inquirers need to pay close attention to who we are in the inquiry and to understand that we, ourselves, are part of the storied landscapes we are studying. Thus, as inquirers, we are part of the landscape and acknowledge that we too make the worlds in which we find ourselves. We do not stand metaphorically outside of, but are part of the phenomenon under study. Narrative inquiry is relational inquiry.

As narrative inquirers, we enter into research in the midst of our own lives, in the midst of participants' lives, and in the midst of institutional, social, familial, and linguistic narratives. We engage for a time, over time, with participants, either alongside them in the living of their lives and in their telling of stories or only as they tell their stories.

As part of engaging in the narrative inquiry with the youth and their families in which Jean and Tara's work is embedded, each narrative inquirer engaged in an autobiographical narrative inquiry that allowed us to tell stories of ourselves and then move to inquire into those told stories in order to better understand our interest in a particular phenomenon, a phenomenon we are trying to understand narratively. As Jean began work with the youth, she engaged in telling her stories of growing up in a small rural community that was not too distant from a reserve and of attending a high school where at least one of her classmates was of Aboriginal heritage. Jean awakened to the social and cultural narratives of people of Aboriginal heritage as "other," narratives in which they were seen as deficit, as less than. Jean's told and retold stories allowed her to position herself in the research and to understand the ways people of Aboriginal heritage are often positioned in institutional narratives such as stories of school.

It is through these autobiographical narrative inquiries that narrative inquirers are better able to frame research puzzles and to justify their studies. Although we initially engage in autobiographical narrative inquiries as we design the study, we know that staying wakeful to who we are in the study is part of the ongoing inquiry work, from living in the field to composing field texts and to composing research texts. We know that who we are in the inquiry will shift and change throughout the inquiry as we too begin to retell and relive our stories of experience. However, the initial autobiographical narrative inquiries allow us to awaken to how we position ourselves in relation to future participants and to how we frame our research puzzles.

5. FRAMING RESEARCH PUZZLES: SHAPING DESIGN CONSIDERATIONS

Through engaging in the autobiographical narrative inquiry, research puzzles begin to become visible. Narrative inquirers use the concept of a research puzzle rather than a research question to hold open the idea that we are engaged in re-search—that is, searching again in deeper ways understand the nature of experience. "Narrative inquiry carries more a sense of continual reformulation of an inquiry than it does a sense of problem definition and solution. As we think about the phenomena in a narrative inquiry, we think about responding to the questions: What is your narrative inquiry about? or What is the experience of interest to you as a narrative inquirer?" (Clandinin & Connelly, 2000, p. 124).

In the narrative inquiry from which the fragments of Jean and Tara's work are taken, we framed research puzzles around the experiences of urban Aboriginal youth and families, particularly in relation to their schooling and educational experiences both in and out of schools. Again, it was our return to narrative conceptualizations of experience and to the three-dimensional narrative inquiry space that helped us frame the research puzzle with attentiveness to the life-making experiences of the youth and their families.

"Come in," she urged, and we entered the school. I saw the large sign telling me that visitors were to report to the office. But I was here as Tara's guest, and although I felt the dis/ease of being in a school without official permission, I followed her through the main atrium of the school and into a room jammed with about twelve young people of Aboriginal heritage, all of them sorting candy into Christmas stockings. "This is my friend Jean," she said. She got me a chair, sat down across from me, and the stocking stuffing resumed. Stockings were passed to me, and I stuffed in a candy cane and handed the stocking to the person beside me. The group conversation began again and the work continued for about twenty minutes until all the stockings were filled. Youth ready for drumming appeared in the room from time to time, and someone who appeared to be the staff adviser bustled in and out. Tara told me a few names of the people who were there.

When the work was finished Tara told her friend Ann to come with us. Ann is of Inuit heritage and comes to school here. We began a tour of the small high school, both of them pointing things out. Tara took me to her locker and retrieved her art notebook and showed me a variety of her drawings, sketches, and studies. "I like it here because of the art," she said. We three walked and talked and returned to the small room where we had begun and sat down again. At that moment, while Tara was speaking with someone else, one of the young male students leaned over and asked, "How do you know Tara?" I responded that we had come to know each other at her junior high school and that she was my friend. I watched his skepticism, but at that moment I felt that Tara and I were friends. I felt that we had begun to world travel, and it was through her invitations for me into her home and school places that allowed me to world travel. (Interim Research Text, December 18, 2013)

As Jean came to spend time with Tara in her new high school, it is clear that much is shifting for Jean and for Tara. Here we see Tara shaping the research relationship, inviting Jean to her place, her school, where Jean is her guest. This move momentarily dispositions Jean as she realizes that she is more accustomed to entering a high school on her terms—going to the school office to announce her presence in the school and naming herself as someone from the university. Tara takes Jean to the room and introduces her and is the one who invites Jean on a tour of the school. Although the other students are puzzled by Jean's presence, Tara assumes a position where Jean is her friend and is welcome in places where friends are welcomed. She positions Jean in relation to herself.

Much has changed since the days of imagining the study. However, what is evident is that the design of the study allowed the unfolding of the narrative inquiry in ways that are congruent with the relational onto-logical commitments of a narrative inquiry.

6. Positioning an Inquiry Within the Scholarly Literature: Shaping Design Considerations

As we design narrative inquiries it is important that we attend to our autobiographical experiences of the phenomenon we are interested in. However, we also know that we need to know something of the scholarly conversations and discussions that are ongoing in the research literature. What is known about the phenomenon from other narrative inquiries is important, and we learn much from it. However, sometimes there are no other narrative inquiries about a particular phenomenon.

Maxine Greene's (1995) description of seeing big and seeing small is helpful to us as we attend to other studies about the phenomenon. Greene writes of seeing small as helping us to discern the patterns, trends, and movements of phenomenon over time and of seeing big as helping us to see the person in their particularity, in their wholeness. Although neither of Greene's ways of seeing are of seeing narratively, she does offer counsel on the importance of being able to see both ways and to see the value in both ways of seeing. We find her work helpful as we think about the importance of attending closely to what other researchers have learned about particular phenomenon.

We also think that attending closely to other research about particular phenomena is important in that it helps us understand and position our work within the ongoing discussions and dialogues in an area. We need to know how other researchers are framing the research and scholarly discussions in order to be able to join the discussions and to add to the larger scholarship. This is important as we design a narrative inquiry and as we prepare to justify our study as important in contributing to knowledge.

We knew something of the ways that youth and families of Aboriginal heritage experienced schooling from our earlier studies and from our experiences as teachers, nurses, consultants, and psychologists and as people composing lives in multiple and diverse places. We also read the extensive literature around youth and families of Aboriginal heritage and knew that the stories foregrounded in that literature were frequently composed around statistics of high rates of unemployment, involvement with the justice system, substance abuse, and lack of high school completion. We also read the calls for more in-depth studies of the experiences of the youth that did not start from a deficit perspective.

We read this literature with concerns around the lack of inclusion of the voices of the youth and their families. Thinking about the studies as ways of seeing small helped us see that there were few studies that allowed us to see big. We also read this literature and wondered about the lack of consideration of the ways in which education was a life-making process that included the whole of a life in the multiple life contexts in which lives are composed, lived, and recomposed. We shared Dewey's distinction about the importance of seeing life as education and of not equating schooling with education. As we framed our research puzzle, we were attentive to the need to imagine our research puzzles differently, being careful not to begin with assumptions from some of the literature we read but to be open to searching again, to trying to understand experience in narrative ways.

7. Justifying Our Work: Shaping Design Considerations

As we design a narrative inquiry, we need to imagine the end of the inquiry and how we will respond to the questions of "So what?" and "Who cares?," questions all researchers need to answer. It is at the outset of our narrative inquiries that we first meet the questions of *so what* and *who cares*. These questions draw us toward the need to justify our narrative inquiries in three ways: the personal, practical, and social/theoretical justifications. In part the autobiographical narrative inquiry work and the close attention to the scholarly literature are ways of beginning to respond to these questions, questions that we begin to answer as we design our narrative inquiry.

Considerations of personal justification draw us to understand more deeply why the inquiry matters to each of us: "Our research interests come out of our own narratives of experience and shape our narrative inquiry plotlines" (Clandinin & Connelly, 2000, p 121). Although this often sounds like an easy and straightforward task, we know how difficult it is to engage in autobiographical narrative inquiry and to understand the complexity of understanding who we are in the inquiry and our purposes and justifications for engaging in the inquiry. We cannot engage in narrative inquiry without considerations of who we are and are becoming in the inquiry and what brings us to the inquiry. However, justifying our narrative inquiry in only personal terms is not enough.

Considerations of practical justifications are also important as we think about how our work will be taken up by others in teaching, nursing, policy making, teacher education, and so on. As we imagine our studies and write about them in final research texts, questions of how we justify our work practically are particularly important. Again, at one level this seems like a straightforward undertaking, but as we have learned, this is much more difficult than it first seems.

Considerations of personal and practical justifications are often not considered of importance to the scholarly literature. As Clandinin and Connelly (2000) wrote, "Although we encourage the justification of inquiry interest in personal terms, the norms of inquiry have it that people should only justify their inquiry in social terms. . . . We need to be prepared to write "I" as we make the transition from field texts to research texts. As we write "I," we need to convey a sense of social significance" (p. 122).

Justifying one's research in social/theoretical ways is often the only justification that appears in final research texts. However, this is not enough for narrative inquirers, and we note that it is crucial for all three kinds of justification to be in evidence in narrative inquiries, even if the personal justifications are sometimes not fully evident in public research texts.

8. Finding Participants and Co-composing an Inquiry Field: Shaping Design Considerations

As we design each narrative inquiry we are especially mindful of who we will invite to participate in the study with us. We want to invite participants into the study whose experiences fit within the criteria we set for each inquiry; that is, we set certain criteria as guides to select participants. Although in one way this seems a straightforward process of setting criteria, this is far more difficult than it seems at first. How we set the criteria for participants shapes who comes to be a participant. For each narrative inquiry, setting the criteria requires us to return again to ontological commitments and the three-dimensional narrative inquiry space.

In narrative inquiries we want to study participants' experiences within a particular phenomenon, but we want to study that experience within the three-dimensional narrative inquiry space—that is, with attentiveness to the dimensions of temporality, sociality, and place. Our intention is not to focus on a particular experience that is torn from the life context of an individual. For example, in our narrative inquiry (Clandinin, Schaefer, & Downey, 2014) into the experiences of teachers who left teaching within the first five years of teaching, we wanted to attend to their experiences over time, attending to the stories they lived that brought them to teaching, to the stories they lived and told while teaching, to the stories they lived and told as they moved out of teaching, and to the stories they lived and told after they had left teaching in public schools. We did not want to focus on the event or time of leaving teaching, for that would not allow us to give a sense of the unfolding and enfolding life experiences of which leaving teaching is a part.

The difficulty is finding ways that allow us to find or identify potential participants that allow participants to imagine themselves within studies. It is as participants begin to see themselves as part of the narrative inquiry that we can begin to negotiate what we call the field. What we mean by *field* is perhaps different from what is seen as the field or site of inquiry in other qualitative research methodologies. In narrative inquiry we negotiate with participants an ongoing relational inquiry space that we call the field.

9. MOVING FROM FIELD TO FIELD TEXTS: SHAPING DESIGN CONSIDERATIONS

As we imagine composing field texts of our experiences in the relational field, we attend once again to the three-dimensional narrative inquiry space. As we imagine those field texts, we have written elsewhere (Clandinin & Connelly, 2000) of the importance of multiple forms of field texts. We indicated a range of possible field texts, including:

field notes of activities in which participants and researchers engage
transcripts of conversations
annals and chronicles of life events
archival photographs that participants share of family, school, other events
purposely taken present day photographs taken by participants or that
    participants ask be taken of them
documents
art work
institutional policy and other documents
researcher journals
participant journals

There are many possible forms of field texts, and what becomes important is that we carefully situate the field texts within the three-dimensional narrative inquiry space.

10. RESPONSE COMMUNITIES: SHAPING DESIGN CONSIDERATIONS

In narrative inquiries we are always in the midst of the inquiry in the sense that even as we begin to plan the inquiry, we are engaged in the inquiry. We enter in the midst of individuals' lives, both researchers and participants, as well as larger social, cultural, institutional, linguistic, and familial narratives. We leave while still in the midst of lives and larger unfolding narratives. It is from within this sense of being in the midst, caught into stories and larger narratives, that response communities are so important to our work as narrative inquirers.

What we mean by *response communities* are those individuals who we ask to come alongside us to read and respond to our field texts and particularly as we move from composing field texts to co-composing interim and final research texts. The processes of composing and co-composing field texts and research texts requires the demanding yet playful work of what Maria Lugones (1987) calls world traveling. Lugones describes world traveling as the task of entering into another's world and, in so doing, understanding what it is to be oneself in one's own world, to be the other in one's own world at the same time as understanding what it is to be oneself in another's world and to be an other in his/her world. This process of world traveling requires us to attend to not only how we construct ourselves in different worlds but also to attend to how we construct others in different worlds. The task is a difficult one that requires much of us—that is, wakefulness and attentiveness to the lives in motion.

As we attend to the multiple stories that live within the experiences of each researcher and participant, response communities can help keep us awake and attentive to who we and participants are and are becoming. Response communities listen to our research texts and urge us to "say more" about the experiences we share. As we move from field texts to interim and final research texts, we are engaging in a process of "unpacking," of attempting to make visible the interwoven and entwined stories that live within each experience. Response communities help us as they "give back" our interim and final research texts, our texts in the making.

We find that response communities can be composed of one or more persons, but they must be people who are in the response community for the long haul, for sustained periods of time. They must be people who come to the work with different experiences but are interested in attending to researchers' and participants' experiences. The work of people in response communities is helping researchers stay awake to what they see but are not awake to, to see what we might miss in the experiences under study.

11. MOVING FROM FIELD TEXTS TO INTERIM AND FINAL RESEARCH TEXTS: SHAPING DESIGN CONSIDERATIONS

Although it is often very difficult to imagine how we will move from field texts to interim and final research texts at the design phase of a narrative inquiry, we need to keep the necessity of this move in the foreground at the outset: "As narrative inquirers we understand that as we co-compose field texts and research texts in more or less relational ways with participants, we are attentive to the temporal unfolding of experience, and to the unfolding of our relationships" (Clandinin, 2013, p. 204). Temporal, relational, and place vantage points make a difference. Even as we make this move from field texts to interim and final research texts, we need to remind ourselves that there will never be a final story. We need to continually remind ourselves that each story of experience opens into new stories to be lived and told, always with the possibility of retelling and reliving. As Downey and Clandinin (2010) wrote,

> Unexpectedness also lives in, and through, the unfolding relationship between researchers and participants. Living one's life in the midst of others' lives opens us up to the possibilities of what this experience will call forth and lead into. This unexpectedness is not only expected in narrative inquiry but is also one of its goals, as inquiring narratively with others opens up the possibility for growth, by which we mean coming to tell and live what at least seem, in the moment, to be better stories. (p. 390)

"Attending to uncertainty and to the ongoingness of lives lived and told over time brings researcher commitment to understanding lives in motion, a commitment to seeing and representing lives as always in the making (Greene, 1995), to the forefront" (Clandinin, 2013, p. 204). We have found that returning to Dewey's concept of experience reminds us of this commitment in the research texts we write. "We always live in our world, living in the midst of a life that won't sit still, one always still unfolding. Experience is just that, the schlepping of our world in the world, a trying or doing that can lead to unexpected outcomes, including a very trying undoing of aspects of our worlds. Dewey understood this as life itself, something to be welcomed and worked with rather than avoided" (Downey & Clandinin, 2010, p. 391).

It is by this continual return to the ontological commitments of a relational methodology that we can begin to imagine the processes of moving to interim and final research texts. As Clandinin (2013) notes, "Holding these conceptual commitments of narrative inquiry mean that the kinds of research texts we create are difficult ones in at least two ways. They are difficult in the sense of composing texts that continue to honor these commitments but they are also difficult because they challenge us to attend in multiple directions and toward multiple audiences" (Clandinin, 2013, p. 205). Responses to the questions of *so what* and *who cares* are not easy responses to make when research, from within the dominant stories of research, is expected to offer truths and certainty. In the quest for certainty, answers, and solutions, narrative inquirers offer research texts that speak for now, that acknowledge that there are the gaps when stories are intentionally or unintentionally not told.

12. RELATIONAL ETHICS: SHAPING DESIGN CONSIDERATIONS

Relational ethics pervade the whole of the inquiry from writing narrative beginnings that shape our research puzzles, to considering the *so what* and *who cares* questions, to being in the field, composing field texts and interim and final research texts and even after the final research texts are written and made public. Building on a detailed analysis of the evolving development of the relational ethics of narrative inquiry (Clandinin, Caine & Huber, accepted), we offer a more detailed discussion of ethics in Chapters 12 and 14.

Chapters 1 and 2 are a kind of summary of what has already been written in books and articles. The following chapters work with these understandings to open up questions of engaging in research with children and youth.

CHAPTER 3

Narrative Beginnings in Work with Children and Youth

As we move more directly into considerations of narrative inquiry undertaken with children and youth, we are particularly awake to the importance of attending to who we are as inquirers in these studies. We know that beginning with inquiring into who we are as narrative inquirers in relation to particular experiential phenomena is part of any narrative inquiry. In this way we become more awake to the complexities of who we are as well as to the personal, practical, and social justifications of any particular narrative inquiry. We also become more attentive to how we imagine ourselves in relation to particular research puzzles. However, we suggest that these autobiographical narrative inquiries are of particular concern in research with children and youth. As we show in this chapter, these ongoing practices of autobiographical work make visible how participating in narrative inquiries have the possibility to shape not only who we are and are becoming but also the children and youth we come alongside.

Our purpose in this chapter is, partially, to make visible aspects of our autobiographical narrative inquiries around children and youth, with particular attention to who we are and who we are becoming. However, through the fragments of each of our autobiographical narrative inquiries we not only make ourselves visible but, more importantly, show the importance of these inquiries as part of our work as narrative inquirers. In sharing fragments of the accounts and our processes of composing them, we develop an argument for the theoretical importance of engaging in the challenging work of autobiographical narrative inquiry through which we compose narrative beginnings.

As shown in Chapter 2, autobiographical inquiries as narrative beginnings have long been central to engaging in narrative inquiry. Our argument for engaging in this work follows the reasoning of Rosiek and Pratt (2013):

The knowing subject conducting social scientific inquiry is no longer assumed to stand innocently outside the phenomenon it studies and is instead understood to play a part in producing many of the realities it purports to describe. Reciprocally, the nature of the knowing subject is no longer assumed to be independent of the processes of inquiry and representation. The process of knowing is understood to ontologically constitute the knowing subject. (p. 578)

Rosiek and Pratt (2013) go on to discuss the methodological shifts from a focus on processes of description to processes of representation, noting that "the term *re-presentation* acknowledges the ontological gulf between description and what is described; it emphasizes the role communities of inquiry play in constituting the objects of their inquiry" (p. 579). Their description of the shift from seeing researchers as describers of situations to committed to a relational ontology makes evident that we are not only describing participants' experiences but are also actively in relation with participants. We are, as Connelly and Clandinin (1990) pointed out, studying our experiences in relation with the experiences of the participants. Thus, as Rosiek and Pratt also highlight, "communities of inquiry" play a significant part in constituting participants (including researchers and those who we more visibly name as participants).

Seeing ourselves as people whose experiences are also under study highlights the importance of new conceptions of inquiry, ones in which we see ourselves as always in the making, as embodying cultural, social, familial, institutional, and linguistic narratives in our past, present, and future experiences. As Rosiek and Pratt (2013) emphasize, what we need are "conceptions of inquiry that embrace the pluralism and the reciprocal ethical obligations made manifest by acknowledging the limitations of our representational practices" (p. 581). Drawing on the work of Jane Addams, they show that in such conceptions, the researcher is also "an agent, not a passive conduit connecting cultures or connecting data, but a person invested in all of the intersecting cultures" (p. 585). Further, they highlight the importance of attending to how the inquiry "works on the inquirer" as the "inevitable and desirable outcome of conducting inquiry" with participants. They argue, as do we (Clandinin, 2013; Clandinin and Connelly, 2000; Connelly and Clandinin, 1990) that "knowledge is ultimately grounded in and must return for its validation to the course of personal experience" (p. 586) and "that the form this knowledge takes most readily or appropriately takes in our lives is that of narrative" (p. 586).

Narrative inquirers do not often use the term methodological reflexivity (Rosiek, 2013), preferring to speak of narrative inquiry as a relational methodology, assuming that the concept of a relational methodology acknowledges that we, as inquirers, are also under study in a narrative inquiry. The importance of self-facing, of turning the gaze upon whom we are and are becoming throughout the study of our experience alongside the experiences of participants, highlights the importance of methodological reflexivity. What we highlight is that although methodological reflexivity is not the term narrative inquirers use, engaging in ways of being reflexive is very much part of engaging in the relational methodology of narrative inquiry.

Making these interconnections more visible also allows us to highlight the shift away from beginning with epistemological questions. Attention is shifted away from a focus on epistemological concerns with the turn toward the ontological and the ontological commitments narrative inquiry entails. A commitment to a relational ontology is fundamental to narrative inquiry.

Narrative inquiry, grounded within the three-dimensional narrative inquiry space, has a strong focus on temporality and the future consequences of processes of inquiry. It is Dewey's conception of experience, with its criteria of interaction and continuity within situations, that draws attention to the importance of temporality and the always-becoming processes of experience and, consequently, understandings of narrative inquiry as partial, tentative, and open to the possibility of otherwise.

What Rosiek (2013) and Rosiek and Pratt (2013) sharpen for us is the importance of a conception of inquiry that embraces pluralism and the reciprocal ethical obligations we share with those we come alongside in our inquiry. This attention to who we each are and are becoming makes necessary an ongoing focus on who we are in the inquiry, as people in relation studying people in relation. Working within narrative inquiry, we, as inquirers, study our own experiences alongside participants. We need, therefore, to re-present our own storied experiences as we enter into each inquiry. These autobiographical inquiries need to be ongoing from the outset of studies and continue through to the aftermath of the inquiry in order to attend to the ways that the ongoing inquiries shape both researchers and participants. As we describe the importance of engaging in these autobiographical inquiries at the outset of a particular inquiry, we need also to remember the importance of ongoing wakefulness as we come alongside participants. Sometimes in the ongoing work of an inquiry memories of earlier experiences are triggered, and we return again to the need for further autobiographical work that allows us to continue to make sense of the experiences of participants and ourselves. We have all experienced moments alongside participants when they say or do something, are in a place with us, or when a song or smell triggers an experience long since forgotten. We deal with the importance of attending to this ongoing turning back on our experiences further in Chapter 8.

We argue in Chapters 1 and 2 that autobiographical narrative inquiries at the outset of each research project help us more carefully situate ourselves in relation to the research puzzles that call us into each study. Through this autobiographical work we become more awake to how we understand our experiences as we frame research and justify in personal, practical, and theoretical ways each particular study. We also come to understand more clearly that who we are, as people and as inquirers, shifts as we move from study to study and as we are shaped by our ongoing participation with children and youth over time.

NECESSARILY TROUBLING: LAYERS OF COMPLEXITY

What at first glimpse seemed a straightforward representation of who we are as narrative inquirers became less clear as we worked to consider how to situate ourselves in this book. While we have all, over some years now, engaged in narrative inquiries with children and youth we were somewhat puzzled by just how we could best show readers who we were, are, and are becoming. We wondered, for example, whether we should only attend to our experiences as children and youth. Should we focus on our experiences at similar ages and situations as participants in the studies? Or should our focus also be on when we first engaged with children and youth as teachers, nurses, babysitters, parents, and so on? Or should our focus also be on previous inquiry experiences in which we engaged with children and youth?

These questions occupied our considerations as we engaged in discussions of narrative beginnings. We know that who we are now has been shaped in multiple places and within multiple relationships. We know that we are each of us embedded within shifting cultural, familial, social, institutional, and linguistic narratives. We are not fixed and frozen but are, as Dewey (1938) and other pragmatic philosophers argue, always in process. "I am what I am not yet," said Maxine Greene (2001). As we worked on writing this chapter, we each wrote many fragments of stories, knowing, as Laurel Richardson (2000) reminds us, that writing is inquiry. As we wrote stories of our experiences, we awakened to new understandings of who we are and are becoming. As we engaged in narrative inquiry into the stories, we puzzled again and again over our purposes and intentions for including narrative accounts of our experiences.

As we thought about these questions and the importance of making who we are and are becoming visible within narrative inquiry, we came to the following ways of re-presenting who we are as narrative inquirers alongside children and youth in this book. We looked backward to our early landscapes (Greene, 1995) and then moved forward to experiences with children and youth and then to the first experiences of becoming narrative inquirers. In what follows we offer narrative accounts of the autobiographical by showing first the shaping of our early landscapes, and then the shaping of our experiences as teachers and nurses, and finally drawing on the shaping of our studies. We thread this chapter together with the importance of the shifting stories we live by (Connelly & Clandinin, 1999), stories of who we are and are becoming. After the brief narrative accounts of our experiences we highlight the important facets of narrative beginnings and, indeed, of the ongoing narrative inquiries throughout each inquiry and across inquiries.

Jean

Early Beginnings: Attending to Experience

A week or so ago I drove down a major highway that passes close to the small town where I went to school. Off in the distance I could see the hills that surrounded the farm where I grew up. It was autumn, a beautiful day with blue skies and bright sunshine. The horizon was marked by a low-hanging band of what might appear to be dust by those unfamiliar with the September prairie grain harvests. As a child of the prairies, I knew the golden dust was the result of the swathing and combining of the crops. The smell of crops just combined filled the car. And with the sweet dusty smell of the fresh harvest, my mind drifted back to other moments.

As a small child, I tagged after my father as he went about his busy fall days, days filled with what I now know was back-breaking labor as the golden crops of oats and barley were swathed, then stooked, and finally loaded onto wagons that carried the stalks to the threshing machine. Amidst the smell of gasoline and the noise of a rumbling, aging machine, grain was separated from stalks.

In those days, when I followed my father before the harvesting began, we walked, mostly in silence, as he looked closely at the grain stalks, at the grains still hanging in golden bundles on the stalk. Sometimes he talked to me, but mostly, I now think he was caught in considering the decisions he faced. I already knew, as quite a young child, that our family livelihood, our very survival in some ways, rested on those slender stalks of grain. Selling the grain bought the groceries and supplies we needed. The straw would bed and feed the animals on our small farm.

I knew to be silent and to listen when he talked, but I also knew to be silent and to watch him as he attended closely to what he was seeing. I learned to read his frowns and to listen carefully to what he said. I learned to notice his expressions as he held stalks in his fingers, rubbing the stalks and feeling the individual kernels of grain. I learned to watch as he looked at the skies and smelled the air, hopeful that the weather would stay warm and dry until those crops were harvested.

It mattered to him, and I knew it mattered to our family. So much depended on the decisions he made about when to plant, when to harvest. I learned to watch what he watched and to watch him watching. In those moments in the fall and earlier in the spring and summer, I watched my father as I followed him on those walks in the fields. I was learning to be attentive, to read the landscape, to stay with what mattered. I learned to be attentive to change, to what was happening to the grain, to the soil, to the weather. And I learned to watch, to notice, to be in some ways a keen observer and to remember what changed, how much changed over time. The soil, the weather, the grain as it grew and turned from green to golden.

As I learned to inquire into my experiences in the landscapes of my childhood, I was drawn to Mary Catherine Bateson. And her words about attention, presence, and care were words that helped me inquire into those early experiences alongside my father. Bateson writes,

> To attend means to be present, sometimes with companionship, sometimes with patience. It means to take care of . . . .Yet surely there is a powerful link between presence and care. The willingness to do what needs to be done is rooted in attention to what is ... I believe if we can learn a deeper noticing of the world around us, this will be the basis of effective concern. (1994, p. 109)

On those walks with my father I had a model of what it meant to attend, to be present, as I watched my father attend to the land, to the grain, to the weather. His was a deeper noticing of the world, and I learned from watching him.

On many hot and muggy early evenings in August I walked silently alongside my father as we walked into the fields, fields that had been filled with healthy green plants just an hour or so earlier. Now, after a few minutes of dark skies, pounding hail and rain, the stalks were broken and crumpled on the ground. I watched my father's anguish, as I knew he was thinking back to the hard work of preparing, seeding, and tending the crops. And I also knew he was thinking forward to the winter months when there would not be enough feed for the livestock and perhaps not quite enough for his family. I knew then to be silent. I knew then what uncertainty felt like and gained my first glimpse of a liminal space, an abyss filled with the certainty of not knowing. I learned early that my family needed to live with uncertainty and improvisation.

Bateson's (1994) words that "Living and learning are everywhere founded on an improvisational base" (p. 9) drew me to consider my living and learning, the ways the uncertainty of living on a small prairie farm drew me to understand what it meant to live in uncertainty, "full of the inklings of alternatives" (p. 8). For when our crops were lost to summer hail storms or early frosts, there were only inklings of alternatives, no certain path forward. For months my family improvised ways forward.

And so in these early experiences I learned about attending to people and to the worlds in which they lived. I also learned about uncertainty and about improvisation as a way to compose a life. It was not until later that I learned about imagination, about the possibility of imagining otherwise, learning from and with Maxine Greene's work.

Shifting Forward: Coming Alongside Youth
As a third-year university student, I was almost out of the money required to continue my studies. I needed to find work and decided to apply to teach in the school district, which surrounded the university I attended. I got the position: teaching grades seven, eight, and nine "oral French" with a prepackaged program "Voix et Image" on Tuesday, Thursday, and Friday afternoons. The junior high school was quite a distance from the university but was not too far from my uncle's house where I lived, so I could make the public transit routes work. I remember my days there vividly: the old brick school that smelled of gestetner fluid, cleaners and sweaty young bodies. I remember my ride from the university, where I spent my days in lecture halls and the libraries. I had learned to be comfortable in school; I knew how to study, how to write essays, how to pass tests. When I went to the big urban junior high school I did not know how to teach French, to talk to colleagues, or to make relationships with the youth. I figured out early on that I did not like the discipline processes that included strapping children for a variety of misdeeds and after-school detentions.

I knew, though, to stay silent and to watch the youth. Watching with patience and openness to possibilities were threads in my stories to live by, stories shaped in those early experiences with my parents. I knew I could not be a teacher without relationships, and I knew I could not begin to shape relationships until I knew something about the worlds of the youth I was to teach. On an October day I remember coming home after 9 p.m. one evening from the university library where I had been studying. Riding in the big transit bus en route to my uncle's home, my temporary home for the year, the bus rumbled down a familiar avenue that linked my home to the school. And then I saw her, one of the girls from class, one of the little girls, someone in grade seven. I watched her and wondered what she was doing on the street so late on a school night. And I watched to see who she was with. An older sibling? A parent? A friend? And then, gradually, I realized she was alone on the street and that perhaps she was waiting to be picked up, perhaps by a stranger. I watched until the bus rumbled away and took me to the warmth of a cup of tea with my aunt and uncle who wondered about my day. As I drank my tea, I realized how much of my world I had assumed was like their worlds. And I realized that I needed to watch more closely, to attend more carefully, to not assume, to try to come alongside.

Shifting Forward: Learning to Attend as a Narrative Inquirer

As a beginning narrative inquirer, I began by situating myself alongside teachers, a positioning that felt most comfortable in part from the way I positioned myself in my doctoral research. I was studying in a curriculum field, and I was studying alongside teachers. As I write these words, memories flood back as I think about those first days in Stephanie's classroom in an urban Toronto school. I was alongside Stephanie; that is, she was the participant in my study around teacher knowledge. But the children's voices and lives almost filled my vision. I remember two twin girls, Natalie and Natasha, girls of African Canadian heritage, and how excited they were as we planted the bean seeds in the soil I carefully dug up from my garden in suburban Toronto. I remember the sticky fingers that grasped my hands, that touched my body, that reached in to stroke my velveteen jacket. I remember their voices, some quiet and some not so quiet, as they called Miss Jean, come see, come look, come help. And so I began this work in classrooms alongside a teacher, Stephanie, but I was also alongside the children. The pull was to them, to their lives, to trying to understand their experiences, experiences so different and yet the same as those of my son who was only slightly older. The times that come forward in my memory now, stories that are barely acknowledged in my dissertation and subsequent publications, are always those alongside the children. For many years after that I was positioned alongside principals, teachers, and student teachers, although there were moments when I found my way again to being alongside children.

And so it was in 2000 when I found myself again alongside a teacher and children, this time in a curriculum-making research project where we intentionally wrote about the curriculum being made by children and families. By then we had developed the concept of co-composing curriculum and the notion of composing coming alongside in the relational spaces as lives met in classrooms. Now, rather than attending to children's lives through my peripheral vision, I could attend more directly, to seeing them and to making more visible to others that I was seeing them.

Of course, as we came to see children, I also saw them in their families, people with mothers and fathers, aunties and uncles, brothers and sisters. This attention took my attention back to those early days as an elementary school counselor when I made sure I spent time with families in their homes as we sought to find educative places in schools. Those mornings and afternoons in homes with mothers were times I so valued, when I could understand a child's life in the complexity of the living. In that 2000 project I was recollecting those earlier memories, but this time it was different. I was different. I had lived more; I knew something more about power and agency and lives.

Now I was more awake to what schooling did to lives, about what it meant to compose a life in school that, in part, did not attend to the lives being composed outside of school. Now I was more awake, but I also knew a bit more about how to talk about that life making, about the complexity of different worlds we each inhabited, about the multiplicity of composing lives.

Sean

Early Beginnings: "Two-Stone Stories."
My given name is Sean Michael Lessard. I am the middle child in a family of five. I grew up in North Battleford, Saskatchewan, on a farm; it was a special place where I learned from the land and the rhythms of life that are nested within the rural landscape. I have many stories of my farm and the knowledge passed on that captures the spirit of the harvest and the relationship to the land. Living life on the farm taught me lessons, showed me how to deal with people honestly, of the importance of shaking hands, of lending help to people when needed, and of respecting the community members who share a common rural purpose. The physical place where I grew up provided me opportunities and a base that continues to shape my identity.

My birth name is Harvey Curtis Settee from the Kingfisher family. I am the youngest member of my family. I have two older sisters and one older brother. My home is on a reserve in Northern Saskatchewan and is situated on a lake surrounded by dense forest; it has many proud stories and traditions that have been passed on. My mom was a cook, and she worked in a bush camp near the reserve. My family members have a long history in this area, and many of them are the political and spiritual leaders of the community. I am learning about life in this place and the values and protocols that exist. I am learning when to talk and when to listen, of the importance of helping and of honoring the older ones, of the power of stories, and of what it means to give and receive gifts. Life in this community has provided me with many opportunities and is adding to my existing identity in meaningful ways.

I started off in life not knowing and removed from the ways of cultural teachings and struggling to compose a comfortable identity. Over time I am learning about the past and my Woodland Cree ancestors. I have started to grow through the teachings shared with me. For the past five years I have embarked on a journey to my shared "homes": a place where I was born and a place where I grew up. Both places provide me opportunities to learn and reflect on the life I am composing, a life in which I acknowledge the multiplicity of who I am as I am becoming (Bateson, 1989). As I think about these early experiences and my multiple home places, Mary Catherine Bateson reminds me to think about the composition of a life and the multiplicity within lives that requires careful attention.

When I go back to the farm, I pay respect to my father's land and take time at an old oak tree. It is in this place where I turn inward and say a few words in honor of a life that has passed on. I try my best when I return home to update my dad on the journey I have been taking and the good and bad that life offers. I spend time in this place back on the farm so I don't forget the stories. This land helps me, it grounds me, it heals me.

After I spend a day at the farm, I continue down the road. As I drive, the landscape shifts moving from the vast wheat fields to the shadows of trees and the traditional territory of my ancestors, the Woodland Cree. When I drive back to my community I often wonder what life was like on the land. I think of the older ones and my ancestors. I wonder whether we were similar people. Were there people like me in this place? Bateson (1989) helps me think about my ancestors and my identity when she writes, "Life is not made up of separate pieces. A composer creates patterns across time with ongoing themes and variations, different movements all integrated into the whole" (p. 109). I linger with these words as I think of the movement required between my home-places and the necessary travel, both metaphorically and physically. I am attending to my life in these places, paying attention to the patterns in both places that are a part of the ongoing multiplicity within my life, never are these separate pieces.

I started my life in foster care, and I was adopted into a non-Aboriginal family. In this way I have multiple families and multiple homes in which I travel. My identity continues to shift, and it is shaped by lived experiences and evolving multiple identities that look to honor both pasts and guide my future journeys.

On the farm, my dad often walked on the land, sifting through the soil, carefully analyzing the future of his crops. In the fields he often found artifacts from the Cree people who once inhabited the land. I remember the two "hammer stones" (mauls) he uncovered. He showed me how they were used as tools to grind down meat and grains. One of the stones was gray and the other brown. I could see how, through time and use, distinct markings and grooves were formed in the rocks. Eventually these artifacts found their place on a shelf in the closet near our front porch. I never gave much thought to the "two stones" that were placed on the shelf in the closet surrounded by hats, mitts, and other rural family necessities. The two stones and the meanings they held for me changed as I grew older. Many years later, when I came home from university for weekend visits, I often had vibrant discussions with my dad about the stories of the past and the history of First Nations Peoples. I was always excited to share the stories I was learning about myself. He always asked good questions in our conversations.

A memory from a weekend trip to my home stays with me. I was getting ready to leave to go back to the city, back to university. I put my jacket on and opened the closet door, and on the shelf were the two stone tools. They were moved to a place that was clearly visible. My dad reached up and gathered the two stones in his hands and told me to take care of them. Like many of our conversations, his message was simple and powerful. Throughout my travels the only possessions I have retained from the memory of the farm are my two stones. I realize how important these two stones are. They represent my worlds, the multiplicity within these worlds, and the shared paths that often intersect in my developing stories of who I am and am becoming.

My dad was not an educated man in the sense of being schooled. He finished school in grade six to start work on the farm. This is the way it was, he told me: there was not an option or an alternate path to take. Despite his lack of formal schooling, he had wisdom that books cannot teach. Most importantly, he understood his kids and the importance of nurturing their individual spirits. As I get older I understand, that my dad knew the power of the two stones and what they would eventually mean to me. I return to Bateson's words yet again: "Concentration is too precious to belittle. I know that if I look very narrowly and hard at anything I am likely to see something new—like the life between the grass stems that only become visible after moments of staring. Softening that concentration is also important—I've heard that the best way to catch the movement of falling stars is at the edge of vision" (1994, p. 104). Perhaps it is the edge of vision that I long for and the ability to see something new by attending carefully in one moment but also letting myself soften my concentration so that I can find new meanings and possibilities in other ways.

Shifting Forward: Learning to Attend as a Narrative Inquirer
To coffee shops, malls, a bus stop, on the reserve, and to different cities I traveled during my first research project, "A Narrative Inquiry into the Experiences of Early School Leavers." I recall the moments of being asked to join a group of researchers on this study. I was asked first whether I thought I could help find some young people to share their experiences of leaving school before graduation. I could do that.

I vividly recall moments before and after joining the research team. Among these memories are moments of not knowing my place within a university. I remember walking the halls at the university and sitting in the cafeteria, waiting for night classes to begin each week. I was clearly an outsider within this place. I took one class at a time, arriving after teaching at a local high school during the day. I remember trying to figure out what I should be studying and what a research question should look like.

There was nothing more that I wanted than a master's degree ... it was a plan I had scrawled down in books for years. I wanted to keep studying both personally and for my community. Earning a master's degree was something I thought I could do that would help me in my understanding of education. Perhaps what I learned would help me in my job as a teacher or help me move to an area of interest like counseling, something similar to the work a mentor did with me long ago in schools. For my master's program I picked a subject area where I thought I could draw on my experiences working with youth in schools and communities. I did not know that in this place of study experiences counted as less and that most of my classes revolved around statistical analysis and theoretical knowledge that was far removed from what I had come to know through working with youth and families.

The invitation to study with a research team provided me a place of connection ... it was a place where I put my backpack down each week and had a cup of tea as I moved from high school teacher to graduate student. The research team consisted of a group of scholars who came from different fields of study and experiences, psychologists, teachers, artists, nurses, policy makers, and poets, in no particular order. The team welcomed me in with a kindness that I had not previously experienced within my studies. I felt at ease in this place almost immediately.

I sat with one particular researcher, Claire, in the early moments of joining the team, and she went through paperwork with me, showing me what ethics information letters and consent forms looked like and helping me understand what we might ask of the youth during our research conversations. The language and how she spoke of research was different from what I had heard. I paid close attention to how she was sharing her knowledge with me. During our early conversations she shared her stories of teaching both in schools and universities. It is through these stories that she shared her interests in language and what it can mean to be a parent in a place of school.

Claire was kind and gentle in her sharing and teaching ... as she took the time with me over many cups of tea in local cafés to explain to me what the research could possibly look like. She did not have one answer or prescribed formula. She helped me think about the research by asking me questions about my stories of school and of how I knew of students who had left school. I recall these conversations as she helped me to think about research in a different way and how we would be listening to the stories the youth would share. I did not know at this time that I was in the midst of something different and that I had found a place and a way of thinking about lives that would resonate so deeply within me. I had found a place and been welcomed into a place where I could think about experiences and start the hard work of inquiring into some of my experiences as I came alongside the youth to learn more of theirs.

Janice

Early Beginnings: Attending to Experience
As I linger with thoughts of my becoming as a narrative inquirer along side children and youth, I am filled with memories of my experiences as a child, shaped by deep respect for the animals, land, plants, water, and people with whom my family daily interacted and upon whom we depended. I am called, for example, toward memories of my experiences with animals such as Mitsy, a horse with whom my siblings and I spent many hours while we were growing up. Especially during the summer months my siblings and I and a small herd of cousins who left their more urban home places to spend time "in the country" filled our days with Mitsy. We rode bareback, but first we needed to attach a rope to Mitsy's halter, and Mitsy was in charge of whether or not we would ride her. If she did not want to be ridden, it did not matter how many children ran up and down the creek hills behind Mitsy, trying to slip a rope through her halter. And even when we did ride, Mitsy stayed in charge: sometimes she lowered her head into the creek so we suddenly slipped forward and off her; sometimes she walked so close to trees that our knees banged; sometimes she ran so fast that we became afraid and jumped off; sometimes she merely laid down and did not move.

I am called, too, toward memories of the Simonette River, which sustained the cattle and calves as they grazed at its shores. In my hands I often still hold the stone, which my dad pressed into my hands when I was very young. He encouraged me to keep the stone because of its heart shape, a stone too special to skip across the water but one to keep as a reminder of that time and that place. I continue to treasure this stone as a reminder of this beautiful river and its place in my life.

I am called, too, toward memories of ways in which my home was filled with diverse people. I remember, for example, Carla and Velma, two sisters of Métis ancestry who lived with my family when I was very young. From late fall until spring their parents and younger siblings moved further into the bush while their dad worked at a sawmill. Carla and Velma's parents wanted them to continue in school. Similar, too, were the dreams of Darcy's parents, a teenager from a far-away city who became part of my family when I was in elementary school. Darcy's mother grew up along the Simonette River, and as she raised her sons in the city and they became teenagers, she grew concerned about aspects of their lives that had not been part of her early life.

These remembered fragments of my life before and outside of school show something of the ways in which I spent my days interacting with places, animals, and people who surrounded me; they were my teachers, slowly, gently nurturing the "spirit within me" (Sewall, 1996, p. 2), a spirit threaded by "stories to live by" (Connelly & Clandinin, 1999, p. 4), of commitment, humility, gratitude, relationship, and responsibility. By the time I became a teenager, I saw ways in which the pulp and paper mill was reshaping the Simonette River. As the birth of grotesquely deformed calves increased, my parents and others lobbied the government to stop the actions of a pulp and paper company that dumped its chemical-laden sludge into the Simonette River. I gradually learned that at times living by stories of commitment and responsibility also meant living by stories of resistance (Lindemann Nelson, 1995).

As I entered into school, I learned that what I knew first, these stories I lived by, were seen as irrelevant in school. Not until grade five, and never afterward, did a teacher ask me what I knew of or thought about concepts in the text and workbooks we studied. It was also only this grade five teacher with whom we ventured outside the building; sometimes we read outside, and often she involved us in interactions with the physical environment surrounding the school as a way to explore concepts. By the time I reached junior high I was well aware that my family and many of the people with whom I interacted daily were seen as less than. My strongest memory of being seen in this way happened in grade three, when a principal told me I would not go to heaven because my parents were not "good people." This principal often told me he thought it was wrong for my parents to allow so many people, especially if they drank alcohol, to live in or to be around my home. In these ways, and over time, I became aware that my experiences in school were mostly intended to change me from who I was and was becoming or to save me from what I knew first.

These experiences, although long past, have always filled me with dis/ease. What I remember most about these experiences are the feelings of tension that took shape in the meeting of my home and community experiences, and my experiences in school. My parents held high expectations for my siblings and me, expectations that included being respectful of and responsible to and with other people and living beings; they also held high expectations for us in relation to schooling, expectations that included that we should each complete high school in addition to some form of postsecondary education. Yet as I continued in school, I often felt caught between conflicting stories (Clandinin & Connelly, 1995, p. 157).

Shifting Forward: Coming Alongside Children and Youth

As I linger with thoughts of becoming a narrative inquirer alongside children and youth, I am filled with memories of recent conversations with my daughter. From a very young age she has loved animals and being outside, and even today, as an almost teenager, she wants to hear stories of my experiences as a child who grew up learning deep respect for the animals, land, plants, water, and people with whom my family interacted daily and depended upon.

My daughter knows stories of the Simonette River; of the stone my father gave me. My daughter knows, too, of the spruce tree place where my family and friends spent much time together—spring, summer, fall, and winter—often gathered around a campfire, sharing stories, laughing, and teasing, all the while filled with sheer gratitude for the possibility of knowing, of dwelling in, and of staying committed to that place.

As a young child I did not know the enduring ways these interactions would shape me. However, as I more presently share stories of these experiences with my daughter, I often find myself understanding more of what Leslie Marmon Silko described as she wrote of the indelible relationship between place and identity.

My daughter also knows of people, people such as Linda who, with her family, over many years worked alongside my parents and family. My daughter knows, too, that my interactions with Mitsy, the Simonette River, the spruce tree place, and people like Linda and her family and others taught me to live by stories of commitment, humility, gratitude, relationship, and responsibility; she also knows that these and other interactions in my life as a child and youth were not always smooth, happily-ever-after experiences and that woven with these knowings are other knowings, knowings of painful family differences, tensions, and secrets; of racial and religious diversity, hatred, and shunning; and of struggles to afford clothing, electricity, and food.

As I shift back to thoughts of my daughter, lingering in relation with some of her experiences in school, I am now filled with wonders of the "intergenerational narrative reverberations" (Young, 2005) that shape my daughter's and my interactions and, in turn, may shape her interactions in school. For some time Mary Young has supported me to begin to attend to the "intergenerational narrative reverberations" that shape unfolding lives. As she was in the midst of her doctoral research, Mary often spoke of and later wrote about ways in which "intergenerational reverberations" are narratively woven into the lives of family members across generations. "We all carry in our bodies, in our memories, in our souls" (Young, 2005, p. 162), the stories lived by our ancestors. In this way these stories shape "intergenerational narrative reverberations" (p. 162) in the lives composed in successive generations.

Shifting Forward: Learning to Attend as a Narrative Inquirer

> Just before I left for the university Karen and I talked with Elizabeth and Sheena. . . . Then I talked with them about how we may not be able to use their "real" names in the written work. I think Elizabeth said it all when she asked, "Why would you want to use our 'real' stories when you can't use our 'real' names?" (Huber, 1992, p. 47)

During my master's research alongside Karen, a year three-four teacher, and the children in the classroom, there was a moment of tension as I began to work with the field texts of the two child participants, Elizabeth and Sheena, with whom I engaged in more intensive inquiry. The field texts included copies of Elizabeth and Sheena's classroom work, such as their artwork, inquiry projects, and math logbooks, as well as transcripts of our conversations and my field notes of participation. When we talked with Elizabeth and Sheena about their selection of pseudonyms, the concept of pseudonyms did not make sense to Elizabeth. She saw her name and who she was as inseparable; it did not make sense to use her stories of experience without using her name, as she was named by her parents at birth, the name around which she had composed her life, first in an African country and more recently in Canada as the oldest child in her family, as a sister of three younger siblings, and as an eight-year-old girl who held dreams of becoming a doctor.

A few days later, as Elizabeth and I were in the midst of talking about one of her writing projects, she said she "just felt hurt that you wouldn't use my real name" (Huber, 1992, p. 88) in my thesis. My relationship with Elizabeth and her family helped awaken me to ways in which children are situated differently by institutional research ethics boards and by the relational ethics of narrative inquiry. Elizabeth's expressions of the importance of respecting her and the ways she wanted to be named in the research text shaped my becoming as a narrative inquirer alongside children and youth.

Vera

Early Beginnings: Attending to Experience
I remember that early fall day in my advanced social studies class in grade twelve, the beginning of the year in which I left school. I remember

the boredom that had accumulated over the years, the arguments with teachers over what mattered most, and also my sense of having to learn a curriculum that was irrelevant to my life and that did not reflect the life experiences of me or those I considered friends. One of a series of social studies exams was happening that day. The exam focused on the curriculum we had studied in the weeks prior, and I remember reading the questions and being left with two options: I could leave and hand in the blank test sheet or I could engage in thinking about the things I felt were important to think about in the social and political climate of Germany and, perhaps, globally at the time. It was a chance for me to take ownership over the curriculum and the instructions, a resistance to a curriculum and instructions I felt were a continuous breeding ground of apathy and disengaged citizens. I choose in that moment to engage in a process of writing back and writing myself into the curriculum. Over the two hours I wrote a set of poems in which I reflected on the experiences of women, of feminist thinkers, of historical practices of witch hunting that, although attributed to particular times, still played out in other ways in contemporary society. I remember trying hard to understand the place of creativity, openness, and spontaneity in developing movements of resistance to increasingly conservative and neoliberal discourses that marginalized girls, difference, and creativity.

I remember the dread of waiting for a response when I submitted the pages. It wasn't long when we discussed the questions within the class context, and I recall how I was asked to provide verbal responses to the questions during that time. After the first two or three responses, the social studies teacher looked at me and asked, "Why didn't you respond to the questions on the test?" I still can hear the puzzlement in his voice, and I remember the feeling of vulnerability in my gut. He didn't get what I had done and what I, in some convoluted way, was asking of him. When he handed the test back I received a blank page with a statement that he will keep the poem and that I had clearly failed the test. I was too troubled in that moment to ask for the poem back or to engage in a meaningful conversation with him about the things that mattered to me. This too was mixed with a strong sense that it didn't really matter. (To this date, however, I wonder why he chose to keep the poem or why he didn't return it to me.) How had his experience with me at this time shaped his stories to live by, I wonder.

This lingering sense that my life and the questions and wonders that were part of my life didn't matter in school continued to stay with me. The wonders written within the poems were wonders that lived large in my life, that were informed by my family stories of war, of loss, of resistance, and also of complacency. They too were generational questions that I heard at the time from my friends and continue to hear, because in large parts they have not been answered, contemplated, or discussed. Returning to the narrative inquiries alongside children, youth, and families in my current life opens for me a metaphorical possibility to trace the lines. The tracing of marks and imprints, yes, I too know from the etymology of the word lines, there is a connection to linen. This knowing carries me backward to my mother's, grandmother's, and great-grandmother's stories, who used linen to cover the inner parts of a garment. I still carry their linen and wonder whether their marks and imprints indeed provide the lines that link me not only with the past but also with the forward-looking stories of my life. The poem written in a classroom space long ago opens up new wonders for me, and perhaps it more so holds the potential to open up spaces of conversations that continue to matter deeply in my own life now as a mother. As I came to learn much later, through the work of Sweetland, Huber, and Keats Whelan (2004), I saw that conversational spaces are spaces that could live "within, between, and among us" and that tensions were part of these spaces.

Although my schooling had created a strong sense of opposition, defiance, and perhaps, at times, resistance, it was my out-of-school experiences that formed my beginnings of becoming a narrative inquirer. The Sunday lunch conversations were clearly important in my life and a place and time that shaped me in profound ways, yet it was the silences that drew me to my work as a narrative inquirer. I only came to name the unspoken and, in very rare moments, whispered conversations, silences after reading Anna Neumann's work. Like Neumann (1998), "my life has been formed in the aftermath of a horrifying human event" (p. 426).

Being the daughter of the youngest of six siblings in my mother's family, I become one of the younger cousins of a large extended family. My mother's five brothers all were teenagers during World War II, as was the husband of one of her sisters. All of them were conscripted to the war very late and experienced prison camps for several years after the war. I know very little about this time from my uncles; I came to know some through my grandmother, mother. and aunt's stories of worry. My uncles did not talk: they did not talk about the war, their teenage years, their bodies that were missing arms and legs, or their escapes from prison camps. Although discussions about the consequences of the war and how Germany's postwar political environment shaped our lunchtime conversations, their experiences were not part of the discussions. We did not ask about their experiences directly, and any attempt to ask was responded to with silence and silencing gestures. I remember Neumann's (1998) words "I think we sometimes live our lives, including our intellectual lives, absenting knowledge of genocide, absenting knowledge of human's capacities for unspeakable horror and destruction. The world with a Holocaust looks different" (p. 427). I often stop and think about what this means, about how it calls me to not only look backward but also to stay wakeful to the ways in which my knowing is shaped and what perhaps we can never know of another's experience.

It was the same strange silence that echoed in the experiences of the women who were part of our Sunday lunches during my childhood. My aunt worked with the women who came to our home. My mother and aunt talked about the trauma, grief, and deep loneliness that marked many of the young women's experiences as refugees from Eastern European countries and Vietnam in the mid-seventies and eighties in Germany. It was in these moments that I wondered whether my uncles' experiences, too, were marked by trauma, grief, and loneliness.

I recall as a teenager being struck by this unexplainable void of knowing the details and experiences of my family's history and the experiences of the women who came to join us often. The silences were profound, as was my fear of touching the wooden leg and arm of my uncle, fear that it would call forth memories and stories I was not supposed to hear. My grandmother, mother, and aunt often talked about how grateful they had been that their brothers had survived the war and their subsequent imprisonment. I wondered many times what surviving meant for them. And as Neumann's (1997, 1998) experiences are situated in relation to the experiences of the Holocaust, there is a resonance that helps me better understand too: "For those who claim to try to understand what it was like, but without having experienced, in themselves, the horror of what it must have meant to survive, that world is beyond conception, beyond utterance, beyond comprehension. It cannot be recalled. It cannot be portrayed in the words of today, for to do so would require the re-creation of the camp itself" (pp. 430–431, 1998). I fall silent as I read her words and wonder how words will carry me in understanding experience, yet I cannot stop to ask, to push, to want to hear more, to find words.

The year my first uncle died was 1991, and I can still recall the soberness at the graveside. My sense was that the memories of his life were cut short by the war and postwar period, as it was not a time one talked about. Although people talked with admiration that he had managed to become someone despite his disabilities, the cause of this disability was never discussed. Silences were present, reinforced, and reiterated in different ways. I left that same year to Canada, filled with a sadness of missing an important part of my own family history. And all I know is that "I can know only in terms of who I am and what I know" (Neumann, 1998, p. 457), and a deep sense of loneliness engulfs me. Neumann reminds me that "our abilities to grasp each other's knowing are bounded" (p. 438). It is the silences that carry a story, and as I dwell and revisit these silences, I come closer to perhaps what it means to survive.

Shifting Forward: Coming Alongside as a Narrative Inquirer

It was not so much the metaphorical and real Sunday table conversations that shaped my life as a narrative inquirer very early but rather the silences. It is now, more than twenty years later, that my uncles have slowly begun to talk, often shortly before their death and in response to a rise in right-wing movements and their wish that we would remember their experiences, experiences that had deeply shaped their personal and political lives. Yet they all had little time left to talk, and their experiences remain fragmented for me. And as I mourn their deaths, I learned through others to not only see that our experiences are bound by place and distance but that they live in places (Caine, 2010).

My early childhood experiences not only shaped some of my early understandings of narrative inquiry but also called me to return to work alongside children and youth much later. My first research as a narrative inquirer was alongside young Aboriginal women living with HIV in Canada, a puzzle that was called forth during my work as a registered nurse in remote northern communities. At that time communities often feared and stigmatized people living with HIV to the extent that people living with HIV were asked to leave their communities or asked to never return home. I wondered in particular about the experiences of women living with HIV and the impact of familial and social stories that shaped their lives in deep ways. As I listened to the women's stories, I began to understand just how much their lives were shaped by their early childhood experiences; these early experiences that, although situated in a different social, political, and cultural context, called me to return home. I not only return to the geographic places of my childhood; I too return to the memories of my experiences of my childhood and youth—the silences and gaps of my own knowing become more visible to me. My early childhood stories mattered. I learned, as I returned, how others had told and continued to tell and retell these early experiences and how their lives were impacted by my childhood and youth and who I had been at that time.

As I traveled between Canada and Germany during the time of my first research, I began to ask different questions and became more awake to the importance of living alongside participants and of meeting metaphorically or in actuality the people who had shaped their early stories, the places in which their early experiences were situated and the social contexts. I recall the long drives to reserves, and places their mothers, grandmothers, and other family members were born, lived, or buried became most important. As I lived alongside Tammy, Deanna, Debbie, and Debra, they helped me see, as Debra once said, "You should have come much earlier into my life." As I move into new inquiry spaces, I remember Debra's words and understand them as her request to work alongside children and youth, as an invitation to puzzle over my own early childhood experiences, and as an obligation to find ways to understand her early experiences better.

What We Know About the Why of Autobiographical Narrative Inquiry

In this section we look across these fragments from our autobiographical inquiries, not so much for the resonances across the stories of experience but with an intention to highlight the importance of the ongoing work of continuing to engage in autobiographical narrative inquiry as we plan each new narrative inquiry, as we live alongside participants through each study, and then as we move forward into new inquiries. Following from our Deweyan-inspired conception of experience, we know that we embody stories lived in one time, place, and set of relationships into further experiences. What the body remembers comes along with us, and we are more or less awake to the ways those stories shape subsequent stories we live.

In this way we become more awake to the complexities of who we are as well as to the personal, practical, and social justifications of any particular narrative inquiry. We also become more attentive to how we imagine ourselves in relation to particular research puzzles.

1. *Openness to thinking with stories through slowing down to attend closely.* As Jean engages in her autobiographical narrative inquiry, she draws forward plotlines that shaped and continue to shape her stories to live by. Her narrative inquiries call forth the importance of slowing down and thinking with stories, something learned alongside her father. As Sean awakens to his stories to live by, he begins to notice the importance of thinking with stories, of recollecting the stories and inquiring into, with, and through them and becoming otherwise. This re-turning back on storied experience is part of narrative inquiry, which is both methodology and phenomenon. It is the study of experience when experience is understood narratively. And part of the importance of autobiographical narrative inquiry woven throughout an inquiry and with such importance at the outset in narrative beginnings is that so much more than methodological reflexivity is at work. We learn to work toward thinking with stories as we slow down to attend closely.

2. *Openness to being disrupted, to moving out of places of comfort.* Jean's sense of attending to others with patience and wonder becomes evident as she justifies her narrative inquiries in studies such as those

with youth who left school early. Watching her father, she knows that schooling is not the same as education, and we see her willingness to see education within broader life understandings and the ways this shapes how she understands children and youth's experiences. Yet we also sense how who she is, is interrupted, and disrupted as she awakens to the experiences of others, like the junior high student on the urban streets and to the children in the urban classroom in Toronto. It is through the work of autobiographical narrative inquiry that we begin to understand that in narrative inquiry we need to live with openness to being disrupted, to seeing the world as otherwise.

3. *Openness to questioning stories of school and other social and cultural narratives.* In the narrative accounts of Vera and Janice we see that they are awake to questioning institutional narratives. They both tell stories of knowing as children and youth that stories of schools—institutional narratives—are not always educative. They also tell stories of being disrupted and of interruptions as what they know and who they are becoming are shifted. We see this too as important to come to understand as part of autobiographical narrative inquiry—that is, this wide awakeness to the social and cultural narratives, to knowing that everything could always be otherwise. Without a sense of wonder and imagination we are not awake to the possibilities of otherwise, to what might be, to what could be. Before we can come alongside an other, this open wondering about the possibility of otherwise needs to be available to us.

4. *Openness to the multiplicity of lives.* In Sean's narrative account we see his father's patient teachings with Sean, awakening him to his multiple home-places, signified by the two stones. Sean's awakenings to the multiplicity in his life are part of how he is able to come alongside, to see each person in their uniqueness, shaped over time and place and relationships. Without this openness to multiplicity of stories, of awareness of the dangers of single stories, we cannot come alongside with the openness that is required of narrative inquirers about their own experiences and the experiences of others. It is beginning with autobiographical narrative inquiries that open each of us to begin to question the single stories around which so many institutional, social, cultural, and familial narratives are composed.

5. *Openness to resisting, to going where lives take us.* We see Janice's willingness to attend closely but also to resist, evident as she struggles to see Elizabeth as who she is, as a person composing a life. As Elizabeth questions why her "real name" cannot be included in the research text, we see how Janice is particularly aware of the need to resist, to question, to change institutional narratives.

6. *Knowing silences in lives, knowing silences as stories.* It is perhaps through autobiographical narrative inquiry that we first begin to become

aware of the silences in our lives. We see how silences work to shape Vera's stories as she lives within silences marked by the events of a world war on her family and on what is said and what remains not said. We see that sometimes the silences are the stories, that they can be stories lived in the silent spaces between.

7. *Knowing that writing is a process of inquiry.* None of us have remained the same, but we can see the silences, patterns, continuities, discontinuities, ruptures, and disjunctures as we write and inquire into the stories of our experiences, both in and out of inquiries. As we write our stories, we see the process of writing as in itself a process of inquiry (Richardson, 2000). It is the writing of our stories of experience and the inquiry into those written stories that help us frame research puzzles and justify our work.

8. *The ongoingness of inquiries.* How we each live alongside children and youth shapes how we enter the next study and reshapes how we tell stories of who we are and are becoming. Clandinin, Lessard and Caine (2013) made explicit what they called recursive reverberations as they described the ongoingness of studies:

> Now as we are in the midst of working with the youth and their families, we stand, look backward and inward, and see that each project recursively elaborates the ones that came before. The reverberations of previously lived stories alongside participants from earlier studies come into our current life living, telling and retelling. The stories of the youth who left school early shaped our stories at the time but also continue to shape our stories as we live our retold stories into the future. Our retold stories shape our reliving as we imagine and live out our current study. The stories of the youth who left school early mingle with ours and allow us to newly imagine this "becoming" conversational space in light of the echoes left behind by those who came before. The reverberations stretch across, and through, lives. (p. 23)

Without autobiographical narrative inquiry that attends to these reverberations across projects, we are not awake to the ongoingness of inquiries, to how who we are in one inquiry shapes who we are in subsequent inquiries.

9. *Autobiographical narrative inquiries keep us awake to how we are shaped by communities of inquiry.* We also know, as we engage in these studies over time, how our work alongside each other has shaped how we each enter into new studies. As we compose our lives as narrative inquirers, we live within multiple interwoven inquiry communities. Although this may not be evident in the individual narrative beginnings we authored, it becomes evident in the stories we share in this book. Being attentive to how we are shaped and shape allows us to make visible our communities of inquiry as we attend to several projects in future chapters.

In this book we highlight the ontological commitments, the mutual shaping of lives that happens when we understand experience as always in the making. We pull forward these nine key points about how we see autobiographical narrative inquiries as centrally important in work with children and youth. We attend briefly to the responsibilities we have that seem particularly profound in narrative inquiries with children and youth. In Chapters 12 and 14 we revisit these questions.

CHAPTER 4

Living Within the Layered Landscapes of Narrative Inquiry

In Chapter 3 we highlighted the ongoing importance of autobiographical narrative inquiry. In this chapter we turn our attention to what we see as the landscapes, the places within which we, as inquirers, are situated, the places within which participants are situated, as well as the places within which narrative inquiries are lived. Marmon Silko (1996) helps us understand that we need to take up the word landscape carefully:

> A portion of territory the eye can comprehend in a single view does not correctly describe the relationship between human being and his or her surroundings. This assumes the viewer is somehow outside or separate from the territory she or he surveys. Viewers are as much a part of the landscape as the boulders they stand on. (p. 27)

Silko's work with the concept of landscape draws attention to how we live within landscapes, not on landscapes. We are, she writes, "part of the landscape."

Over several years we worked to develop a narrative conceptualization of landscape in the sense that these landscapes we live within are shaped by plotlines (Clandinin, 2006), marked by intergenerational reverberations, and shaped by the particularities of place. Following Dewey, this understanding of landscapes reflects an understanding of patterns of change and development that are visible in plotlines; in this way continuity and interactions are central. The landscape, composed of cultural, institutional, linguistic, political, economic, and social plotlines, is shaped by and shapes experience over time; lives and landscapes are interwoven (Clandinin, 2010).

We try to capture the complexity of this narrative understanding of landscape by drawing attention to temporality, to distinct places, to the interwoven narratives that shape these landscapes we live within. We do this by drawing on a metaphor of layers, suggesting a kind of layering as the stratified layers of landforms. Stratified layers of different materials, solid stone, aggregate stone, soil, and so on are built up over time. The layers can be distinctly different or can be more or less blurred as the different materials mix together. It makes a difference how different materials form into layers, how different materials can be ordered. The ways events form layers are unique; layers can be disrupted by erosions, violent eruptions such as those in volcanic eruptions, or smashed apart by external events such as earthquakes. Thinking of landscapes as layered in this way draws attention to the temporality, the unique structures of layering, and of the possibility of changing the landscape layers through gradual processes or abrupt violent processes.

Drawing on this metaphor of layered landscapes highlights how difficult it is to understand, to make sense of what is visible, what is hidden, how and why the layers are shaped, and the possibilities for time to work in different ways on the landscapes. The complexity of such layered landscapes is difficult to grasp. And it is even more difficult as we find ourselves entering into these landscapes more or less awake to who we are, how we story ourselves, and how we are storied as narrative inquirers. In trying to understand experience, we situate ourselves in relation to the landscape and its multiple plotlines through writing narrative beginnings that make visible the plotlines in our lives and that begin to hint at the landscapes within which we have lived, continue to live, and are entering into as narrative inquirers. Our narrative beginnings reflect not only our autobiographical traces in relation to the phenomena under study but also how we are positioned in relation to the landscape.

As we showed in Chapter 3, Sean's early experiences were lived within a multiplicity of familial, cultural, and social narratives that he shows in the "two stones" stories and that allow him to understand the multiplicity of landscapes and the layers of each landscape as he moved within and across landscapes. Attending to these multiple layered landscapes requires an ongoing wakefulness. Sean's ways of telling who he is and who he is becoming draw us back to thinking about our childhood experiences and makes evident the multiplicity of tellings and retellings that might be possible. Thinking with Sean's narrative beginnings, we begin to see the landscapes in which his life is embedded, and we also become awake to the multiplicity of possible experiences. This requires detailed attention to what is happening and what might happen.

As we noted in earlier chapters, who we are and are becoming as narrative inquirers is always a process that draws experiences forward from previous experiences and shapes what we experience in the future. For example, when Vera, Jean, and Sean worked with others to imagine a new study with youth and families of Aboriginal heritage, we knew we were shaped by earlier experiences in our lives, including what we had come to know in our study alongside youth who left school early.

Beginning to participate in a new study required us to return again to inquiring into our narrative beginnings. As we began to name the phenomena of the new study, a study alongside Aboriginal youth and families, we purposefully involved community members, Elders, and service providers who were part of the ongoing life experiences of Aboriginal youth and their families. As the study unfolded, Sean came to know Elders and guides on different landscapes; for Sean this is a reminder of how he received his name Muskwacicy.

MUSKWACICY

As I travel back in memory I think closely with a name I have come to know over time. "Your name is Muskwacicy … a bear's paw," he said to me. It is a moment I recall vividly, a moment when this name was first given to me. It is a name that has meaning within it. It is a name I hold closely as I continue to understand what it might mean as I compose my life in the present. This name, Muskwacicy, was gifted to me in ceremony by a Cree Elder and a friend. I wonder, as I travel back to these memories of being gifted with this name, what this name might mean and how important it is to seek to find meanings within a name as I story myself into the future. What does it mean to be gifted with a name through the beat of a drum and through songs and stories alongside Elders and friends I have come to know?

Through long walks and visits alongside Elder Bob Cardinal, I continue to think of the meaning within this name. It is through visits to his home place and through stories he shares of his family that I begin to understand the significance of a name. It is through this name, Muskwacicy, that he continues to teach me and to take care of me in a different way. I travel back to early memories as I think of my name, its meaning. I continue to wonder why he chose it for me. There is knowledge from the teaching and learning alongside an Elder that sustains me in the present. It is relational knowledge connected to a place of teaching that matters. There is a certain wisdom in not knowing for now; a wisdom of wondering and learning from the experiences of not having it figured out or clearly defined that stays with me in the present and shapes me into the future.

Sean's early experiences within a rural context helped him see not only the importance and significance of this rural home but also his sense of community in who he is and is becoming. However, there is also a sense of the importance of attending to the layered landscapes and plot lines that shape different landscapes. Elder Bob Cardinal, through his gift of the name Muskwacicy, opened up new spaces that allowed him and Sean to travel together as Sean engaged with the Aboriginal youth who became part of his doctoral research (Lessard, 2013).

As I close my eyes and think with the name, Muskwacicy, and the stories of being alongside Elder Bob, I have an image in my mind of a bear.

The bear is moving slowly, carefully after a long seasonal rest. The bear, muskwa, was asleep, but in the reawakening time that is spring, he slowly wakes. The bear moves out from his resting place deep within the surrounding trees. He takes steps that are, at first, slow and measured. His bear paw markings leave imprints on the land, the mud and grass sink with each step, the tree branches snap, and memories of this place start to become clearer; his memories remind him that he has traveled here before. The smells, the sights, and the land are increasingly visible with each slow step. After such a long seasonal rest, the bear looks in all directions, moving slowly, surveying the landscape. It has been a long winter; snow still covers the ground and trees in some areas. In other areas trickles of water are heard. One step at a time, movement—the hunger draws muskwa out. The bear has been here before. This he knows deep within himself.

It is important for Sean to share these experiences as a way to show how he was shaped by and lives within a layered landscape. Attending closely to who he is and is becoming allows Sean to also make visible the relational aspect of coming alongside both Elders and communities in narrative inquiries. Sean wrote about and then inquired into his experiences of being named as a way to help him think about his negotiation of relationships as part of various research teams and what these experiences might mean going forward.

As Sean inquires into his experiences alongside Elder Bob Cardinal, he shows that his experience of coming alongside was a slow process, one composed over time. It was not a fast process of being given a name. The commitment to return often and to honor multiple ways of being, the conversations necessary to engage in this way alongside Elders, such as Elder Bob Cardinal, and community are visible between the written lines. Sean's relationship with Elder Bob Cardinal emerged and grew over more than eight years. Elder Bob Cardinal's teachings, shared with Sean, create spaces that allow Sean to pause and slowly begin to understand what Elder Bob Cardinal might be sharing with him. In his field notes Sean writes,

The answers I desire around the meanings of Muskwacicy are not readily available. Elder Bob responds to my queries around the meanings with the words, "That is what you will have to find for yourself." His response, as open as it is, leaves space for understanding and to slowly move in my understanding and the way I am thinking about the gift of a name. This experience and my stories of it continue to provoke imagery within me, imagery that sustains me, as the teachings and the experiences shared alongside one another in a naming ceremony are especially important to me. They are important as I find myself in a new city and negotiating a new landscape as a teacher educator and researcher.

What Elder Bob Cardinal offers Sean is a way forward as he lives within multiple landscapes. Sean is reminded that what he has come to know in one place does not necessarily have the same meaning in a new place. Sean returns often to his experiences through which he was gifted the name Muskwacicy by Elder Bob Cardinal, a Cree Elder from Alberta. For Sean it was important to know that

> *what I can be sure of and call on in one place to try and understand and negotiate a landscape cannot be met with the same certainty or conviction in a new place. So now I am met with varying degrees of uncertainty in a new landscape ... there is haziness in this negotiation of a new place.*

As Sean inquired into his storied experiences, he was reminded that Elder Bob Cardinal frequently reminded him that the ways we attend are crucial and that paying attention is significant. Most importantly, Sean now understands, is that paying attention requires him to slow down. As the bear emerges from hibernation, he moves slowly. He slows down, and Sean is reminded of possible meanings of his name Muskwacicy. Although at times the bear may move quickly, it is also important to move slowly into new landscapes.

MOVING SLOWLY INTO UNFAMILIAR LAYERED LANDSCAPES

While the research study alongside Aboriginal youth and families was coming to an end marked by the final negotiation of research texts, Sean began a new position as an assistant professor at the University of Regina. As Sean returned to Saskatchewan, the Canadian province where he grew up, he realized that the name Muskwacicy may have different meanings for him as he re-entered the layered landscapes with which he was once familiar. This change geographically was significant both in his ongoing relationships with the youth he had come to know in the study but also in his life alongside Elder Bob Cardinal and other Elders he had come to know while in Edmonton.

> *I find myself in Treaty 4 territory in the present as a university professor. I am in a place with Nakoda, Dakota, and Cree people. I find myself in a landscape that is markedly different. I think of the rolling hills in the valley and the connected lakes that flow into one another. The grasses grow differently in this place as I drive straight for some distance and suddenly the road shifts. The landscape weaves and dives and moves slowly ... jutting ... and finally I find myself in the valley ... the dotted trees with the yellow, red, and orange of possibility. The connected water ways tell a story ... the hills high up above comfort the water around them ... there are stories that live on this landscape ... within those hills and within the markings. I am both visible and invisible in these places. My name means different things here. My name, Muskwacicy, may not have the same meaning in this place. It is through the inquiry and the coming to know that I become*

awake to the shifting meanings. What my name means in each place is significant.

As Sean engages in his inquiry, his stories remind us to not assume that who we are in one landscape will stay the same on another landscape. He reminds us, too, to move slowly. For example, as Sean moved, he found himself in the midst of renegotiating his relationships with research participants. From the physical distance of another place, in another layered landscape, Sean writes about his experiences of being away from Lane, a research participant, in a piece he entitled, "Are You Alright, Little Brother?"

> *Research relationships can shift dramatically, and what seems a straight line becomes filled with movements that were not anticipated or planned, a certain blurriness that requires action mostly filled my thoughts. Lane had been going through difficult moments in his twelve-year-old life. He had been crying out for help, reaching out in different ways to express emotions that were deep seated, somewhere in those places between hurt, anger, and confusion. He was like the winter weather ... blanketing the urban landscape with fury. Snow has the ability to play tricks with the eyes, impede the vision, but mostly it demands change and a response to how I interact with the world around me. I moved a little slower, paid more attention, and planned my actions with more detail on days when the wind met the snow in those faraway places above me. But all I seemed to be thinking about was ... are you alright, little brother?*
>
> *The prospects and thoughts of Lane living between places—"couch surfing," some even say sleeping outside—hurt me in ways I had not expected, in places that move beyond the objective realities. The silence and the inability to contact Lane for a few weeks, despite my best efforts, left me with a feeling of hopelessness in this new landscape. All I had at my fingertips was a cryptic message that asked, "Can we meet?" ... and then silence. I was unable to connect. I had no way to help him, despite my best efforts to put these troubles on my shoulders. I was walking through the snow ... a slow walk on the city streets of Regina, far from Edmonton, with these thoughts weighing me down in different ways. The heavy snow and wind pulling at me was just fine because all I could think was ... are you alright, little brother?*
>
> *Sometimes I don't know in my heart, in those inner places, when a relationship has changed. It just changes over time, and I can only see the change in those moments that push at the edges. It preoccupied my thoughts when I was unable to find Lane, contact him, or see him. It became more difficult for me when I started to think of how hard it must have been for him to negotiate the life he was trying to make, mostly in solitude. As I imagined this during my morning walk, the winds picked up, the snow started to lose its gentle and playful touch and began to swirl, making it impossible for the birds to even sing their morning songs. The weather was heavy out there this morning when I heard about him going missing. He finally came back to the school, but only to stay long enough to cry out for help in a different way. All I could think about as I walked*

and as my movement became more difficult and my path was blanketed over was ... are you alright, little brother?

I guess Lane brought a toy gun to school. But I believe, and now I know, that he was asking for help in a different way. A friend of his told the school staff about the toy gun; they reacted to the situation by calling authorities and relaying information to the crisis line. "Workers" then took him out of his home. They told him they were sending him to a farm or to a group home and that the choices were no longer his. He spoke from his heart when he said he was "tired." He was done ... he just wanted the difficult parts of his life to stop. He told me he "can't see a way out in his life anymore." He was so hurt. He was so angry. But he was mostly just calling in a different way for his mom, his dad, the people in his life. He told the worker he would only talk to me. This once again changed our relationship, as I was now looked upon as the counselor ... which most definitely I am not. Despite the titles and role definition, the response and reaction, all I could think was ... are you alright, little brother?

I spent most of the week that followed in meetings, writing, advocating to find a space so we could listen more carefully to Lane. In many ways it seemed so simple to spend those days alongside ... listening to some stories over a soda. The space between relationships was so important for me to continue to think about as our research relationship shifted once again and asked me to participate in such different ways. The week was filled with twists, turns, and the raw emotions of a life turned upside down. As the snow fell, coating the trees and the ground in a twisted sort of way, feelings of worry challenged me. But all I could think in that moment of distracted thought was ... are you alright, little brother?

As Sean entered a new landscape and began to physically leave the landscape where he was engaged in his doctoral work, who he was began to shift in multiple ways. He was no longer able to be alongside Lane in the ways he had been. Sean's question—*Are you alright, little brother?*—helps us see the shifts as Sean moves between layered landscapes and attended not only to the landscapes but also to who he was and was becoming in the landscapes.

SLOWING DOWN, ATTENDING TO LANDSCAPES AND WHO WE ARE AND ARE BECOMING AS RESEARCHERS

Moving carefully and slowly, as we attend to the landscapes in which we work and to who we are and are becoming in narrative inquiries is not the dominant plotline shaping present-day university research landscapes. As we attend closely to who we are and are becoming in new landscapes, we begin to see how previous experiences shape not only our memories but also how we attend to the plotlines that structure the landscapes within which we find ourselves. Sean shows how his experiences with Lane and with Elder Bob Cardinal become inquiry sites for thinking about and with these storied landscapes. Our tracing makes visible ways in which this commitment has at times rubbed up against the dominant plotlines shaping the research landscapes where we work.

Just Get Started

For over a year now colleagues and I at the University of Regina have intentionally moved slowly in our negotiation of relationship as we thought about ways in which to engage alongside urban Aboriginal youth and their families. Community members within the City of Regina had asked us to create a place/program where Aboriginal youth and families can meet outside of school and engage in wellness activities. As someone new to the city and with very little knowledge of the context and place, it was important to not rush into the invitation to "start the work." What we knew from previous narrative inquiries was to pay careful attention to the landscape within which we are situated and that negotiation of relationships comes over time and through thoughtful attention and planning.

As Sean shared this writing, he also remembered that, despite the eagerness within their research team and the larger institutional pressures of writing, researching, and publishing, he and his colleagues resisted—by design. Past experiences in narrative inquiries helped them in their negotiation of relationships and continued to guide their research design and questions. One area in particular that Sean's experience highlights is the invitation from community to create a place or program for Aboriginal youth. The invitation from the community as well as attached funding was an important negotiation to consider as Sean and his colleagues thought of the long-term commitments to the youth and the community; they also attended to their desires to be researchers, not programmers, who come alongside the youth and community in the co-creation of a wellness space. Sean was also mindful of how he was storied in this new landscape as a strong researcher and a researcher of Aboriginal heritage, perhaps one who could connect other researchers to Aboriginal peoples.

The wisdom in walking alongside and paying close attention to the research landscape not only helped us to negotiate relationships with the community but also guided us in our process of thinking about who we are in relation to the people and the places we are coming alongside in the research. By moving too quickly in this process and accepting funding that had more of a focus on interventions around wellness and required answers to questions that reduced the lives of youth and community members within the neighborhood, we could have moved far away from the ontological commitments of narrative inquiry.

As we reflected on Sean's experiences in the present, it became visible that as Sean and his colleagues listened to various community members, there were external pressures for a quick fix around wellness, and that as invited researchers, they could unintentionally become positioned as expert knowledge holders who could change the lives of youth within this particular community. These were not Sean and his colleagues' intentions. It was through processes of ongoing wakefulness to who they are and are becoming and an attentiveness to the layered landscapes and who they are within the landscapes that they were able to slow down and listen more carefully to what other possibilities might be imagined alongside one another, possibilities that were attuned to the ontological commitments of narrative inquiry.

Just Get an Elder

The words "just get an Elder" remain fixed in my mind as I consider nego-
tiating relationships with Elders and community. "Just get an Elder" was
the suggestion from a community agency as our research team considered
potential grants. I believe the statement was a response to grant require-
ments to have Elders and traditional knowledge keepers' roles within the
research as well as grant requirements that asked for demonstrated affili-
ations with Aboriginal organizations as requisites for funding. We also
experienced these requirements as part of institutional ethics forms and
questionnaires. What is the percentage of time that Elders and traditional
knowledge keepers will be involved in the project? What are the duties in
which Elders and traditional knowledge keepers will participate? How
will Aboriginal community organizations benefit from the proposed grant?
The questions are all relevant in negotiating the layered landscapes in ethi-
cal and relational ways. However, with the pressure to do this quickly, I
experienced a sense of a rushed and empty process.

As Sean reflected on the statement that the research team should "Just get an Elder," he began to inquire into his experiences of coming to know Elders in his life, Elders who helped him think carefully about what it means to walk alongside youth and families. He drew forward stories of his experiences of Elder Bob Cardinal and his experiences of being named. He slowed down to inquire into who he was and was becoming within these new landscapes. Moving slow was part of the process. As Sean wrote the words "just get an Elder," he was drawn back in memory to earlier research experiences alongside Elder Isabelle Kootenay.

Elder Isabelle and Sean met over tea and work with a local school board. She was hired as a school district Elder to guide processes around the Stoney language and development of curriculum. Sean and Elder Isabelle came to know each other slowly over a year through tea and conversation. Sean recalls the first time they met: "We met at a meet-ing about five years ago. I greeted her before sitting down at the table. I felt immediately welcomed in through her warm smile and gentle handshake."

It is this experience that Sean calls forward as he is advised to "just get an Elder." In their first meeting Elder Isabelle asked Sean where he was from. Sean remembers that as he shared about places he was from, Elder Isabelle also shared stories of people she knew in Sean's home places. As they shared, Sean began a conversation about her territory, her home places, and the people who lived within them. As Sean had taught at a local high school, he awakened to understanding that many students who had moved to the city were from Elder Isabelle's community. Sean had taught many of her relatives, her nieces, nephews, and grandchildren. These relationships shaped connecting points for Sean and Elder Isabelle. As they continued to work together over years, their conversations continued to weave back and forth between them. Sean knew their relationship was different; he knew he had met someone with whom he would continue to think.

As Sean inquires into these past experiences alongside Elder Isabelle, he also looks forward, thinking of who Elder Isabelle is and is becoming in his life. As Sean tries to name who Elder Isabelle is in his life, he realizes that after five years of relationship, she is more than an Elder in his life but is now a grandmother to him. Sean and Elder Isabelle have, since their initial conversation, been involved in various research projects and have written together, creating and sharing their lives through not only words but also events and projects. Elder Isabelle helps Sean think about what he is doing within the community and what protocols and rhythms mean in different places. They have spent time on long walks in the trees, as Elder Isabelle explains to Sean the teachings she knows, teachings that have been passed down to her. Their relationship has shifted over time and places, and Elder Isabelle is now a guide to Sean as she awakens him to the layered landscapes and to who he is and is becoming within the landscapes.

It is inquiry into the relationship lived over time that Sean awakens to what was not visible to him initially. He begins to see that his relationship with Isabelle is shaping who he is as an Aboriginal person working hard to learn about himself and who he is in relation within multiple layered landscapes. Through his inquiry into his relationship with Elder Isabelle Sean bumps against how difficult it is to even think about what it means to be told to "just get an Elder." The advice shapes a bumping place for him as he negotiates a way forward within new landscapes at the university and within the community. Sean did not come to know Elder Isabelle through "getting an Elder"; their relationship took root through years of working within landscapes and attending closely to who they each are and are becoming. They remain deeply connected through teachings that are sustaining Sean in the present. Sean has learned that there is a commitment involved in this process, as Elder Isabelle welcomes Sean into her family and the teachings that have been passed on to her. Memories of Elder Isabelle are called up through the lighting of sweet grass and sage, medicines that invite Sean to a place of reflection. For him, Elder Isabelle remains present, and Sean knows that Elder Isabelle is standing close by, always, through these teachings once shared.

ATTENDING TO MULTIPLE LAYERED LANDSCAPES AS WE ENGAGE IN NARRATIVE INQUIRY

We tell these stories of attending to who we are as we move into new layered landscapes with participants in narrative inquiries for several reasons. First, we need to be attentive to the layered landscapes within which we live and to which we need to be attentive as we begin to think about engaging in narrative inquiries. As we begin to move forward into narrative inquiries, we enter these layered landscapes, which are in the midst of ongoing social, cultural, familial, institutional, and linguistic narratives. Wide awakeness to these shifting landscapes is part of what we hope to show. However, we also need to be attentive to who we are and are becoming as we enter the layered landscapes. This is more complex than merely naming ourselves, for we too are in the midst of our own stories within these larger narratives.

And it is important to remember that we, as narrative inquirers, are also storied into other stories by others living within the landscape. As Sean makes visible in his stories, he is storied by community members as well as by other researchers as he moves into these multiple layered landscapes. Being wakeful to how we position ourselves within the landscape as well as how others position us within it is necessary.

Sean's careful inquiry into his experiences of living the name gifted to him, Muskwacicy, shows the importance of how we need to move slowly into new layered landscapes even as we need to attend to how we are each always shifting as we move from one place to another and, in that move, shift who we are and are becoming. As Sean moves into a new landscape, who he is also changes how he is positioned in relation to his other landscapes, landscapes within which he is no longer quite so present.

Sean shows the importance of having guides to help us understand and inquire into who we are in multiple landscapes and how carefully and slowly we need to move into relationships with guides, letting them know us over time and coming to know them over time. These relationships cannot be rushed but need to be developed over time. Guides cannot be picked up and installed as "apps" into our computer GPS systems in the layered landscapes about which we are concerned.

In this chapter we tried to show the importance in narrative inquiry of attending to the interwoven nature of lives composed within multiple layered landscapes, landscapes shaped over time, place, people, and events. These understandings of research rub up against the dominant plotlines for research. Mapping the landscape prior to and during narrative inquiries with children and youth is important; so, too, is staying attentive to who we are and are becoming in relation with the landscape and child and youth participants. Narrative inquiries require slow living. Although slowness has often been connected with adjectives such as inactive and sluggish, living slowly in narrative inquiries shapes possibilities for wakefulness (Clandinin & Connelly, 2000), in storying and restorying lives and landscapes as we and participants together imagine forward-looking stories.

Although the upcoming chapter continues this thread of living slowly within the layered landscapes of narrative inquiry, it does so with particular attention to ways in which we locate and come into relationships with child and youth participants, both in and outside of institutional contexts.

CHAPTER 5

Finding Participants Within and Outside Institutional Contexts

One of the persistent concerns when engaging in any narrative inquiry is participants' location. We know that engaging in a narrative inquiry requires participants to make a long-term commitment to work with researchers over time and in multiple meetings and, depending on the research design, may involve having researchers live alongside them in their familial, school, institutional, and community contexts. We know that this frequently raises concerns with possible participants and sometimes results in them not agreeing to be participants. What is asked of participants in narrative inquiry is more than completing a survey, answering a questionnaire, or participating in a structured or semistructured interview; engaging in narrative inquiry means that participants and researchers are in it for the long haul. This sense of engagement over time raises and complicates finding participants. This concern becomes even more problematic when we seek to find participants who are legally under age and who are frequently seen as part of a vulnerable population. So how do we find child and youth participants who are willing to engage in narrative inquiry?

Often it seems we make initial connections with children, youth, and families through institutions. In a review of the literature of narrative inquiry in early childhood research (Clandinin et al, 2015), we learned that most narrative inquiries with young children are undertaken when children and families become involved with institutions. Very few narrative inquiries appear to be outside of institutions such as hospitals, childcare settings, schools, and clinics. We realize that most of our narrative inquiries with children and youth involve negotiating our participation through an institution. We have, however, also worked with children and youth who we have located outside institutional contexts.

A STARTING POINT: RESEARCH ETHICS BOARDS

Regardless of whether we propose to find participants through institutional contexts or outside of institutions, our first meeting place with

71

institutional narratives comes, of course, as we work through the universities' ethical review boards. We realize that these boards are shaped by understandings of ethical relations founded, we believe, in Kantian understandings of rights as well as the legal concerns of research-intensive universities (Clandinin, Caine, & Huber, accepted). As we work through the processes established and required by ethical review boards, the relational ethics at work in narrative inquiry often become visible. In addition, we increasingly find that large school boards and hospitals have additional institutional review or approval processes in place. Although ethical approval is required, the institutions also have review processes to determine whether the research fits with the institutions' mandates. Nowhere is this more evident than when research with children and youth is being proposed.

Although we find the ethics review boards of universities and of other institutions appropriate and important, as narrative inquirers we find ourselves challenged by the forms, processes, and questions asked from those who are positioned within institutional narratives. We are often asked to provide samples of instruments, interview questions, and information about the amount of time required of children and youth. These aspects are not easy for us to respond to as we struggle to explain the relational processes of narrative inquiry in our requests to come alongside children and youth both within and outside institutional contexts. The amount of time, for example, is negotiated with children and youth we work with.

Research ethics boards hold powerful influence over what research is allowed to go forward. The questions raised about the participation of youth and children who are in institutions such as schools are often about how their participation in the research will influence their experience within the institutions. Because schools are shaped by considerations of instructional time, physical structures, student learning, and outcomes, questions frequently are asked about benefits to student learning and influences on instruction. There are ethical concerns around whether research involvement will in some way interrupt or change ongoing teaching and learning. In health care settings, similar ethical concerns are raised around interruptions to care, increased staff time or responsibilities, and about liability issues for hospitals and other care settings. Sometimes the questions appear more substantive as ethical considerations are interwoven with what might seem more methodological questions. For example, research ethics boards have asked questions such as the following when we seek approval for working with children and youth. "Tell us again what your research questions are? How much time are you asking to spend with the youth? Will you be in classrooms? Will you use instructional time? What are the benefits for children, youth, and the school?"

We are also asked to be clear about the involvement of families and others as consent givers and about the children and youth as providing assent for their participation. We are also asked to clarify where conversations and researcher involvement will occur and how long these conversations will take. If other people who are not research participants, such as other children in classrooms will be present, we are asked to make clear that they are notified and, in some cases, that they give consent.

We deal with those differences in more detail later. However, negotiating with university ethics boards is only the first place we may become entangled in institutional narratives when we engage in narrative inquiry with children and youth. In designing our narrative inquiries and specifying the criteria for selecting participants and in undergoing ethical reviews by the university research ethics boards and boards of other institutions, we have begun to discern possible ways to locate potential participants.

FINDING PARTICIPANTS: A PROCESS OF ONGOING NEGOTIATIONS

As part of this chapter we look more specifically at several narrative inquiries both within and outside institutional contexts where researchers identified and negotiated relationships with youth and children after ethical and organizational approvals have been obtained. Finding children and youth participants within and outside institutional contexts is an ongoing negotiation. What we do in this chapter is to try to pull forward several threads that we can draw on to animate the process of finding participants, serving as gentle yet helpful reminders for proposed narrative inquiries with children and youth. It is with careful and intentional steps that we consider coming to research alongside youth and children. We turn now to considerations of finding participants who are located outside institutions, such as in the study with the youth who left school prior to graduating.

Finding Participants Outside of Institutional Contexts

I sat in the local bus station restaurant sipping on old coffee and anticipating that I could see this family at any moment. It was going to be great to reconnect for the first time in many years. I had waited too long. I wondered what Skye even looked like now. Would I recognize her? I wondered how she was doing in life. What type of job did she have? As hours passed I began to wonder whether I might have missed Skye or perhaps I hadn't quite understood the departure times her family had shared with me. Even though I felt like going home after waiting so long, I decided I would sit and wait just a while longer. There was one last bus leaving in an hour. There was a chance to still see them, and I was determined to follow through.

As the clock crept closer to the last bus leaving for her destination, her family suddenly appeared at the sliding doors. The wait was worth it! I immediately packed up my belongings and made my way to greet them. I was happy to see them. There were hugs all around, first to Arnie (dad) and then to Daphne (mom). We laughed about the mix-up in times and we laughed harder when I told them how many cups of coffee I drank while I was waiting. After several minutes of laughter and reconnection, Skye made her way through the sliding doors. It was great to see her on this day. I had many questions, but they would be for another time.

We both laughed when we saw each other. This is the way it used to be, and it was like old times in this moment. We sat down and talked, all of us together, sharing as much as we could in the limited time. I told them about my work at the university and about how I wanted to talk to Skye about her school experiences. Skye reassured me that she would be happy to participate. She was concerned we would not be able to set the next opportunity to talk, as she now lived in a new city. Skye's parents helped us with this next part. Arne and Daphne said they were hosting a round dance in honor of Daphne's father. A round dance is a way of honoring and celebrating life in their Aboriginal community. They explained that it was the fourth and final round dance for this important family member. I heard them say, "Come and visit. You will learn all the kids' stories. We invite you." With these simple but powerful words I knew what had to be done. I sat with Skye's parents as she boarded her bus, making her way down the road to her new adult life. It was so good to see her family on this day. I am glad I waited. I wonder how the story would have changed if I had left. (Field notes)

In this field note fragment Sean describes an experience at a bus stop while waiting for what seemed to him a very long time. He is in the hopeful process of finding a participant, Skye, in the study of the experiences of students who leave school before graduation. In this fragment Sean is located within a community setting, outside of an institutional place, quite literally at a bus stop. What is not visible in the field notes about finding a participant is the ongoing relationships Sean has with Skye, Arne, and Daphne. Caught in the midst of living their lives, the possibility of having Skye as a research participant is the start of the renegotiation of their relationships. Sean first met Skye in his work as a teacher within a public school in an urban setting. He met her parents through knowing Skye. Sean had now moved from high school teacher to graduate student and beginning narrative inquirer. He wondered whether and how his prior relationship with Skye, a possible participant, and her family will shape the research relationship. Sean has been storied by Skye and by her parents as a teacher. Sean has also storied Skye and her parents. Their relationships were shaped initially by the institutional narrative of school and by the ways teachers and students are storied in relation to each other in stories of school. This wide awakeness to the stories participants have of us and of how we story participants is an ongoing necessity in narrative inquiry from the first moments of searching for and finding participants.

When Sean joined the research project and decided to situate his master's thesis study within the larger study, he remembered Skye and began to imagine her as a possible participant. He learned she has moved on, both physically and metaphorically, as she now lives in another city than the one where they knew each other as teacher and student. As Sean waits at the bus stop, it has been two years since she left school. The return to earlier experiences through the study focus on youths' experiences of leaving school prior to graduating is important as it may shape how uncomfortable or difficult this particular research study potentially could be for Skye and her family.

Sean also drew forward other experiences that shape who he is and is becoming in this layered landscape. He drew on his earlier experiences as a youth worker and community worker to reconnect with this possible participant. He knew the importance of reconnecting in safe places, such as a local bus station, that are not inhibited and allow space for possibilities and negotiation over coffee and food. Sean knew that to create a safe space for a new relationship to emerge from within the ways they knew each other, he needed to acknowledge the relationship he had once built alongside her family. Sean carefully shared his research intentions and explained ways that he was curious about Skye's experiences of leaving school. He began these explanations by talking with her parents. This wide awakeness to knowing that new relationships are needed in a narrative inquiry is visible in Sean's actions. This would now be a different relationship and a different type of conversation from their earlier relationships.

Sean is also aware that he and Skye and her family are people of Aboriginal heritage. Sean is an Aboriginal person from a small Cree community in Saskatchewan. Skye and her family, Stoney Nakoda people, are also from a small Aboriginal community. Sean came to know Skye's family over time through cultural and community settings as well as through friendships and kinships that connected them. In the field notes it may not be visible that Sean was acknowledging that Skye and her family lived within particular linguistic, cultural, and social narratives. Sean's knowing of these narratives were, in part, what he knew needed to be negotiated. Sean offered protocol in the form of tobacco as an expression of thankfulness and openness. By bringing tobacco, he was being respectful of the evolving relationship between himself, Skye, and her family. Protocol in this case came in the form of tobacco, which Sean brought to start the conversation and to build a relationship. It is a symbol in many ways of helping us to think about what it is we are asking and to come with this from a good place. Elder Francis Whiskeyjack asks us to bring tobacco wrapped in print cloth, which he will then use in his own way and within his own ceremony and teachings. It is a sign of respect for what we are asking in this situation and honors this process of coming to understand. Protocol is different depending on place, relation, and context.

Although this shared identity grounding as Aboriginal peoples has been present in Sean and Skye's relationship from their first meetings in school through to this new meeting, Sean is awake to how his purposes and intentions may be storied differently now that he is positioning himself as a narrative inquirer in relation with Skye and her family. Within the new research relationship Sean would no longer be a teacher, and Skye and her family would no longer be a student and parents of a student. Sean knew that the research had the possibility to shape the life of not only Skye but also her family as well as their home place and community. The reverberations could be felt in many places and could shape multiple lives.

As he considered the ways he would invite Skye and her parents' participation, he moved forward in ethical ways to create a space where Skye and her family could decide to respectfully choose not to participate in a research relationship. As we consider how Sean framed the invitation to participate, we are not suggesting that there is one way to find participants or a cultural pathway to be followed; rather, we highlight that Sean was paying attention to the experiences he understood that shaped the lives of Skye and her family. As we engage in narrative inquiry with children and youth, we need to make visible the importance of attending to the multiplicity within the lives of children and youth and to the ways their lives are interrelated with familial and community experiences. Attending to the multiple contexts of children and youth and their families allows us to move forward into research in respectful ways.

By beginning with this particular field note and by the inquiry into the field note, we show the complexity of the beginning processes of finding child and youth participants outside of an institutional context. Frequently these considerations around the initial moments of finding participants are not considered in depth. Without careful attention to the layered landscapes and to the ways that people are positioned within the landscapes, finding participants can result in moving forward in unethical and harmful ways. The mundane details that shaped finding and beginning to negotiate a research relationship shaped the research relationship into the future that Sean, Skye, and her family developed.

Although finding participants from within already-known networks of people is one way of finding participants, this is not the only way to find participants. The process of finding participants is not a fleeting exercise or whimsically organic in nature. Sometimes, although it may seem serendipitous, as we find children and youth participants to engage in studies, we need to be intentional and thoughtful as we seek participants.

Naming Participant's Experiences: Considering Terminology

The narrative inquiry within which Sean and Skye participated was a study of the experiences of youth who left school early. The criteria for participants was set in part by the funding agency, the Alberta Centre for Child, Family, and Community Research, which asked that participants be youth who had left Alberta (Alberta is a Canadian province) secondary schools. The research design was one we describe as beginning with telling stories (Connelly & Clandinin, 2006), that is, it was a conversational study with nineteen youth. We located the youth participants from outside institutions. There was no one institution that could allow us to find such youth, as they were composing their lives in different ways and within multiple institutions, such as retail outlets. Although we did locate some of the youth participants through previous relationships and through working through networks of friends and colleagues, we also located participants in other ways. As we think back to this study, it becomes more visible how the context of the study required a very careful and perhaps gentle negotiation of the location of and initial and ongoing research relationships with youth participants.

One of the ways we awakened to the importance of a gentle and wide-awake process to locate youth as participants was through the use of particular terms and concepts—that is, the terms and concepts used to locate participants and how these terms would shape the study. The most frequently used term in local policy, school, and community discussions to describe youth who left school without graduating was *dropouts* or youth as dropping out. Although the language around naming youth who left school was somewhat more nuanced and contested in the literature (Clandinin, Steeves, & Caine, 2013), the most frequently used term to refer to this population was *school dropouts*. As we came to research design conversations around the study and locating participants with the importance of attending to the youths' experiences, we were also influenced by the importance of naming the phenomenon under study. As a diverse group of researchers from different fields of study, we designed and considered these questions of terminology as we framed the research study. Through dialogue with each other and through a literature review on and about youth who leave school early, we recognized that researchers named the phenomenon in different ways over time and across contexts. We were attentive to the importance of recognizing and disrupting notions of protective factors and risk factors and how these definitions were prescriptive and narrowed how lives could be understood. We were awake to how, if we began conversations with youth with these narrow ideas in mind, we risked possibilities of not attending to their narratives of life experiences in diverse ways.

We wanted to locate participants from across the province of Alberta, from different life contexts, and from different geographical contexts. One of the ways we decided to locate youth was through the use of posters in English and French, Canada's two official languages. Despite a carefully designed poster that used inviting font, we asked the question to potential participants, "Are you a high school dropout?" and went on to give ways to contact us. We also designed a second poster with the question: "Do you know someone who is a high school dropout?" We posted the posters in multiple cities, towns, and rural settings in places that included businesses, libraries, bulletin boards, malls, and other such places. We also posted the invitation on social media sites, including Facebook. It was because our posters yielded some but limited responses that we began to consider how the term dropout closed rather than opened possibilities for participation.

Through continued conversation with those outside our research team we began to awaken to how our framing shaped the process of finding participants. We shifted our approach to a description focused on those who left school prior to graduating. We began to speak of the importance of framing the invitations to participate in narrative inquiries as a process that allowed participants to imagine how the study would fit into their forward-looking stories. As we learned from the participants, many of them did not tell stories of dropping out but of not being in school for now.

Finding Participants Within Institutional Contexts

We have engaged in other narrative inquiries where we have located children and youth participants outside institutional contexts. The narrative inquiry with youth who did not graduate from high school was one where we began to attend closely to multiple landscapes and to the ways we are positioned in landscapes. In another study Sean and two colleagues, Lee Schaefer and Brian Lewis, shaped a time and place for youth of Aboriginal heritage to participate in physical activities after school as a beginning place for finding child and youth participants. We realize that there are few narrative inquiries that do not in one way or another locate participants from negotiating within institutional contexts. We turn now to finding participants within institutional contexts before we turn to tensions we experience as we find participants within institutional contexts.

In many of the narrative inquiries with children and youth in which we have engaged, we have located children and youth through institutions such as schools, hospitals, daycares, and organizations and through involving service providers. We found participants through spaces shaped by the institutions in which children and youth attend, gather, and/or participate. In these situations we first negotiate through institutional processes of organizational approval (some community organizations also have ethical approval mechanisms, whereas others rely on the ethics approval obtained through research ethics review boards situated at universities and are primarily concerned with organizational impact and approval). We try to stay awake to how institutional protocols and policies shapes the inquiries along the way both directly and indirectly. We know the importance of considering how inquiries might be shaped through the institutional landscape within which we are negotiating. We need to stay wakeful to the ways the institutional landscape may shape the ways we might find participants.

We draw first on our experience with designing and finding participants with the children, youth, and families of Aboriginal heritage. We highlight the processes of finding a school setting and of the negotiation of relationship first through a principal within a school district. There were several levels of negotiation before we were able to find a junior high school setting in an area of a city with a high population of urban Aboriginal youth. However, this was not the starting point for locating participants for the narrative inquiry; rather, we considered the following key processes.

Starting with Communities: As we began to plan for and design the narrative inquiry, we reached out to community members to listen carefully and to attend to what we saw as a research puzzle with which many people had experiences. We wanted to hear multiple stories of experience as we designed the study and as we considered the experiences of urban Aboriginal youth and their families outside of school. We found it critically important to think with others within various communities as they helped us shape and reshape the research puzzle. Within this openness in the narrative inquiry process we came to learn more from those around us. These intentional processes acknowledge not only the larger personal and social contexts within narrative inquiry but also the ways people's experiences are nested within larger social, institutional, linguistic, and cultural narratives. Through multiple conversations we came to understand the possibilities within the research puzzle as we sat with service providers, Elders, community program providers, teachers, administrators, parents, and Aboriginal leaders throughout the province. We recall gatherings with government agencies, school board leaders, and even with elected Aboriginal leadership and Chiefs at national meetings. Through these conversations we built relationships and developed research partners who guided our study and shaped how we began to locate participants and how these opening considerations shaped and shifted the study. Although we do not provide details here, we note that these intentional processes shaped how we situated the study and how we found participants.

We turn back to the considerations of moving slowly into landscapes, which we discussed in Chapter 4 to underscore the importance of mapping a research landscape and carefully considering the steps taken well before we begin to search for participants. The beginnings of a narrative inquiry shape and reshape the ways in which the inquiry unfolds, even shaping the possibilities for how the inquiry can unfold. As we moved into the layered landscapes, we frequently sought out guides and friends who we thought might help us be more awake to who we were and were becoming and how we were being storied. Sean sought out school board friends and Elders he knew in schools. Jean sought out school principals and teachers. Vera turned to previous research relationships and people she knew who worked with peoples of Aboriginal heritage. All of these guides and friends helped us move more wakefully into the study.

Starting with Research Ethics Boards: As we engaged with the communities about the research we were also mindful that we needed to satisfy the requirements of the university ethics board and the school district approval board. In our design we had already determined that we did not require instructional time nor time in classrooms with students except for the brief time when we would make students aware of the possibility of participating. However, we did want to meet junior high school–aged students as well as locate a physical place in a school for the weekly art club meetings. We realized this meant that participants in the research needed to be students at a school in order to participate. At first this did not seem problematic, as we agreed to this parameter that participants in the study would be students in the school. This became more problematic as students moved out of the school but we still wanted to have them participate in the after-school club. Some of the issues we encountered were that both students and we needed to follow all school regulations, as we were still on school grounds. As we worked within this parameter in this study, we were mindful that we would be more awake to such requirements as we negotiated future narrative inquiries.

Gaining Approval to Work in a School: Several members of the team, Jean, Sean, and Vera, knew from work and research relationships people in a particular school district. There had been other studies and other times spent in schools, and although we may not have known the particular people with whom we were meeting, we were known on the storied landscapes of the school and district. Sean had a relationship with the school administrator, so when the district administrators suggested this school, it seemed that working in the school would allow us to engage in the narrative inquiry in the ways we had imagined. In June of the school year with a hoped-for fall start, we met with the junior high school principal to inquire into the possibilities of developing a relationship with the community and the school. We met in the school staff room. We were attentive to how we might be perceived within the institutional place and how the principal and school staff might perceive us moving forward. We only had an opportunity to meet the principal, but we were listening carefully to how he might story our work that would shape, we knew, how youth and their families understood our intentions. We knew that how we were storied would shape how we would eventually find participants and negotiate the research relationships. As we noted in multiple field notes and conversations after that first meeting, we felt the junior high school principal opened up the school in a welcoming way and was eager to share what the school staff had been working on throughout the year and how the school's programs were part of a larger district-wide focus on Aboriginal education and programming.

We wondered about what was important to him as a principal and about how he perceived us as he identified the importance of programming for Aboriginal youth and the importance of Aboriginal students within the school. As we prepared to enter research relationships, we wondered how these initial thoughts, shared through an afterschool conversation, might shape the way we entered the research landscape of the school. In this example we see more clearly how the layered institutional landscape, a school within a school district with particular objectives set within a province within Canada with its particular geography, are all relevant to the processes of narrative inquiry. Paying close attention to who we are as narrative inquirers in the midst of a beginning research relationship is part of a larger process that we consider and reconsider carefully at various points throughout the research.

In these ways, as we negotiate our research into the institutional landscape, we are in the process of shaping how we come to and find participants. As we work through these processes it is akin to a filtering process to which we need to be attentive. We need to be able to, at each point in the process, name and understand what is happening to research plans and to us. If we do not remain awake or cognizant of the filtering processes, we may not be able to find and negotiate relationships with children and youth in the ways that help us inquire into the proposed research puzzle.

Finding Child and Youth Participants in the School. In the above description we have not yet found the children and youth who were to participate in the narrative inquiry. We had imagined a kind of space situated within what the school offered as after-school club time, a time after official school hours had ended. It was working within that space that we hoped to find the children and youth who would become participants. We hoped some of the children and youth would agree to be participants and would, in their own ways, both metaphorically and physically, take us home where we could hear their stories and their families' stories of experiences. As part of the study, our intentions were to come alongside families and youth outside of school.

Through the establishment of what became known as the art club at the school, we invited students who were interested to join us. We met each Wednesday afternoon after school for approximately ninety minutes over two years. We were very consistent, and at least two of us were always present as researchers on any given Wednesday afternoon. We informed the teachers about the club and visited classrooms to invite children and youth to attend. We and the first students who attended made posters to invite other youth. We also worked with a person from an agency who worked in the school on a part-time basis with Aboriginal youth to invite youth. As we came to know youth in the art club, we gradually invited them to participate in more intensive conversations with us. Even though all of the youth did not participate in the more intensive conversations, they continued to attend the art club. In Chapters 1 and 2 we introduced Tara, who became a participant in this study. In subsequent chapters we introduce Chris, Lane, Jason, and Donovan and learn more about their stories of experience in the study.

STAYING WAKEFUL: TENSIONS OF THE SHAPING INFLUENCES ON RESEARCH DESIGNS

We experience many uncertainties as we design narrative inquiries and begin our search for participants. Staying wakeful to how we begin narrative inquiries requires an ongoing attentiveness. Some months ago Vera was contacted by people within a community agency who sought support for children and youth at risk of being sexually exploited. The community agency was desperate to find a program that would help to interrupt the sexual exploitation of children and youth. As Vera met with people from the agency she heard many stories. One story was of an eleven-year-old girl who had a sexually transmitted disease yet was refused treatment by a doctor. Another story was of youth being forced into human trafficking as a way to support their families. As she listened to these and other stories, Vera recognized that many of the children and youth, faced with no place to sleep, no food and clothing, were using their bodies as a way to meet their basic needs.

However, as a narrative inquirer, Vera lived in this conversation tentatively. In part, the sexual exploitation of children and youth was a reality about which Vera was deeply concerned, given her earlier narrative inquiry alongside women who had experience working in the sex trade. A thread made visible in that inquiry was the very young ages at which the women began to experience sexual exploitation. In this and subsequent early conversations with people at the agency Vera and her colleague Margot Jackson were able to get the agency to agree that any kind of program that might be offered needed to be shaped and led by the children and youth. Janice also joined the research team. They proposed the possibility of a narrative inquiry in which they, as part of a larger, interdisciplinary team, might come alongside children and youth in ways that could shape openings for understanding their experiences and, through this process, co-imagine and co-make ways forward that would support their life making in good ways.

Vera, Margot, and Janice, through negotiating with the policy makers and workers at the agency, were awake to the necessity to shift the intentions of the agency away from a starting point of intervention—that is, of intervening in the lives of the children and youth so that there is no longer the reality of, or risk for, any of the children and youth to be living experiences of sexual exploitation. Without the shift from intervention, it is not possible to imagine a way forward that would allow us to work within narrative inquiry. The intervention is imposed, no matter the congruence or coherence with the lives of the children and youth. Without coming alongside the youth in narrative inquiry, it is not possible to begin to imagine and co-compose forward-looking stories with the children and youth. How we think about our lives shapes how we might begin to negotiate entry with children, youth, and their parents.

NEGOTIATING ENTRY WITH CHILDREN AND YOUTH IN NARRATIVE INQUIRIES

Our focus on lives in the making and multiperspectival inquiries has meant that we engage alongside children, youth, and families not only in school and institutional places but also in the places they gradually take us outside of school, such as places in the communities where they live and, sometimes, their home places. Engaging in narrative inquiries outside of institutional places still requires completion of university research ethics and ongoing negotiation of the relational ethics that shape narrative inquiries. As with narrative inquiries lived out alongside children, youth, and families in institutional places, we also begin and live in the midst of not knowing, of not knowing in advance or with any sense of certainty the kinds of possibilities, complexities, or tensions we might experience. In this midst, as in all narrative inquiries, we continue to focus our attention on maintaining mutual, reciprocal relationships as we live alongside participants.

Staying with Participants: Ongoing Negotiation of Participation

There is not a clear line in narrative inquiry between locating participants and negotiating entry into research relationships. In the study with the youth who left school early, it was the first time that many youth had shared their experiences of leaving school. They did not tell of their experiences of leaving school as a singular act or a moment in time. In a similar sense, research relationships were an ongoing negotiation of locating participants and beginning to negotiate who we were in relation to each other. In a narrative inquiry it is not simply a case of finding participants, starting conversations with youth at a fixed beginning, and then exiting at the end the conversations with the desired research outcomes. In narrative inquiry finding participants requires careful mapping and a slow entry into the research landscapes, attending closely to who we are and are becoming and paying close attention to the three-dimensional narrative inquiry space at all times. As we located participants through multiple means and entered their lives in the midst of theirs and our lives, we did not have a clear sense of where the study would take us. We wondered how participants perceived us at the outset and then each time we met. We wondered at the shifts over the course of the research study. We wondered about the cultural, social, familial, institutional, and linguistic narratives that required careful attention as well as the attentiveness to ongoing negotiating processes between researcher and participant. We have learned that we need to stay wakeful. We turn our attention now to the negotiation of relationships that begin somewhere in the processes of finding participants and negotiating entry.

CHAPTER 6

Negotiating Entry with Children and Youth

In Chapter 5 we showed the complex processes that were necessary as we worked to locate children and youth as participants for our narrative inquiries. Although in some ways the processes of forming relationships with children and youth are akin to the ways we form relationships with older participants, there are added layers of negotiation. We might assume that all we need to do is acknowledge that children and youth are legal minors and then work in ways that allow us to negotiate participation with them as individuals as well as to seek family or guardian permission for their participation. However, there are further complications to negotiating entry with children and youth.

There is much at work as we negotiate entry into the field, particularly when a field is understood as a relational space between researcher and participant as it is in narrative inquiry. Negotiating entry into a research relationship with children and youth takes place over time and with careful attention to the storied experiences of each child, youth, families, and us, as narrative inquirers. To suggest either that there is a single moment that counts as negotiation of entry or a prescribed pathway for negotiation between researcher and participant is quite simply not possible.

One of the challenges of locating participants that we made evident in Chapter 5 was in finding ways to name the experiential phenomena that is the focus of the study. Naming the experiential phenomenon without creating a category that boxes in or creates fixed categories of participants was one concern in the processes of locating children and youth as participants. However, as we engaged in processes of locating youth in narrative inquiries, we realized that locating youth and children as potential participants is only the beginning of negotiating ways to invite them into a narrative inquiry and of negotiating their ongoing participation. In this chapter we discuss processes and challenges of negotiating entry in narrative inquiries with children and youth. As we consider ongoing negotiation of entry into research relationships with children and youth, we look back at several studies to animate the discussion.

We briefly outline the three narrative inquiries we draw on in the next section and then return to draw forward more complex tellings of the processes of negotiating entry with participants.

NEGOTIATING ENTRY WITH PARTICIPANTS

Ravine Elementary School. Drawing on a study with teachers and children in Ravine Elementary School, we show how we worked first to negotiate ethical approval through the university ethics board and then sought approval through a school district. We then negotiated entry into the particular school, Ravine Elementary School, and subsequently negotiated entry with particular teachers within the school. When we entered classrooms we then gained parental consent for our involvement with each child and gained assent from children to participate. All of this is part of the processes of negotiating participation with individual children, teachers, and families.

As we worked through these layers of negotiation, we awakened to how children construct us and how we began to construct them, and we began to make visible how research puzzles began to shape-shift through the negotiation of entry. In our narrative inquiries at Ravine Elementary the children, teachers, and parents positioned us, as researchers, as teachers/teacher helpers and friends of the teachers and principal. We positioned ourselves in this way as we explained our presence in the school to teachers, parents, and children. It gave us and them ways to tell of who we were in the classroom and school contexts. We return to this study below as we explore the unfolding negotiations of entry that Vera experienced as she began work within the narrative inquiry at Ravine Elementary School.

Engaging with Children and Families of Aboriginal Heritage. Drawing on the study with the children and families of Aboriginal heritage, we made visible in Chapter 5 the multiple layers of negotiation of entry. Initially we negotiated an after-school time and unused classroom place in a school with school staff and administrators. We then negotiated the participation of youth who came to the after-school art club and parental/family consent for them to come to the club. After we came to know the youth, we began to negotiate one-on-one research relationships with particular youth and their families. In this study we were also attentive to how our negotiation of entry shaped how we were positioned in the stories of teachers, administrators, families, and children and youth and how we positioned ourselves. However, despite the careful attention to how we attempted to position ourselves in the inquiry fields, there were still multiple questions around who we were in relation with children, youth, and families. (Copies of consent and assent forms are included in Appendix 1 as an example.)

Engaging with the Youth in the Early School-Leaving study. Drawing on the narrative inquiry with the youth who left school (all of whom were over eighteen), we did not locate them through institutions nor did we need parental consent to work with them. Through posters, friends, and community connections, we eventually negotiated entry into a relational field with nineteen youth. As we noted in Chapter 5, we became particularly attentive to how we named potential participants, as we initially advertised for youth who had dropped out of school and for people who knew youth who had dropped out of school. It was in coming alongside the youth that we became sensitive to how our naming of the youth as dropouts did not fit with how they named themselves. They did not respond to our posters because, as we later learned, they did not see themselves as dropouts.

We also awakened to how the intentions of participants in the inquiry shaped their participation in the inquiry. We were awake to what brought each of us to the narrative inquiry, and we were attentive to how our stories shaped the research relationships we established. For example, Sean was a former teacher/youth worker. He knew some of the youth who became participants. Some of the youth came to the inquiry because they wanted to reestablish connections with Sean. Other youth sought us out because they wanted their stories told. We began to attend more closely to participants' intentions for participating in the research and how their intentions shaped the negotiations of entry.

NEGOTIATING ENTRY: REVISITING VERA'S NEGOTIATION OF ENTRY AT RAVINE ELEMENTARY SCHOOL

Turning to the negotiations of entry shifts our focus to the relational commitments we have to those who might join the proposed study. However, it also calls forth a commitment to attend to who we are and are becoming alongside participants in the early processes of negotiating entry with participants. In Chapter 3, in her narrative beginnings, Jean wrote of her experiences within her early landscapes, called forth on an autumn drive through the countryside close to the farm where she grew up. She drew forward the narrative threads of attending closely and of walking alongside threads rooted in the embodied stories shaped by her experiences alongside her father. Jean described how drawing on Mary Catherine Bateson's words about attention, presence, and care helped her inquire into those early experiences alongside her father and to who she was, is, and is becoming as a narrative inquirer. Through her autobiographical narrative inquiry, Jean awakened to what it meant to live in uncertainty and the need to live within the imaginative possibility of improvisation.

As Jean shared these stories of her early landscapes, Vera was drawn into recollecting her experiences of negotiating entry to Ravine Elementary School as part of a SSHRC-funded project (Clandinin & Connelly, 2001) called School Landscapes in Transition: Negotiating Diverse Narratives of Experience. Jean, Shaun Murphy, Anne Murray Orr, Marni Pearce, Pam Steeves, and Marilyn Huber were researchers in the narrative inquiry at Ravine Elementary School. Vera entered the project somewhat later when an additional teacher asked that she and her students be included in the project. Vera expressed an interest in working alongside children and teachers in the narrative inquiry.

In the weeks prior to Vera's arrival Jean and the other researchers received ethics approval from the university ethics review board, followed by institutional approval from the school district. Jean knew the principal, Jeannette, from earlier studies. Jean's interest, shared with Jeannette, was in exploring the idea of working together on a narrative inquiry into the ways that the diverse identities of children, teachers, and families were shaped in school curriculum-making places. Jean, Shaun, Anne, and Marni met with the principal at the end of the school year to discuss ways they could participate—that is, be positioned as narrative inquirers—in the school. The research design for the overall narrative inquiry involved each researcher participating in a classroom with the intention of coming alongside more intensively a few children in order to understand their experiences in school. Three teachers volunteered to work alongside Shaun, Anne, and Marni. In the late August start-up meetings of the new school year the four researchers, including Jean, were participant observers with all of the teachers and the principal at Ravine school. It was at this meeting that another teacher approached Jean and wondered whether it would be possible to work alongside a researcher in her grade 2/3 split classroom, a classroom designated for children with learning challenges. It was in this way that Vera became part of the narrative inquiry.

Vera had recently attended a workshop by Wendy Ewald at Duke University where she learned about the possibility of engaging children in photography work using large-format film cameras, dark rooms, and the possibilities of using the photographs to create books. Filled with ideas about what might be possible in working alongside children, Vera, a doctoral student at the time, was hoping to have the opportunity to become part of a research project. Jean and the principal, Jeannette, felt that Vera could become part of the grade 2/3 classroom given that the grade 2/3 teacher wanted to participate.

As the possibility became real, Vera knew that not only was she negotiating entry into the lives of children and their teacher but that she was
also in a process of negotiating entry into a school, a site of practice
not familiar to her. Although Vera has been in schools in her professional life, she entered schools as a public health nurse and not as a
teacher or as a researcher. Jean's reminder of improvisation in times of
uncertainty in her autobiographical narrative work created a space for
Vera to remember how much she felt out of place as she thought about
classrooms. As Jean shared her autobiographical narratives of experience, Vera was reminded of the importance of attending to the need to
improvise, to imagine possibilities as part of the process of negotiating
relationships with children and youth. There was no sure path forward,
but there was the need to be open to new imaginings and what might
be possible. Vera was attentive and reached back to her memories. She
recollected the following from her field notes:

> I was apprehensive and nervous about walking into the school. I was dis-
> mayed that I had asked to engage in the study and, for the long moment
> of walking between the school parking lot and the front door, won-
> dered about my soundness of thinking. As a nurse, I had come to dislike
> institutional spaces, spaces that seemed governed by rules I never quite
> understood. Despite my excitement to work alongside children in a pho-
> tography project, I could hardly believe I had volunteered to become part
> of a school and classroom space for the next year. Opening the front door
> of the school didn't bring any relief to my fears of having made a terrible
> decision. What made me open the door was a sense of commitment to
> Jean and to colleagues I valued as well as the excitement of being able
> to engage in the photography work from the work with Wendy Ewald.
> The bright orange of the school, together with the linoleum floor and the
> obvious signs that pointed to character education brought no relief to my
> worry. The front office was placed right next to the school's front door,
> and the sound of the voice asking me whether I was here for the meet-
> ing, reinforced the sense of commitment I felt—someone expected me to
> "show up." I was invited into the principal's office, an office filled with
> teddy bears of all sizes and shapes. A boy sat in a chair, avoiding eye con-
> tact. I wondered once more what I had agreed upon, yet I too recall being
> curious about the young boy. Why was he in the principal's office? Why
> did he avoid eye contact with me? What were his stories of school? In this
> moment I realized just how much I would have to learn to shift my sense
> of being out of place to one who could improvise in order to negotiate
> entry into the school and a classroom alongside children and a teacher.

Jean's writing was a reminder about the importance of Bateson's ideas
to understanding what it means to negotiate entry with children and
youth. Jean shared the following from her autobiographical inquiry.

> These experiences in the landscapes of my childhood live deep in my body.
> I know how they shape my practices as I think about and live narrative

inquiries with children and youth. Attentiveness to each moment, to the movements of bodies, to the expressions that move swiftly across or linger on faces are part of composing relationships with children and youth. And not only the movements and expressions on the faces of the other but a deep attentiveness turned inward to my own bodily knowing, to what is happening to me in the moments. These living practices of wide awakeness and watchfulness are important as we begin to work with children and youth. Alongside the importance of watchfulness are the practices of patience, of waiting, of not rushing into the research. Bateson helps me see "the willingness to do what needs to be done is rooted in attention to what is."

As Vera listened carefully to Jean, she began to see that the negotiations of entry begin long before we meet children and youth and that they are shaped by who we are and are becoming. As Jean learned to watch the landscape and attend to her parent's worries about their lives on the small farm, Vera had become distrustful of institutional spaces of school at an early age. Vera recounts the following early childhood story.

It was in our grade 3 classroom in the middle of the school year when stories of someone stealing people's lunch and money started to circulate through the elementary school I attended. Seconds after Lydia left the classroom to go to the washroom, the classroom teacher asked me to see where she had gone. Without thinking much about the request, I obliged. Skipping down the hallway, I was relieved to be out of the classroom for a few minutes. To my dismay, on the way to the washroom I found Lydia in another classroom. She was the only one present and was just going through someone's desk—my eyes caught Lydia's, and I know she saw me watching. I still remember that moment even now, almost forty years later. I remember the classroom, the hallway, and her eyes. Lydia did not know I had been asked to look for her. When I returned to the classroom without Lydia, I stayed silent and, even today, I remember wondering what was I to do? What I do remember is that my relationship with Lydia and my relationship with the teacher changed forever.

Standing in the principal's office that day at Ravine school, watching the young boy, Vera remembered the moment of catching Lydia's eyes. What would happen at Ravine school, Vera wondered? Would teachers request students to spy on their classmates? Would students be asked to reveal information to teachers that made them feel uncomfortable? What would discipline be like at Ravine school? How did teachers at Ravine school think about their impact on students? And most of all, who was the teacher she would be working with? At the same time, as a researcher, Vera worried about how the teacher and children would perceive her. Who would she be seen as standing alongside? And how would she negotiate tensions of which she was yet unaware?

In these initial moments Vera thought much about who she would be in the moments of negotiating entry into the relationships with children.

Yet in the long walk from the principal's office, where Vera met with the principal and Jean, Vera wondered how she and the children and teacher would negotiate their relationships. How would each child position her? How would the teacher position her? And as she engaged in the self-facing work of narrative inquiry, she wondered how she would position each child and the teacher? How would her stories of silence in her narrative beginnings (see Chapter 3) and her stories of not belonging in schools shape the stories she lived alongside the children and the teacher?

NEGOTIATING ENTRY: REVISITING ENTERING LIVES IN THE MIDST ALONGSIDE YOUTH AND FAMILIES OF ABORIGINAL HERITAGE

In Chapter 5 we described how the processes of finding participants shifts into the negotiation of entry, making visible that there is not a sharp divide between when we try to locate or find participants and when we begin to negotiate entry. Acknowledging that the processes of locating participants is part of—indeed shapes—the negotiation of entry is important in narrative inquiry. As we show, it is also important to attend closely to how we enter lives and places in the midst of ongoing stories.

Drawing on the study with the youth and families of Aboriginal heritage, we note that there were many ways in which our undertaking to find participants shaped the negotiation of entry with participants. However, as we engaged in setting up the narrative inquiry we negotiated a time and place within a school but outside of school hours—that is, in the time allotted for school club meetings after school hours. We were not in relationship with the teachers who taught the youth before they came to the art club; however, we were physically in the place of school, in a classroom surrounded by other classrooms and hallways lined with the kind of lockers that are common in Canadian junior high schools. We signed into the school each day as we stopped at the school office and greeted the secretary and sometimes one of the administrators. The classroom where we engaged with the youth was filled with worn desks, displays, and materials left by past and current teachers. The classroom connected to a foods classroom, with its multiple cooking stations. Sometimes administrators and other teachers came into the classroom while we were with the youth to look for certain children or to see what we were doing. It both was and was not a classroom place in the school.

As we began to meet possible research participants, we were mindful we were entering their lives in the midst of their ongoing experiences as well as being in the midst of our own lives. For us this is important to recognize, particularly as we often ask for extended amounts of time and involvement with participants. Clandinin and Huber (2010) note,

Narrative inquiry is a process of entering into lives in the midst of each participant's and each inquirer's life. What this draws attention to is the importance of acknowledging the ongoing temporality of experience when it is understood narratively. Narrative inquiry always begins in the midst of ongoing experiences. In this process, inquirers continue to live their stories, even as they tell stories of their experiences over time. Inquiries conclude in the midst of living and telling, reliving and retelling, the stories of the experience that make up narrative inquirers' and participants' lives, bit individual and social. (p. 438)

We see this acknowledgment that possible participants and we are always in the midst as central to our negotiation of entry. The year we started in the arts club made us think often about how we negotiate entry and, particularly, about how places such as schools are also situated within the midst of institutional narratives. We knew that we would be entering a busy junior high school, a school that hosted some after-school programming and where many students were bused to school or took the regular city buses. As we imagined our entry, we knew some students would be in the midst of adjusting to a new school, whereas others would already be thinking about leaving the school and negotiating their move to a high school. Vera recalls one of the first days of the arts club:

> We arrived at the school more than an hour and a half before the last school bell rang for the day, around 2 p.m., in order to set up the after-school arts club. The school doors were unlocked, and Nancy, the school secretary, kept a watchful eye on who was coming and going. Other than the watchful eyes of Nancy, who followed Vera as she signed in at the school, the hallways seemed deserted. A couple of students were lingering in the hallways, hallways that were lined by rows of lockers and the occasional paper or pencil on the floor. In order to get to the room that was to become the designated arts club room, we had to walk through the entire school. It was a room tucked away in the corner of the school. Yet it was also right next to another set of outside doors. Trudy, Simmee, and Shauna (other researchers) had been there the previous week and had tried to set up the room in a way that the children and youth could engage in some activities. In the far corner of the room was a place where we set out the snacks, the food we had prepared for the youth. The room felt awkward, and although we tried, it continued to feel much like a classroom.

What Vera draws our attention to in this field note is that while we were in the midst of our lives as researchers, graduate students, and professors, the youth and school staff were also in the midst of their ongoing lives. They lived their lives each day, in part, in the particular school. We were entering their place and were trying to re-story one classroom into a research site, a place that made it no longer a classroom but an art club. We were mindful of the location of the classroom, at the edge of the school. As we noted, there was an outside door adjacent to the classroom, but we knew that part of the story of school is that visitors, such as us, had to enter the school through the main door and to sign in, an indication that we were in the school and were guests in the school. As we negotiated entry, we realized that we were positioned by place, time, and school rules within the story of school, an institutional narrative. This positioning of us, in the midst of our own lives, was also a positioning of us within the institutional narrative. Over the two years of working within the arts club, we were frequently reminded that we needed to continue to negotiate our entry with the youth and families in school because of how we were positioned in the institutional narrative, the story of school.

NEGOTIATING ENTRY: REVISITING THE EARLY SCHOOL LEAVERS STUDY ATTENTIVE TO THE WAYS THAT RESEARCHERS ARE ONLY PART OF THE NEGOTIATIONS

In the narrative inquiry with youth who were early school leavers, youth participants came to the research from outside the institutional landscape of school. They were no longer located within schools. As we came to know them through the negotiation of entry into the study, we saw them as people composing their lives as cooks, clerks, parents, sales people, restaurant servers, and so on. They were all in the midst of negotiating life stories, all in the midst of the possibilities of lives unfolding.

Beginning to negotiate entry—that is, as we negotiated initial research relationships—we knew the youth from within previous relationships, from within their imagined stories as they responded to posters and from within invitations from others. As we negotiated their entry into the relational field space of narrative inquiry, we made visible how the context of the study required careful and gentle negotiation of entry into the field of the study, which is the research relationship with each youth. Within the careful negotiation of language and the context of the study, it is evident there was an ongoing negotiation of relationship within the research conversations. It was a careful and gentle process of meeting over time, as many of the youth had not shared their experiences of leaving school. Sometimes in the first meetings that were part of the negotiation of entry—the youth told us that leaving school was not a singular act or a moment in time. For some youth these stories emerged later, over time and as relationships deepened. As we met in the midst of negotiating entry and as we moved into research conversations, we were awake to the importance of beginning in different places as part of the negotiation of relationship and experience. What comes out of this ongoing negotiation of the research relationship is the necessary attentiveness that slows the inquiry down and helps both the researcher and participant think carefully about what might be taking place and exploring the possibilities that might emerge through narrative inquiry.

The negotiation of entry became, in this study, part of the ongoing negotiation of who we are in relation to each other. As the process of locating participants and negotiating entry shifted to the ongoing telling of stories, we found ourselves in the midst of a shifting research relationship akin to the process described by Thomas King (2003) of taking care of stories. We awakened to the ongoing life-making processes in which the youth were engaged, and we realized that, as we entered their lives, we were interrupting their life making by asking them to pause, to go backward and forward in time, to places in schools and to relationships that may not have been educative for them. As we negotiated entry, we knew we were asking them to dwell in experiences that, at times, may have been smoothed over and may have been left behind or silenced for the moment.

Each time we meet in the midst of research conversations we are imagining that we begin in different places as part of the negotiation of relationship and experience. We are forever shifting between positioning ourselves as researcher and participant, exploring different moments within lives, and through this process we move through the experiences together. What comes out of this ongoing negotiation of each research relationship is the necessary attentiveness that slows the inquiry down and helps both researcher and participant to think carefully about what might be taking place and exploring the possibilities that emerge through narrative inquiry.

As we reflected on the negotiation of entry with youth, we awakened to how it is not only that researchers select participants for studies but also that potential participants select us and make us part of their lives. Sean, Vera, and Jean were all part of the early school leavers study, a study that profoundly shaped each one of them. In locating participants and negotiating entry with them, we continued to think about who we were in relation to them. In conversation Jean recounts,

> I am reminded of another moment of watching as I stood in the doorway of my office in the Centre for Research for Teacher Education and Development. In that moment Sean was introducing me to Truong, a young man who was a possible participant in our narrative inquiry with youth who left school early. Sean had known Truong for many years and knew that he fit the criteria for the study. Sean convinced Truong to come to the university to meet me. In that moment of meeting I knew that much depended on watching and waiting, on being attentive to his expressions and mine, on being attentive to his body and mine, and to a deeper noticing of how that moment was being composed. So many stories were present in the moment, the stories of a youth of South Asian heritage and

a white older woman; of the different stories of family immigration to Canada separated by more than a hundred years, of a body marked by tattoos and one unmarked except by age. And the watching as he watched and I watched, a moment that seemed to last far longer than a moment. All of this lived in the moment of meeting, a moment marked by silence and by words. The handshake that lingered, eyes that locked in a look and the searching for a deeper noticing. It was important to wait, not to rush, not to judge but to wait.

Part of the watching and waiting was that familiar feeling of uncertainty, of not knowing what would happen next, the need for improvising ways forward that allowed Jean to be open to responding to the multiple inklings of alternatives that the moment opened up. There was a certainty that something would happen, that the moment would lead to other moments. What was uncertain was what, out of a range of possibilities, some imagined, some not imagined, would happen. What was certain was that if it were to open into a relational inquiry space, it was not all on Jean's terms as a researcher.

That moment was a moment of negotiating entry. In narrative inquiry it is moments such as this that begin to shape what we see as beginning to create spaces to come alongside children and youth in narrative inquiries. What started to become visible to us as narrative inquirers is how the negotiation of entry is not a one-way process. Although we may have criteria for participants, we are not solely in charge of the negotiation of research relationships. Participants are choosing us, choosing how much and what they will tell us, choosing whether or not they want to participate, their intentions for joining the research also shapes the research processes.

As we engage in negotiating entry into research relationships with children and youth, this wide awakeness to the mutuality of the relationships is heightened. Their intentions for participating are part of the watching process, them watching us to see how we fit into their unfolding stories, and us watching them to see how the processes of negotiating entry and research relationships might unfold.

NEGOTIATION OF ENTRY AS AN ONGOING PROCESS

As we look across past studies, we see that these processes of negotiation of entry are very diverse. There is no one way to negotiate, and no one entry is like the other. We highlight the importance of attending to how, as we enter into a new context, a new geographic place, and in the midst of ongoing lives, we are in the process of negotiating entry and beginning the negotiation of research relationships. What seems to echo across our studies is that each entry is often marked with anticipation, an eagerness to form new relationships, yet also a sense of uncertainty, of not knowing how our work will unfold. Particularly when we enter into relationships alongside children and youth, we are mindful that we, too, enter the lives of their families and lives that are embedded frequently in a community of friends and peers.

As we begin these research relationships, participants open up new puzzles, and we are attentive that we are negotiating entry into relational places, places that are shaped by both researchers and participants. These ongoing processes of negotiating entry shape the need for a constant wide awakeness to the multiplicity of stories we are entering.

CHAPTER 7

Ongoing Wakefulness to Multiple Stories to Live By: Ripples into Lives

Throughout the book we draw attention to the importance of narrative inquirers' continuing attention to the complexity of the lives of children and youth. Children and youth compose their lives in many differing places—in classrooms, schools, places in between school and home, home and community places, and so on. We also understand that children and youth are increasingly composing their lives within the places created by social media. Being wakeful to these multiple places shaping their lives also means becoming wakeful to multiple people, relationships, and situations in which children and youth find themselves. Children's and youth's interactions in multiple and often very diverse places, relationships, and situations shape their becoming, the multiple stories they live by.

As we engage in narrative inquiries alongside children and youth, we too become part of these interactions. We become part of these complex interactions in more or less awake ways—that is, by attending in wide-awake ways to our presence in the places where youth spend time and in the midst of their relationships. The multiplicity of our lives as nurses, teachers, university researchers, mothers, fathers, and so on also shape the relational spaces of the children, youth, and families who are participants in the narrative inquiries. Although we are attentive to how our presence is shaping the lives of the children and youth and the lives of their families and peers, we also need to be attentive to how our participation is shaping our lives as people and as narrative inquirers.

Thinking in these ways is far different from thinking of ourselves as only researchers with a research question that we are trying to answer. To be involved as a detached researcher is part of a dominant narrative of research and was the dominant narrative when Jean engaged in her master's work. In that work children's scores on two different tests were correlated. Neither Jean's life nor the lives of the children whose scores were correlated were at play in the research (Clandinin & Connelly,

2000). Perhaps it mattered that she was a teacher and counselor at the school in the relationships with the children and their families. But identities, stories to live by, were not visible in Jean's master's research. Not so in narrative inquiry, where the lives of both researchers and participants are always at work, always in the making.

In this chapter we turn back again to particular experiences Jean, Sean, and Vera lived during the narrative inquiry alongside the youth and families with whom they connected through the art club. However, we first turn toward experiences that Jean and Vera lived during a narrative inquiry alongside others at Ravine School, a site of inquiry of a larger Social Sciences and Humanities Council of Canada (SSHRC)–funded study introduced in the previous chapter. Our intent in this chapter is to make visible the importance of being wide awake to multiple stories to live by, ours and participants, and to the ways that narrative inquiries create ripples into lives. We forefront the concept of "world"-travelling (Lugones, 1987) in this chapter as a way to understand the work we are engaged in as narrative inquirers.

Ongoing Wakefulness Through Narrative Inquiry at Ravine School

Thinking about ongoing wakefulness to the multiplicity of stories to live by as we engage in narrative inquiries with children, youth, and families draws us back to memories of Ravine School. In one aspect of this narrative inquiry Jean and Vera participated alongside a principal, a teacher, and children and families in a grade 2/3 learning strategies classroom at Ravine school. Their presence at Ravine school was shaped through years of relationships and earlier narrative inquiries that Jean lived with Jeannette, the school principal of Ravine school. Jean knew Jeannette through a smaller research project they had coauthored in a different school where Jeannette was the principal. Jean had supervised Jeannette's master's work, and they had maintained a close connection over many years. There was a sense that this study was a part of a co-composed story of continuing research together.

Throughout the study Vera and the other researchers in the school were mindful that Jean had a long history alongside Jeannette and that this narrative inquiry in the grade 2/3 classroom was a study that would lead to other studies. This shared understanding, though sometimes more tacit than expressed and discussed, shaped our ongoing lives as researchers, principal, teachers, and others. In this way Vera understood the study as one of many studies yet to come and that the relational and long-term commitments to both Jeannette, the teacher, Kristi, and the children and families mattered in significant ways.

Vera came into the classroom in the context of the new SSHRC grant (Clandinin & Connelly, 2001) developed around puzzles of the experiences of teachers, children, parents, and administrators as their diverse stories to live by met in classrooms and schools. The 2001–2004 study was part of a series of grants from the Social Sciences and Humanities Research Council of Canada that Michael Connelly and Jean held since the 1980s with a focus on teacher knowledge and its expression in curriculum making. The 2001–2004 study was not specifically aimed at a particular subject matter but was more oriented at the life-making experiences within school curriculum making (Connelly & Clandinin, 1988). Literacy was a key aspect of the curriculum making at Ravine School and one that mattered to the principal and the teachers. Jean, in conversation with Jeannette, knew that the school focus was on literacy education, and that was a district priority at the time. As Jean and Jeannette discussed the possible narrative inquiry and Ravine Elementary School as a possible site, they recognized that if they focused on literacy, it would enable school district approval for the study more readily. They were aware that in order to gain approval to engage in the study, it would be important to align the study with school district and school priorities and be able to show that the study would be of benefit to the children and families in the school. They also needed to be able to show that the study would not disrupt the school curriculum making but would, rather, enrich the curriculum making. The research team was aware of the importance of being engaged with children and teachers from the outset, both from the research design and from the negotiation of entry. This need for wakefulness is part of the ongoing entry into layered landscapes and negotiation of participation with a research site, with teachers, and with children and families.

Inquiring into the Need for Ongoing Wakefulness

As we think about engaging in relational narrative inquiry with children and youth, we wondered about how we learn to engage with children and youth so we are wakeful to their complex lives, lived over time, in multiple layered landscapes. We often turn to the concepts of "world"-travelling woven with the concepts of arrogant and loving perception developed by Lugones (1987) to help us consider ways to understand how we can attend to the lives of children and youth as we engage with them in narrative inquiry. We introduced her concepts briefly in Chapter 2 and return to develop them in more depth here.

Lugones described her experiences of having "been the object of arrogant perception" (p. 4) and of perceiving others with arrogant perception. Drawing on Frye (1983), Lugones described arrogant perception as "the failure to identify with persons that one views arrogantly or has come to see as the products of arrogant perception" (p. 4). As Lugones described the ways in which arrogant perceptions shaped the early years of her life, she wrote of her gradual awakening to the need for "world"-travelling, a process she described as occurring when someone perceived as "the outsider has necessarily acquired flexibility in shifting from the mainstream construction of life where she is constructed as an outsider to other constructions of life where she is more or less 'at home'" (p. 3). Although Lugones saw this shifting or "flexibility" as "necessary for the outsider," she also urged that "those who are at ease in the mainstream" also "willfully exercise" this way of being (p. 3). Drawing upon her coming to "world"- travel within her own life as she shifted from arrogant perception to loving perception in relation with her mother, Lugones wrote,

> To love my mother was not possible for me while I retained a sense that it was fine for me and others to see her arrogantly. Loving my mother also required that I see with her eyes, that I go into my mother's world, that I see both of us as we are constructed in her world, that I witness her own sense of herself from within her world. Only through this travelling to her "world" could I identify with her because only then could I cease to ignore her and to be excluded and separate from her. Only then could I see her as a subject even if one subjected and only then could I see at all how meaning could arise fully between us. We are fully dependent on each other for the possibility of being understood and without this understanding we are not intelligible, we do not make sense, we are not solid, visible, integrated; we are lacking. So travelling to each other's "worlds" would enable us to be through loving each other. (p. 8)

Lugones recommended that "world"- travelling "be animated by an attitude of "playfulness":

> Playfulness is, in part, an openness to being a fool, which is a combination of not worrying about competence, not being self-important, not taking norms as sacred and finding ambiguity and double edges a source of wisdom and delight. So, positively, the playful attitude involves openness to surprise, openness to being a fool, openness to self-construction or reconstruction and to construction or reconstruction of the "worlds" we inhabit playfully. Negatively, playfulness is characterized by uncertainty, lack of self-importance, absence of rules or a not taking rules as sacred, a not worrying about competence and a lack of abandonment to a particular construction of oneself, others and one's relation to them. (p. 17)

Through this process, by consciously living in these ways, Lugones imagined significantly changed relationships among people:

> Without knowing the other's "world," one does not know the other, and without knowing the other one is really alone in the other's presence

because the other is only dimly present to one. Through travelling to other people's "worlds" we discover that there are "worlds" in which those who are the victims of arrogant perception are really subjects, lively beings, resistors, constructors of visions even though in the mainstream construction they are animated only by the arrogant perceiver and are pliable, foldable, file-awayable, classifiable. (p. 18)

We draw on Lugones's thoughts on arrogant perception, "world"-travelling, playfulness, and loving perception as important to our work as narrative inquirers as we work to understand children and youths' experiences as well as our own. It is, as we noted earlier in this chapter, important to attend to who we are and are becoming as we come alongside children and youth as narrative inquirers.

As narrative inquirers come into relation with children and youth, particularly if these relationships are initiated and sustained within institutional places, we need to remember that who the child or youth is and is becoming is nested within larger narratives. What we may see, hear, or come to know in, for example, a classroom, a school, a day care, a health care unit, a medical clinic, and so on needs to be situated within larger narratives and within larger networks of people. The child or youth is in relation with many people, relationships that have unfolded over time and place and through many diverse situations. The narrative inquiry in the grade 2/3 classroom helped us to attend more closely to the multiple places shaping children and families' lives. We saw the importance of becoming wakeful to multiple people, relationships, and situations in which children and youth find themselves as well as to the stories they carried within their memories. We also became attentive to the larger cultural, social, and institutional narratives that shaped the lives of the children and families as well as our lives as narrative inquirers. We drew on Lugones's concepts to help us find ways to understand how to think about our work as narrative inquirers.

Vera and Jean often think about their work at Ravine school in relation to "world"-travelling and who they were and were becoming alongside Jeannette and Kristi and, most importantly, alongside the children. Elsewhere (Caine, 2010) Vera notes that

The composition of this learning strategies classroom was marked by diversity, both in terms of intellectual abilities as well as cultural background. The classroom had been created by the principal as a response to some children's struggles to fit into regular school classrooms, children whom the principal thought would benefit from extra attention and from working with a teacher who was trained as a special education teacher with many years of experience. Throughout the school year I was unable to determine all of the reasons why individual children had been placed in this learning strategies classroom. I wondered many times about the

gender composition of the classroom (all boys) and about the stories that
were told about them on the landscape of school. (p. 494)

Thinking about "world"- travelling within this context meant also
understanding the institutional context of the children's and family's
lives, a context that, to Vera, appeared arbitrary and discriminatory. Part
of the mandated curriculum focus in grade 3 social studies was, at the
time, studies into community—that is, studies into the nature, functions,
and purposes of community. As part of the work in the school the children created community alphabet books, using both photography and
writing, to show and inquire into their understandings of community.
The children worked together in small groups to explore different letters
of the alphabet and to find words that reflected their understandings of
community. The words were then enacted by the children and captured
through carefully composed photographs. The photographs were large-
format negatives that the children could then scratch and write on, further develop, and, in some cases, erase. Vera and the children developed
these images in a darkroom and then created written text alongside the
images. This yearlong process was very intense. Each week Vera and the
children spent dedicated time together.

Throughout the process it was visible that tensions existed between
what many of the children understood as community and the mandated
curricular focus on community. Where the mandated curricular focus
appeared to be on goods and services, needs and wants, and natural and
person-made places, the children focused on relationships and families in
homes and other places and the responsibilities of being part of a community. Community was understood from the children's understandings
of community as both moral and relational. This long-term engagement
created a playfulness as Vera and the children came to know each other
well and began to trust each other with the stories of their experiences
in their schools, homes, and other places. The complex layers that began
to become visible, including who the children were on the landscape, the
mandated curriculum, the children's complex lives on and off the school
landscape, necessitated the need for Vera and the children to "world"-
travel to each other's worlds and to their own. This "world"- travelling helped them to stay wakeful throughout the work. Only much later
did Vera recognize how living alongside the children in ways that made
"world"- travelling in relationship possible could shift social agendas.
As the school year came to an end, Jeannette asked whether the children's work could become part of a planned penny carnival. She wanted
to make visible the work that Vera and the children had created in the
classroom. Vera notes (Caine, 2010),

The children's final images and texts of the community alphabet were displayed at the school's year-end event, amidst penny carnival stands, silent auction items and bake sales, to which all the students and parents of the school were invited. Interestingly, their work was the only academic work that was displayed during the activities. I still recall my initial reaction, one of fear and hesitation—displaying the work amidst penny carnival stands had a circus feel to it, and I was not at all sure that it would honor the children's hard work. Yet, the children were excited at the opportunity to show their work. As the day and evening progressed the responses of the school community were marked by amazement and awe—peoples were pulled to the exhibit. Perhaps it was the dis-positioning context, shifting who the children in the learning disabilities classroom were, their abilities and insights, as they shared their understanding of community. The children had been able to shift the commonly held story of their classroom; they had shifted the stories of who they were in that moment of the exhibit. For many this was the most important part, to begin shifting institutional practices of labeling to more open conversations of possibilities and inclusiveness. At the end of the school year the teacher indicated that all of the boys would become part of a regular classroom, that their school had re-thought special classrooms; I am left to wonder how much of this was due to the insightful and amazing work the children had done all year. After the children received their own hardbound copies of their community alphabet, I received an email note from one of the parents indicating how this work had allowed her son to finally be heard and that they as a family would treasure this book forever. The children helped others to re-imagine their understanding of community, and notably they helped me see how important it is that as a narrative inquirer I need to be attentive to the possibilities for reflection, action and change; that research could lead to social action (Lewin, 1946). The use of visual narrative inquiry within a classroom opened up the possibility for a deeper understanding of the children's understanding of community, and the possibility to challenge the mandated curriculum, as well as to change classroom practices. Through inquiring deeper into their own understandings of community, the children advanced the social agenda of their school, and their community. (pp. 492-493)

The need for ongoing wakefulness to what is happening in lives, including our own, is part of what we learned was central to being and becoming a narrative inquirer alongside children and youth. In the work alongside the children in the grade 2/3 classroom, Vera began to understand how who she is and is becoming shaped her interactions with participants. This entanglement of the experiences, of the lives of narrative inquirers and participants, is an important thread in narrative inquiries.

Drawing on the concept of "world"-travelling (Lugones, 1987) allows us to attend more closely to the ways in which we are wide awake or at least to the need to strive toward wide awakeness, to the multiplicity of lives and the ways in which engaging in narrative inquiry ripples into multiple lives. In what follows we return to the work alongside the children and youth of Aboriginal heritage in the arts club.

Ripples into Lives: Being Attentive to Our Participation Alongside Children and Youth

As Vera, Jean, and Sean worked with children and youth in the art club, we constantly reminded ourselves to be aware of the ripples we created in children and youths' lives by our participation with them in narrative inquiry. We were mindful of how our presence could shift their lives in multiple ways. Our experience in earlier narrative inquiries, such as Vera's involvement with the grade 2/3 children at Ravine Elementary, had heightened our attentiveness to the ways lives could shift.

As we enter into the work with children and youth in narrative inquiries we realize that we are becoming, in some ways at least, part of their lives. We meet them in school classrooms, in out-of-school places, and in other institutional places. It makes a difference who we are in our complex lives, which are always at work in the relational spaces. Attending carefully to who we are as we engage in the relational work of narrative inquiry is an ongoing and always negotiated process across the multiplicity of places in which we engage with children and youth. We need to be attentive to who we are as we live alongside the children and youth over months and, perhaps, years. Certainly we are attentive to how we continue to have long-term relational responsibilities to the children and youth.

Multiplicity of Stories We Live By: As we, a group of researchers, worked together in the art club, we were aware of the multiplicity of who we were and how working in the arts club drew out aspects of our stories to live by, sometimes in complex ways. Jean's stories to live by are shaped by her work in schools alongside teachers, children, and families and by her work of testing and assessing children when she worked as a special programs teacher and psychologist. Although schools are a place where she often feels she does not belong, she is familiar with finding places on the edge of classrooms. Vera's stories to live by are shaped not only by her work as a nurse but also by her school experiences in which she often lived stories with plotlines of resistance to the ways schools did not attend to the lives of the children and youth who attended.

The place of the art club, the place where we first met the children and youth, called forth our stories to live by, shaping who we were in the place and with the youth. For example, the youth and other researchers often called on Vera when questions of health emerged. They often turned to Sean or Jean when questions of school policy or practice were at issue. As a person who knew schools and school policies and usual practices, Jean felt at ease around drawing attention to possible difficulties the youth might face. When other teachers came to the classroom they often sought out someone who was recognizable as someone who knew schools. Sean, situated as a part-time consultant with responsibilities for students of Aboriginal heritage and as a researcher in the art club, was called to attend to questions of student placements and regulations around school attendance and also seen by the students tara teachers as a teacher and person of Aboriginal heritage. The experiences alongside the youth were ones in which our multiple stories to live by were called forward and became more visible to us and to the youth.

However, in the living in the art club we were intentional in trying to come to know the stories of experience of the youth, and we worked to not be constrained by the stories of school that shaped lives in school. This was frequently challenging work, as we often were somewhat unaware of the embodied stories that had been "planted in us early or along the way," as Okri (1977) wrote. Jean became increasingly awake to a story that she lived by of completing projects and working until there was a finished product. This story to live by was threaded not only around her childhood stories but also around her stories of teaching, where she knew that schoolwork needed to be completed in order to have work products that could be assessed. As she engaged with the youth, these stories were often called forth. Vera became more awake to her stories to live by of feeling dis/ease in the place of school. Sean became more awake to the importance of coming alongside the youth without needing to intervene through school district programming. As we became more awake to what working in the art club pulled out of our knowing, it helped us become more awake to the need to "world"-travel to the lives of the youth and to what they were helping us see about their experiences in schools.

As we engaged with the children and youth, we needed to be able to "world"-travel to who we were and were becoming as we came alongside the youth. We wrote field notes and studied photographs taken during the art club to see what we could discern about not only the youth's experiences in the art club but also their experiences in schools and out of schools. As we co-composed field texts alongside the youth and inquired into the field texts, we came to learn how who we each were and were becoming shaped the experiences of the youth and how the experiences with the youth shaped each of us. The ripples of these interconnected stories shaped the lives of the youth and the lives of each of us. The meeting of our lives in the art club became an opportunity to inquire into the ways lives were shifted and shaped.

Participants Story Us into Their Stories: We introduced Tara in Chapters 1 and 2. We return to stories of her experiences alongside us to show how our stories became entwined with hers. Tara attended the art club

when her other after-school activities made it possible for her to participate. However, she frequently came to seek Jean out at times of family
deaths or to share stories of difficulties she was experiencing with friends
and/or family members. Tara also came to the art club for short periods
of time to celebrate what she was doing in other activities such as her
cheering club and when plans were being made for the grade 8 trip to
Europe. Jean continued to meet with her for one-on-one conversations.

At the end of Tara's grade 8 year, Tara came briefly to the art club
feast and celebration for friends and family who the youth wanted to
visit, a time when we marked the end of the Wednesday afternoon art
club times. However, even though the Wednesday afternoon art club was
completed, as researchers, we continued to meet youth for one-on-one
conversations. Jean and Tara met several times during Tara's grade 9
year at the school. They met again when Tara invited Jean to her high
school, as described in Chapters 1 and 2. It was during that visit that
Jean wondered, as she sat with Tara in the small room in the high school,
whether who she was in Tara's story had changed. Tara introduced
Jean as her friend, suggesting that Jean was someone she cared about,
someone whom she was comfortable to bring into her place in the high
school. Was Jean still a researcher in her story? Over these months and
years Tara and Jean had co-composed a relationship that was both of her
making and of Jean's. She was comfortable in the new high school having an older white woman as her friend. Was Jean wakeful to who she
was becoming in this new relationship? And yet the ripples that we were
making into each other's lives were significant in who we were becoming. This attentiveness to who we are and are becoming as we engage
with children and youth needs to be always something in the making,
always something we are awake to.

Ongoing Wakefulness: Learning to "World"-Travel as Part of Narrative Inquiry

As we engage in narrative inquiry alongside children and youth, we are
called to "world"-travel, which requires an ongoing attentiveness to
who we as narrative inquirers are and are becoming. At the same time
we need to engage in ongoing attentiveness to who the children and
youth are and are becoming. We highlight the importance of learning to
"world"-travel with loving perception rather than arrogant perception.
Had Jean, Sean, Janice, or Vera engaged in continuing processes of arrogant perception as they "world"-travelled alongside the children, Kristi
and Jeannette at Ravine school or Tara or other children and youth, the
relational work of narrative inquiry would not have been possible. It is

Lugones's (1987) concepts that help us see that "Without knowing the other's 'world,' one does not know the other, and without knowing the other, one is really alone in the other's presence because the other is only dimly present" (p. 18). Had we traveled with arrogant perception, we could only have seen the children and youth as "pliable, foldable, file-awayable, classifiable," (p. 18) all ways that children and youth are often constructed in institutional narratives.

By trying to live out Lugones's concept of "world"-traveling with loving perception in relation with the youth and children and they in relation with us, we were enabled "to be through loving each other" (p. 8). It is in these ways that we can more fully understand the importance of the wide awakeness required of us throughout narrative inquiries. In the next chapter we continue to explore the importance of wide awakeness as we explore the nestedness of lives within familial contexts, over time, over places, and within multiple relationships.

CHAPTER 8

Coming Alongside Children and Youth in the Field Within Familial Contexts

In this chapter we make evident our understanding of what it means to live alongside children and youth in the field. We also show, as we come alongside children and youth, that their families—however children and youth define their families—are part of their lives. We cannot live alongside children and youth without an understanding that families are part of the visible or invisible contexts of their lives. We are reminded again of the layered landscapes within which lives are nested. We begin by describing what we mean by "living alongside." We then show aspects of what living alongside entails in the living of a narrative inquiry as we think with an account of Vera and Tammy's living alongside one another, over time, place, and shifting relationships.

UNDERSTANDING LIVING ALONGSIDE

It is important to understand what we mean by *living* and what we mean by *alongside,* as these concepts are touchstones of narrative inquiry work (Clandinin & Caine, 2013; see Chapter 13). Narrative inquirers' commitments to be part of the living—that is, to be part of the lives of participants as they unfold—are central to what we mean by living and alongside. In the "living out of stories" (Clandinin, 2006, p. 47), we are attentive to the experiences of both participants and ourselves as researchers.

What Is the Field in Narrative Inquiry? The field of each narrative inquiry is the relational space shaped between participants and researchers. This relational space, already in the making even as initial conversations about the study and consent forms are signed, continues to become—that is, continues in the making—as the inquiry unfolds. Participants' and researchers' lived and told stories are at the heart of this space. Living together within the continuous co-making of this relational space keeps us attentive to the relational responsibilities (Clandinin & Connelly, 2000) of narrative inquirers.

Ongoing questions of who we are and who we are becoming in relation with participants are always present in the field of a narrative inquiry.

What Do We Mean by Living Alongside in the Field? Our conceptualization of living in this relational space is partly derived from the etymology of the word living. From as early as the fourteenth century the meaning of living entails "the fact of dwelling in some place"; in this way living is linked to life. Life, in terms of etymology, shows the connection to existence, to the conditions of being, to the body, and to continuance and perseverance (Online Etymology Dictionary, accessed October 24, 2014). As we connect *living* with *alongside,* we highlight the importance of dwelling in the living, of understanding experience as it is lived. As we live alongside, then, we spend significant amounts of time with participants. We often visit places where they live or want to show us. In the living we meet others who participants want us to meet. Living alongside, over time, places, and multiple relationships and situations, makes visible our commitments and responsibilities to participants. Living alongside also means experiencing uncertainty and improvising who we are and are becoming in ongoing relationships with one another.

These aspects of living alongside also make visible the nested nature of stories lived and told. As earlier noted, our living alongside children and youth in narrative inquiries has sometimes started within and mostly stayed situated within institutional contexts, such as within a school context. We see that in the studies undertaken at Ravine Elementary School and at City Heights School. Other studies with children and youth have sometimes started within schools and have gradually shifted to other places in their lives. We see that in the narrative inquiry with the youth and families of Aboriginal heritage. Some studies have stayed outside of institutional contexts, in the home and community places of children and youth. We see that in the narrative inquiry with the youth who left school before graduating. Regardless of the starting place, families are always part of the lives and, therefore, are part of the lived and told stories of children and youth.

In the following account we make the nestedness of stories visible as we enter into the relational space shaped by Vera and Tammy's living alongside one another over many years and multiple places. Tammy and Vera first met nearly twenty years ago when Tammy became a participant in Vera's master's study.

TAMMY AND VERA: LIVING ALONGSIDE IN THE FIELD WITHIN NESTED FAMILIAL CONTEXTS

Standing at the side of the road that leads right through the graveyard, Vera remembered the last time she and Tammy had been there. It was well over fourteen years ago, and much had happened since that time. Tammy has given birth to two more children since then, and Geraldine, who was less than a year old at the time, is now a beautiful young woman. It was a difficult visit then, and Vera recalled her walk through the rows and rows of graves trying to find Tammy's mother's gravestone, remembering it was not too far from a big tree in the southeast corner of the graveyard. Today when Tammy asked Vera whether they could go and visit her mother again, Tammy mentioned that it was time to introduce Aidan, her two-year-old son, to his grandmother. Over the past few months Tammy talked often with Vera about how Aidan has saved her, how he has helped her stay away from substance use and sex-trade work over the past year. Tammy also talked about how hard she has worked during this time. Tammy wants to show Aidan to her mother because he is such a big part of Tammy's unfolding life.

As Tammy and Vera drive to the graveyard, Vera looks in the rearview mirror. Later, in her field notes, she writes of what she saw in that backward glance:

> I can see both Aidan and Felix. Felix is our nine-year-old son. In that moment of looking in the mirror I thought about how Tammy has become part of his life too. I remember how exhausted I was in the weeks after he was born and how Tammy responded at that time and made me aware of how little I knew of what it means to become a mom. She was trying to teach and reassure me. Several years prior to this I was part of the birth of her daughter Geraldine. It was in the midst of the narrative inquiry for my master's study, a time when I first became more wakeful to what it means to live alongside people within the contexts of their lives. Tammy, who was actively using substances at the time of Geraldine's birth, had called me when she went into labor to help her negotiate what she knew would be a difficult story. Although Tammy knew I had entered her life as a researcher, she also knew, because my study was a narrative inquiry, I had a long-term commitment to being alongside her. I smile as I think about the many years that have marked my work alongside Tammy and how lucky that Felix and Aidan have become part of this.

Turning back to the present, Vera can see that Aidan loves the big tree and, most of all, the wide-open field at the graveyard. He pays no attention to graveside markers, as he chases invisible and real animals, while Felix chases to keep up with him. Aidan loves to run, the faster the better. A smile is always on his face. His long flowing hair, sometimes braided and sometimes tamed only by streaks of water, is blowing in the wind created by his speed. There are moments when Vera seems to hardly remember what two-year-olds do. Felix loves Aidan's energy. Eventually, though, Felix throws his hands in the air after running after Aidan with the stroller for some time and says, "I don't think I should be the one looking after him." Both Aidan and Felix carry smiles on their faces, and each glance from the corner of their eyes helps them notice when the other would move his body again—to chase and be chased.

As Vera shows in this account, in living alongside we follow our movements in relation with each other over time and place and shifting relationships. All of the many moments have shaped how Vera thinks about what it means to live alongside children and youth in the field and how much of each of their lives are both nested within and shaped by their familial contexts. Although Vera may not still understand many of Tammy's experiences, Vera has come to see how much of who Tammy is and is becoming is shaped by her mother's life and her own mothering experiences. Vera writes,

> I remember her tears and cries when Geraldine was born, tears and cries for her mother. As I stand by the side of the road alongside the graveyard, I think about these long-ago cries and start to sense why we are here and, perhaps, why I am here as part of Tammy's stories of experience. It is Tammy's stories that connect at a deeper level with my current experiences alongside Aboriginal youth in and outside of schools. Tammy, intentionally or unintentionally, asked me to listen in different ways, in ways she felt would help me to understand not only her experience but also the experiences that continued to shape her children's lives. Tammy knows that lives are nested within places and are unfolding over time. It is important for Tammy to be visiting her mother's grave, to be in the city where all of her early life has taken place. Although it is not her ancestral home place, it is the place she grew up. Tammy and I have talked often about the importance of place in her life, not only in ways that ground her but also in ways that some places make it easier for her to return to a life of substance use and sex-trade work that she no longer wants in her life. Place continues to be a hard thing, and the absence of knowing her ancestral home through her familial stories has left a deep emptiness.

Tammy participated in a narrative inquiry with Vera long ago. Tammy has now joined in another study alongside Vera. Although Vera thinks often about Aidan and Tammy, she also thinks of Geraldine, the daughter born during Vera's master's study. Geraldine is now a teenager and lives in a foster family with her younger brother, who is four years older than Aidan. We see in the long drive to the graveyard where Tammy's mother is buried how important this place is to Tammy. This is the second time Tammy has wanted Vera to take her to her mother's gravesite. Now she wants to show Aiden, her two-year-old, to her mother. The complex web of relationships, a web composed over time and shaped by the lives of Tammy, her three children, Vera, and Felix, Vera's son, are all present in this moment of living. This moment of living shows how we understand living alongside the ongoing negotiation of the relational field within narrative inquiry. This moment, not unlike many others, is a moment when narrative inquiry has called Vera to the living, to watch, to linger, and, in many ways, to partake in the experiences that mark our inquiry into lives alongside participants.

As narrative inquirers we also sense the importance of the nested relationships that families create for and with children. As we shift our vantage point to the experiences of children and youth, we wonder how those nested familial contexts shape the experiences of children and youth. We wonder how the experience of being taken to the graveyard of his grandmother might shape Aiden's stories into the future, of how he will make sense of his brother and sister who do not live with Aiden and Tammy.

Of the importance of attending to the lives of children and youth within nested familial contexts, Vera writes,

> I wonder what stories Aidan and Felix and also Tammy and I will later tell about this moment and what memories we will each have or which ones we will remind each other of in the future. I remember the drive home, how we pulled away very slowly from the graveyard with a promise to return. I realize that in living alongside Tammy and Aidan that I have come to understand Aidan's experiences differently. I also think about how much I have come to know of them—that is, of Aidan and Tammy—through knowing Tammy. I wonder: How much of who Felix is and is becoming will others know without knowing who I am? How much would others know of Felix without knowing the experiences of those whose stories his experiences are nested within? How much can I understand about children and youth without asking about who their families are? And I wonder about who each child and youth names as his or her family. Who does each child and youth see as important in having shaped who s/he is and is becoming?

As we continue to think with Vera's account of her experiences in relation with Tammy, Aidan, and Felix, we pull forward a number of threads that are important in order to understand how the lives of children and youth are nested within the visible or invisible familial contexts. These threads we pull forward are threads that are necessarily important to understanding the ways that the lives of children and youth are nested within familial contexts.

ATTENDING TO PLACES WITHIN THE NESTED FAMILIAL CONTEXTS OF CHILDREN AND YOUTH'S LIVES

Years ago, when Tammy and Vera first met and began to live alongside one another in a narrative inquiry, they did not know the many ways in which a place or places would become central in their negotiation of the field of their inquiries. In the first narrative inquiry Vera came to know of particular places that, at that time, were shaping the stories of substance use and sex-trade work Tammy was living and telling. She also came to know of Tammy's mother's gravesite and of the familial within her unfolding life.

Now, many years later, the gravesite is still present, still influencing the stories Tammy lives and tells as she and Vera story with one another their lives as mothers. Their recent visit to the gravesite of Tammy's mother shows something of this, as do Vera's wonders about the possible shaping influence on who Aidan is and is becoming as the gravesite of his grandmother becomes part of the familial context shaping his life. So too does Vera become awake to how the street places of substance abuse and street work shape Tammy's life making as Tammy seeks ways to stay away from these places.

We drew on Marmon Silko's (1996) work in Chapter 4 to show our understandings of how place is woven into our becoming as people. Who we are and are becoming cannot be separated from the places where we are or have been. Places shape and live in us, flowing into the stories we live and tell. As narrative inquirers living alongside children and youth, trying to understand something of the life the child or youth is composing, requires that we are always attentive to place(s). As familial contexts are always nested within a place or places, in order to understand something of the shaping influence of familial contexts on the lives of children and youth, it is important that we try to understand the children and youths' experiences of the places they story for us.

Vera's account gives a powerful sense of this. These places may be geographically near; they may be far away; they may be places that the child or youth has never visited but still connects with through knowing the stories lived and told within familial contexts. For example, although neither Tammy nor Vera have been in Tammy's ancestral home place that continues to shape the familial contexts of Tammy's life, it is important for Vera to understand the meanings Tammy held of this place as a child and as a youth as well as the meanings she holds of them today as a young mother. Understanding these meanings and the ways there have been shifts in meaning for Tammy continues to deepen Vera's understandings of the familial contexts in which Tammy's life is nested. Coming alongside in this way depends on the "world"-traveling that both Vera and Tammy undertake over multiple years.

ATTENDING TO THE INTERGENERATIONAL WITHIN NESTED FAMILIAL CONTEXTS OF CHILDREN AND YOUTH'S LIVES

Over time Vera gradually came to realize some of the intergenerational aspects of Tammy's lived and told stories. Although Vera never met Tammy's mother, she feels a sense of being in relationship with her as a result of her relationship with Tammy. This sense of being in relationship was, in part, shaped through Tammy and Vera's visits to the gravesite and graveyard where Tammy's mother is buried. Stories of Tammy's mother were woven into Tammy's lived and told stories since she and Vera first began to live alongside one another. Along the way Vera began to sense that Tammy needed Vera to know stories of her mother if she was to be able to understand her life and the lives of her children, Geraldine, Aidan, and another son. Vera too, as she reflected upon the recent experience of visiting Tammy's mother's grave, wondered about this intergenerational thread when she questioned how someone could possibly understand her son, Felix, without understanding something of who she is and is becoming in relation with Felix.

As we linger with the ways in which this thread of the intergenerational is woven into the familial contexts in which the lives of children and youth are nested, we think with Mary Young's (2005) attention to the "intergenerational narrative reverberations" (p. 162) that shape the life composing of successive generations within families. In this way we understand that the stories lived and told by family members can and often do live on in the bodies and experiences lived by present generations.

Attending to the intergenerational threads that become visible in the lived and told stories of children and youth has deepened our understandings of their lives and the constant presence of their familial contexts in which their lives are nested. However, attending to, coming to know something of, and then of trying to understand ways in which this intergenerational thread dwells in the familial and in the lives of children and youth has been neither fast nor simple. Our understandings are always only partial and always for now.

In Sean's inquiry alongside Donovan (see Chapter 11), it was in living alongside in the midst of one situation that an opening was created for Sean through which he glimpsed something of the familial contexts in which Donovan's life was nested and shaped. As Donovan was making a drum and learning to play songs that accompanied the drum in the art club, Donovan began to share stories of his early life. As Sean listened to Donovan's stories, Donovan told stories of his experiences of loss that he felt since the passing of his Kookum Muriel (*kookum* is a Cree word that means grandma or grandmother). Sean slowly learned, as Donovan told his stories, that Kookum Muriel was an important presence and teacher in Donovan's life, a teacher in his familial contexts who continues to shape who Donovan is becoming, even though she is no longer alive.

As we learn from Vera's experiences alongside Tammy and from Sean's experiences alongside Donovan, becoming wakeful to and following these intergenerational threads requires imaginative "world"-traveling. Vera will never be able to meet Tammy's mother, nor will Sean be able to meet Donovan's Kookum Muriel. Yet each person has been and continues to be influential in the lives Tammy and Donovan are composing. This imaginative "world"-traveling is important if we are to understand the intergenerational threads that shape the familial contexts of children and youth.

ATTENDING TO MUTUAL VISIBILITY WITHIN NESTED FAMILIAL CONTEXTS OF CHILDREN AND YOUTH'S LIVES

As Vera began to attend to the nestedness of Tammy's life within familial contexts, the visibility of the nestedness of Vera's own life in familial contexts also gradually grew. Often it was aspects of Tammy's life that turned Vera's thoughts and wonders back upon her life nested within her familial contexts. At the beginning of Vera's account she remembers how Tammy reached out to and supported her when Felix was born. Although in differing ways, both Tammy and Vera were away from their mothers when their first children were born. They found ways to support the other: Vera as she stayed alongside Tammy while Geraldine was born and Tammy as she talked with Vera about her experiences as a mother.

Vera continued to live alongside Tammy as they visited Tammy's mother's grave a second time. This visit was shaped, at least in part, through Tammy's desire to show Aidan, her small son, to her mother. It is in the midst of this visit, in living alongside Tammy and Aidan, that Vera wondered about herself and Felix and the children and youth with whom she is currently engaged in narrative inquiry. We see something similar at work in the relational space shaped by Donovan and Sean. As Donovan continued to tell stories to Sean of the presence of Kookum Muriel in his life, Donovan also shared stories of his community and, in particular, the farm where she lived and where he visited. As Sean thought with these stories of Donovan's life and how much Donovan loved being in that particular place with his Kookum, he was drawn back in time and place to memories of his experiences of growing up on a farm.

What this growing mutual visibility of the familial contexts between Tammy and Vera and between Donovan and Sean helps to foreground is that, as described in more detail in Chapter 3, our autobiographical narrative inquiries are present throughout narrative inquiries. As Vera lived alongside Tammy and Sean alongside Donovan, there were many moments that called them to inquire into their own lives and into the nestedness of their lives in their familial contexts, both the familial contexts of their lives as children and youth as well as their contexts as parents.

These methodological aspects of place, the intergenerational, and the growing mutual visibility of the nestedness of our lives in familial contexts are not easily separated in the living of narrative inquiries. As we work within the three-dimensional narrative inquiry space, we need to understand that the shaping influences of Tammy's mother and of Donovan's Kookum are interwoven with the places shaping the familial contexts in which their lives, past and present, are nested.

ATTENDING TO BUMPING PLACES AS WE TRY TO COME ALONGSIDE WITHIN THE NESTED FAMILIAL CONTEXTS OF CHILDREN AND YOUTH

In what we have so far written it may seem that the process of coming alongside children and youth and to understanding that their lives are nested within familial narratives may be easy and straightforward. This is not our intention, as in our experiences this process is never easy; it is an aspect of our narrative inquiries that we stay awake to during the entire unfolding of an inquiry. In what follows we give a sense of some of the complexities we have experienced as we have come alongside children and youth within their nested familial contexts.

In our work alongside children and youth in the arts club we knew the participants were the ones with the agency that would enable us to come alongside them; it was not all up to us. In Chapters 1 and 2 we showed how it was Tara who finally made it possible for Jean to come with her to her home and to her new school. Without Tara creating the space for Jean to come alongside in these ways, it was not possible for her to "world"-travel to Tara's worlds.

In some of the relationships with youth in the arts club some youth did not create openings for us to come alongside them in their familial places. Through not sharing phone numbers, missing agreed-upon meetings, and making themselves inaccessible outside of the art club times, the youth made it visible to us that they were not open—or at least not yet open—to allowing us to understand their familial contexts. We knew how important it was to honor their sense that they did not want us alongside in those ways.

We also know the importance of being open to knowing when there is an opening to come alongside. Sometimes in a murmured invitation or an off-hand comment there was a brief opening to come alongside into a familial context. It was only as we stayed wide awake enough to catch the possibility that we were able to come alongside.

We also came to understand that although sometimes the youth did want us alongside, there were other institutional narratives that prevented us from coming into their familial contexts. We knew that sometimes, for example, youth wanted us to meet a parent or a family member, but constraints imposed by institutional narratives such as social service agencies did not enable us to meet people the youth wanted us to meet.

GATHERING THREADS ON COMING ALONGSIDE CHILDREN AND YOUTH IN FAMILIAL CONTEXTS

As we turn to think again about the importance of recognizing that the lives of children and youth are always nested within familial contexts and about the importance of coming alongside children and youth to understand this nestedness, we remind ourselves of the importance of staying alongside long enough to understand something of the lives in the making. We know how there is the possibility that we will shape their lives, but we also know how coming alongside will shape our lives. As we come alongside, as we and they begin to shape each other's stories to live by, we are reminded to attend carefully to the ways life stories are told and retold and relived in new, previously unimagined ways. We return again to Coles (1989), who reminds us to attend closely to "what we say," as "we owe it to each other to respect our stories and learn from them" (p. 30).

As earlier noted, this aspect of narrative inquiries with children and youth is never easy or finished; it is an aspect we need to stay attentive to in each moment as we and children and youth are in the midst of an inquiry. Not ever feeling certain alongside unending questions of who we are and who we are becoming in relation with children and youth and their families are ongoing throughout the inquiry.

CHAPTER 9

Co-composing Field Texts
with Children and Youth

Over many years of engaging in narrative inquiries we have shaped many methods for co-composing field texts (see Clandinin & Connelly, 2000 for a discussion of the use of field texts to replace the concept of data in narrative inquiry), including engaging in one-on-one conversations; engaging in group conversations; composing annals and chronicles; writing field notes of events in and out of institutional settings; collecting work samples; collecting documents; composing art work; taking photographs in diverse places; using artifacts and memory box items, including photographs as triggers for stories; working with photographs (family and self photos), digital photos, and Facebook photos; writing researcher journals; having participants write journals; and, as Clandinin and Connelly (2000), noted, using almost any methods that allow us to understand the experiences of participants and researchers. In this chapter we show the importance of understanding that field texts are also composed and collected within the relational field of narrative inquiry. With the relational ontology of narrative inquiry it is more appropriate to refer to co-composing of field texts than of composing field texts. As we co-compose field texts with participants it is important that we continue to dwell within the metaphoric three-dimensional narrative inquiry space, with its dimensions of place, temporality, and sociality.

In our studies alongside children and youth we have also composed multiple ways to compose and co-compose field texts. They include many of the methods listed above, but in some ways how we live them out with children and youth may be somewhat different. In what follows we draw from multiple narrative inquiries to show the range, the kind, and the possibilities of co-composing field texts with children and youth.

By dwelling in the processes of co-composing, we find ourselves drawn to different times within research relationships and how the co-composing is shaped by multiple contexts over time. The processes of co-composing field texts begin at the outset of a narrative inquiry—that is, as we design studies, undergo ethics reviews, begin to locate and negotiate entry with participants, and move into the ongoing inquiry relationship, which is the field of narrative inquiry. The processes of co-composing field texts are shaped by the ongoing narrative inquiry—that is, possibilities for co-composing field texts are opened, made visible, closed, and reopened as the relational field of narrative inquiry is shaped.

The physical place(s) of inquiry within which field texts are co-composed shape the field texts. As we consider the co-composition of field texts with children and youth, it is our intention to highlight examples of field texts that have been co-composed in previous narrative inquiries. However, we also look back on the process of co-composing field texts with children and youth in order to unpack the relational aspects of co-composing field texts, exploring tensions that shape the processes of co-composing.

In what follows we show the co-composing of field texts alongside children and youth in several narrative inquiries, although our main focus is on the narrative inquiry into the experiences of Aboriginal youth and their families.

CO-COMPOSING FIELD TEXTS ALONGSIDE ABORIGINAL YOUTH AND FAMILIES

We have already introduced readers to the narrative inquiry alongside youth of Aboriginal heritage. We described the research design, the processes of negotiating entry, and the processes of finding participants and of negotiating relationships. The art club was, as we earlier described, within a time (outside of instructional hours) and a place (a seldom-used classroom within an urban junior high school). It was in the art club that we began to meet youth on a weekly basis, each Wednesday, immediately after the dismissal school bell rang, consistently over two school years.

As we described earlier, each week the members of the research team purposefully worked to transform the classroom place into a place where the youth who attended could engage with each other, with art materials, and with members of the research team. Each week, as we engaged in transforming the classroom place, we came to understand that who we are as narrative inquirers shaped the ways we designed the art club. For some of us, the ways we imagined the place was designed by memories of other conversational places, such as kitchen tables and circles for conversations. Others, more caught in memories of classrooms, imagined table groups and center tables. We intentionally worked with different compositions so the art club place would not too strongly resemble a classroom. Chairs were placed throughout the room, no longer in rows. We intended the space to allow youth and researchers to explore, in various ways, the art supplies neatly presented each week. Paintbrushes, canvases, pencil crayons, and paper in different sizes and compositions and colorful assorted beads were present as we invited the youth into the space.

As we worked together to design the place, there was uncertainty, but there was also intentionality. We knew we were disrupting the institutional narrative of school as we worked to redesign the classroom into a place that was congruent with our research intentions. Although initially we were only partially awake to how our narratives of experience shaped the ways we designed the place, we were aware that the place the youth experienced would shape the ways we would be able to come alongside them. The undertow of rules, routines, structured time, assessment, participation, and projects were present in the embodied knowing of the researchers and pulled us to shape the place, sometimes not quite awake to how the place would shape our interactions with the youth, their interactions with each other, and how we could come alongside them.

The physical place shifted as the youth began to enter. It was as the youth began to enter, to test out who we were and what the place might provide to them, that the processes of co-composing field texts began. Over time the youth helped us understand the processes of co-composing the art club as well as the field texts that we could co-compose with them. The arts club became a co-composed place where the youth and the researchers slowly came alongside one another. Perhaps, we thought, the arts club place itself is a kind of field text that was co-composed with the youth.

CO-COMPOSING THE ART CLUB: CONNECTIONS BETWEEN PLACE AND CO-COMPOSING FIELD TEXTS

There was a great deal at work as we, a team of researchers, worked to compose the art club and even more at work as the youth began to work with us in the art club. It has been through attending closely to the field texts that we have been able to see the co-composing processes at work. Initially the members of the research team wrote autobiographical stories that we shared with each other. In the processes of sharing these autobiographical stories we began to understand more of who we were and becoming in relation with each other as well as who we were in relation to school and the processes of transforming the classroom place. There existed a certain uneasiness and tension in the unknown, in what we saw in the liminal spaces, as we prepared to meet the youth for the first time within this particular narrative inquiry. As we recorded field notes on early meetings, we wondered who and how many youth would attend. What stories would they tell of what brought them to the art club? We wondered how they would spend their time in the art club. Was an art club even the most appropriate place to come to know youth? Was a gymnasium or other place more appropriate? These were just a few of the many wonders we noted in field notes. There were also many silences that we each held close in those early days.

As we began to meet the youth who came to the art club, our field notes also recorded how uncertain many of the youth initially felt. They too were uncertain about who they could be within the art club. As a team of researchers, our experiences were ones of liminality, and we felt the need to improvise ways to engage the youth and to continue to transform the classroom. Our field notes recorded that the food we prepared each week was important to the youth. Although initially we brought small snacks and small juice containers, the youth showed us that they needed more food, such as sandwiches and hot dogs rather than cheese and crackers. They needed several servings of juice rather than small juice boxes. Quite simply the youth, twelve- to fifteen-year-olds, were hungry. We realized that we could, literally, sit alongside them as we ate, drank, and had conversations each week. We began to bring heartier food, and the place and the possibilities for co-composing field texts shifted.

There were other shifts in the transformation of the classroom place as the youth began to be part of co-composing the place. Initially there was a table with containers of beads used in traditional beading activities; a table with paints, paper and painting supplies; a table with writing materials; a table with craft materials. One youth shifted the place from a focus on the small, more traditional beads as she brought larger, more colorful beads reflecting the latest fashion trend. As the youth and we began to negotiate the place and the activities within the place, the youth noted she wanted to bead with the larger beads, not the "native" beads. These beads moved beyond dominant cultural constructions of what beading might look like for Aboriginal youth. However, some youth continued to bead with the small beads, and we learned to take the containers of beads out each week as some youth sought out that table frequently.

Our intention was not to shape the place by our stories of what were seen as culturally appropriate activities. Sometimes, as with the beading, the youth expanded the possibilities of what we had initially imagined. Sometimes youth asked for certain activities, such as the youth who indicated they wanted to make drums. As the youth worked with us to co-compose the place, some youth already knew the need for protocol—cultural teachings that live within land, place, and peoples within a Cree community context—with drum making. They worked with us to co-compose the place so protocol was part of drum making. Protocol in learning to build a drum moves beyond the building of a drum to include the learning over time and in relation to knowledge keepers and Elders who help us understand the responsibilities and teachings that accompany drum making.

Mask making, video cameras, cameras, computers, and materials for drum and rattle making also became part of the possible art-making activities in the art club as the youth came alongside us. Making what the youth saw as appropriate materials available became part of our weekly acts of improvisation as they offered us new ways to co-compose field texts.

What we are drawing attention to is the ways that the co-composition of field texts was part of the co-composition of the art club place. This linking of place with co-composing field texts became increasingly important. As part of the relational aspects of engaging in narrative inquiry, the co-composing of field texts often emerges out of the place (s) we find ourselves negotiating in the midst of research alongside youth and children.

As we became more attentive to the complex interwoven layers of the research place, with who we were and were becoming in the place, and with who the youth were and were becoming, we also began to attend more closely to co-composing field texts. Each week, after the youth had left the art club, members of the research team stayed behind to clean up, to talk about the events in the art club, and to plan for the next week. In those conversations our research puzzles began to shift as we noticed events and relationships we had earlier not been awake to. Although the youth were not co-composing these sessions, we were co-composing with each other in the conversations and later in the flurry of e-mail messages that went among team members. Often these e-mail messages spoke to the tensions we were experiencing around who we were and were becoming as narrative inquirers alongside the youth.

These co-composed field texts, the after-club conversations, and the e-mail messages captured a sense of the fatigue and dis/ease we felt being alongside the youth in a kind of liminal space for them and for us. We were attentive, then, to the importance of holding open the art club as an inquiry space that allowed the youth and us to continue to improvise the purposes of the club and, more intentionally, shift our research purposes, our field texts, and our eventual understandings of experience. We came to realize that our fatigue and dis/ease was partially because of the uncertainty of holding open improvisatory spaces.

CO-COMPOSING DIFFERENT KINDS OF FIELD TEXTS
WITHIN THE NARRATIVE INQUIRY WITH THE YOUTH

As we engaged in the narrative inquiry with the youth and with each other, we engaged in co-composing multiple kinds of field texts. Some of the field texts were co-composed in the art club with the youth and included mask making, print making, memory box making, creating ear rings and other jewelry, beading, photography, and collages. These were art-making activities that engaged the youth and, in part, triggered the stories the youth told. For example, as Tara engaged in making masks, she drew attention to the ways girls and women often portray themselves as pretty. Photography was a way that some of the youth chose to co-compose field texts. Some youth took photographs of themselves in the room where the art club was held as well as in the hallways and other places in the school. Some youth took photographs of places that were important to them in the school, such as the art classroom, the bathrooms, and their lockers. Some youth also chose to take cameras home to take photographs of out-of-school places that were important to them. The youth also brought family photographs to the art club to share with us and to tell stories of their lives and relationships outside of school and in other places of importance to them.

Other ways field texts were co-composed was through using video camera equipment. For several weeks a number of youth worked on writing and filming a video of life on the "rez," complete with sets the youth prepared and painted. As Sean arrived at one point the youth invited him to be an actor in the video, and Lane, one of the youth, cast him as "Chief Chits-a-Lot." The co-composed field notes on the activities around the video were important as the youth spoke of being able to tell their stories of their experiences in their home reservations.

Some of the co-composing of field texts was undertaken with the youth in one-on-one conversations such as when we invited the youth to make annals of their life experiences. We say more about that later in the section on timeline art. Other examples are visible in the narrative account that Sean co-composed with Donovan (see Chapter 11).

The youth also began to invite some researchers to their Facebook pages and used that medium to stay in touch and to send personal messages. Other youth provided us with their cell numbers, and there were text messages sent back and forth. These were also ways of co-composing field texts. These field texts also served the purpose of staying in contact. Sometimes long periods of time passed when we did not hear from the youth. Sometimes we did not hear back from them, and silence became the relationship. Silence also became a kind of field text.

The youth also invited us to out-of-school events such as Tara's invitation to Jean to come to see her in cheering competitions in local malls. There was other co-composing of field texts outside of school in the ways that Donovan invited Sean to do things outside of the club, such as sharing a song that he learned with Elder Whiskeyjack.

An Example of Co-composing Field Texts Alongside One Youth

Timeline Art: Co-composing Annals. In what follows, Sean describes his processes of working alongside Cedar, one youth who participated in the study. Although Cedar was initially part of the art club, she moved out of the school shortly after the art club began. Sean continued to meet with her in other places. Sean was particularly interested in how Cedar's experiences outside of school were a life-making process. Sean often met Cedar in the institutional place of school. When he arrived at the school where she moved after leaving the school where we held the weekly art club, he checked in at the office and was provided with a place, a round table in the cafeteria, to meet with Cedar. This place had some limiting constraints, as it was physically within the institutional place of school. Teachers and other students walked by. This could have closed off the possibilities to engage in research conversations, making it extremely difficult to co-compose field texts alongside one another. However, Sean and Cedar both felt that this place allowed them to talk in ways that may have been more difficult if they were in a closed room in the school.

As Sean and Cedar began to co-compose field texts, Jean suggested Sean begin with asking Cedar to co-compose an annal, a kind of timeline (Clandinin & Connelly, 2000), with him. Sean sat beside Cedar as they worked to sketch an annal of her life that included experiences in the many places in which she lived, including schools, homes, communities, and so on. Co-composing the annal shifted the conversational space between Sean and Cedar and provided an opening to begin to share experiences. The annal was something physical they could shape, draw, and design alongside one another as they thought about their life experiences.

In subsequent meetings they returned to the annal and worked on it again, continuing to situate events, relationships, and places within it. The annal became a place to connect and reconnect when time elapsed between their research conversations. As they worked together, Sean was attentive to the three-dimensional narrative inquiry space, which he used to think about the co-composing of the annal, paying particular attention to temporality, place, and sociality.

It was through the dialogue and the writing out of memories on the annal that Cedar and Sean recalled untold stories. As they drank their tea, the conversations unfolded in relation to the co-composing of the annal. In the beginning moments of co-composing the annal Cedar's experiences outside of school became visible mostly through the stories of school. It seemed, for a time, the stories of school were the safe places to linger and dwell within.

Sean recalls that the co-composed annal was at first neatly designed in some ways, moving from school to school. Cedar took the pencil and moved it backward and forward with relative ease, forward as she explained her school places, backward as she told of early moments in school and of travel to new schools. The focus of her experiences in these early conversations was mostly about school subjects and her achievements in school. She told the stories with good stories in mind; the safe stories of school where her pathway was relatively defined in a trajectory of moving between grades and places with upward mobility.

However, over several conversations her annal began to slowly take different shapes. Suddenly her eraser smudged the lines, and she drew little juts into what had been a smooth line in order to share other experiences of family, places, travel, and her community. The annal was now marked by different movements, and the smooth directional patterns were now less certain as her stories shifted as she told and retold them. The smooth story of a strong academic student that she had at first told was now no longer as evident in conversations or within the annal. Her stories to live by in school as the "solitary academic student" and "leader" were difficult stories for her to continue to tell through co-composing the annal.

The stories of family within her life were less visible than they had been in their early moments of conversation. Perhaps Cedar has learned to stay silent in school about family stories. Perhaps the school cafeteria reminded her that she was still in school and that some of her family stories should stay secret, even from Sean. However, as there were more conversations, she began to tell more stories of her life outside of school, and stories of family started to weave their way throughout the conversations.

Sean recalls the moment when she quietly shared, "So much happened because of so many other parts of my life. We were driving back and forth from the reserve to the city every day, it's a one-hour drive, Lessard." Sean circled this point and the name of the school on the annal. It was the school where the art club was situated, the school where the research started. "I remember the exact day," she said quietly. Sean asked, "How could you possibly remember that? How do you know exactly when you moved?" She looked down and replied, "Because it was on my birthday that we were out of places to live. So many family problems, but I am still getting an education, Lessard." As Cedar and

Sean talked over multiple conversations, co-composing conversational field texts alongside the annal field text, the points, marks, and lines were not always smooth. At times they took on features of wildness, a certain amount of chaos crossed the page, jutting off in various directions. No longer were the stories straight-line tellings.

Through the research conversations their relationship continued to shift and move in unexpected directions. Cedar was slowly beginning to allow Sean to "world"-travel to her worlds to see how she constructed herself in her worlds and how others constructed her. She took care of her stories of family in the conversations. She shared the ways that she was storied by those in schools when she said in reference to teachers and administrators, "They were not understanding how hard we worked to come to school when I was having family problems." When Sean began his first research conversations with Cedar, she shared that "In this year we lived in four different places, but I still came to school ... always." As the research conversations continued, Sean began to understand her experiences as so much more complex.

As the weeks grew into months, Sean arranged to meet Cedar again to begin to read some narrative fragments he wanted to weave into a narrative account of their work together. Cedar's request to have her younger sister join the conversation shifted Sean's plan. Initially he was reluctant, worrying that her sister's presence might shift the dialogue and limit the sharing. Cedar responded to his worries, saying, "Sean, it will be fine." They sat in the school cafeteria; no one was around. Sean ordered a little take-out food to ease the formalities, perhaps to ease his worries about sharing the fragments. Sean began to share some of the story fragments, which shaped something of an interim research text. However, as we show in what follows, the sharing of interim research texts sometimes opens up to the co-composing of new field texts. As we noted in Chapters 1 and 2, the process of narrative inquiry is not a linear one but rather a reflexive recursive one.

Sean started off slowly, reading the opening of the interim research text, a prologue, a beginning. With words he tried to honor Cedar's family and the stories shared over the past year. Both girls listened intently as Sean read. They nodded from time to time. Sean glanced over the top of his computer every once in awhile to try to imagine what they might be thinking, trying to get some reassurance to keep on reading. This was not the way they had interacted before. Now Sean was reading retold stories written from his inquiries into field texts. It felt odd at first—no longer laughter, Sean's voice serious, the tone noted by the sisters.

As Sean finished reading, the girls looked up. He asked, "Am I close? Is this what I am hearing?" "It is good, Sean. We didn't know you liked writing. Our mom told us you wrote, but we really like that story." The response made him dance inside, and he remembers that he blushed but tried to keep them from knowing.

They sat together then and talked. He wrote small snippets, little words and scribbles that might cue him later and help him remember how special the conversation was. As Sean noted,

> It was remarkable how two junior high girls could carry me in conversation, transport me in that "world"-traveling sort of way. Those stories, those good stories they shared, painted images in my mind of my own growing-up places, filled with small and big images of a different time. Stories and memories were brought back now because the three of us sat together in a moment in time and read together. We were sharing a little about what I thought I might know. It turns out that I didn't really know much at all. (Field notes on the conversation)

Sean left the conversation that day filled with ideas and with feelings of wanting to know so much more. He felt good energy to keep on writing, to tell the stories, to share the words Cedar and her sister shared. Sean describes Cedar's little sister's presence as a further co-composing of field texts as her presence gently helped them with the stories. Cedar brought her to the conversation because she knew her sister could help Sean with his "homework … the stories … the experiences." Cedar's sister remembered her own stories along the way, and her presence helped to create a feeling of ease (Lugones, 1987). Sean felt the opening up of a different space between the three of them. Her quiet humor and remembering-back style made the lives so much more visible to Sean. Their relationship was wonderful to be a part of, even though it was not quite what Sean expected, as it did not fit his initial plan.

Sean co-composed annals with each of the three youth—Cedar, Lane, Donovan—he engaged with in this narrative inquiry. The co-composing of the annal with each youth provided ways forward in the conversations. Sean noted that the conversations were sometimes marked by silences, and these are also spaces where we can come alongside in "world"-travelling. Silences are sometimes indirect conversations or "sideways conversations" that create spaces to think, feel, and explore.

Co-composing annals, as a kind of field text, was particularly powerful in this narrative inquiry as Sean used it as he moved from field texts to interim research texts. As Sean noted, he could physically hold the paper and, in some ways, physically retrace the lines to recall the specific memories the research conversations evoked within him. It provided a way he could temporally turn to inquire into the shared experiences. The annal also became an opportunity to turn inward and created moments of pausing with a return to the ontological commitments of narrative inquiry as he thought with the stories of each youth.

CO-COMPOSING FIELD TEXTS ALONGSIDE THE YOUTH WHO LEFT SCHOOL EARLY

We travel back to the day we met at their elementary/junior high school. There were five of us that day—Truong, Christian, Sean, Vera, and I—all of us working in the narrative inquiry into the experiences of youth who left school prior to graduating. As we climbed the steps of the school, we were drawn to the physical features of the building. It was a castle of sorts, one of those old schools made of red brick and an architecture beckoning back to an era in the early 1900s. One entrance marked boys, the other entrance marked girls. In between these markers, embedded within the physical structure of the school, the year 1911 is stamped. Truong and Christian asked us to come to the school that day, although both of them were long out of that school and now out of any school. They wanted us to come with them, to be in a place where they remembered school as fun. It was like coming into a memory box for them. (Sean's reflection on visiting a school)

This is a reflection on a visit to a school with two youth participants. They were part of a narrative inquiry conceptualized around the experiences of early school leavers. In the midst of a series of one-on-one research conversations with participants, this visit to the school was another way to think of co-composing field text. While we were in the midst of co-composing one kind of field texts—that is, one-on-one conversations—the possibility of another kind of co-composed field text appeared.

It was the youth who suggested the possibility of visiting the elementary/junior high school they had both attended. In research conversations they told us of the significance of the school to each of them, the significance of the neighborhood where they grew up, and some of their experiences within this school place. They told us stories as they recollected memories of baseball games on the school field; they told us intimate details of early friendships; they told us stories of many people, including stories of various teachers they remembered from the school; they told stories of participating in clubs, of attending community events, and of playing on sports teams. The youth attended this school at roughly the same time.

As they told their stories of experiences of attending high school, they told of how their experiences were different from their experiences of school in the elementary/junior high school. Each youth, in separate one-on-one research conversations, spoke of a school home place within their community, a place where they felt at ease. The stories of this school place were a significant part of their school stories and early beginnings. The stories were of youth at ease within a school community. However, in their stories of later grades they told us how their stories bumped up against experiences they had in other school places. Each research participant attended a different high school. Each youth told different stories of leaving high school. As Vera, Sean, and Jean talked about the youth's experiences and of their invitation to revisit the school with us, we began to see the possibilities of co-composing a different kind of field text alongside these youth participants. When these two youth participants made it possible for us to re-enter their favorite school, it was an opportunity to co-compose field texts in new ways. Because they invited us to travel with them to a place, we had an opportunity to come alongside in different ways.

This visit to the school was an opening to come alongside the youth to the school and to the neighborhood in which they had grown up. The invitation was an invitation to travel with them to places where they felt at ease. In the conversations we had heard their stories, but being physically present in the school where the storied events occurred allowed us to be alongside in another way. We stood at second-floor windows as Truong pointed out the school fields where games were played, the corners where gang members waited to beat up some youth, the gymnasium wall where winning team banners were displayed. Christian pointed out new water fountains that were now in place that had been in the planning phase when they were in school. He showed us the stairs between floors where particular events happened (Clandinin, Steeves, & Caine, 2013). The field notes we composed as another kind of field text was enabled and enriched by their willingness to take us inside this memory box of a school. We saw this school visit as offering a different type of possibility for inquiry into their experiences of school.

We have described the overall narrative inquiry in more details in other places in the book. As we have noted elsewhere, it was sometimes difficult to ask them about their experiences within school and their experiences of moving out of school. Recollecting their stories of experiences brought them back to experiences that, perhaps, they did not want to revisit. This visit to the school allowed Truong and Christian an opportunity to revisit places they wanted to revisit.

This willingness to accompany the youth to different places is an important part of co-composing field texts. Sean describes how he and one of the other youth in the narrative inquiry, Leanne, searched for a place where they both felt at ease to hear the difficult stories of leaving school before graduating. They eventually settled on a meeting place at a local mall where they could sit at the same table and order the same beverage each time they met. As the stories began to unfold, Leanne invited Sean to play basketball with her brothers. In that meeting he was able to reconnect with her family. What became clear as they co-composed meeting places and field texts was that Leanne took the lead in shaping the places of meeting and who they were meeting. As Sean and Leanne co-composed the field texts and the eventual research text, the co-composing made it possible for them to open up an inquiry into her experiences of leaving school early, experiences that conflicted with the family stories of graduating.

Field Notes and Other Kinds of Field Texts

As we noted at the outset of this chapter, there are many kinds of field texts that can be co-composed with participants. Many of the kinds of field texts we co-compose are visible in the narrative accounts and fragments of narrative accounts that are part of this book. However, we want to draw attention to one very important kind of field text: field notes.

Field notes are those carefully detailed and particular notes that we keep of events, times, relationships, feelings, and responses to ongoing events. These field notes are written with attentiveness to the three-dimensional narrative inquiry space. As Sean notes, "Field notes are more pronounced with details and edges that provide more clarity when I am looking and trying to make sense of what I could not see and could not understand." Although we appreciate that field notes require an enormous commitment of time and careful recollection of our experiences alongside participants, we cannot overemphasize their importance. As we continue to come alongside participants over time, we frequently cannot remember with the clarity and detail that field notes offer us. We described field notes in detail in other places (Clandinin & Connelly, 2000; Clandinin, 2013), but we see their particular importance in narrative inquiries with children and youth, where so much change is frequently ongoing.

In addition to other kinds of field texts, we find the use of photographs as field texts increasingly important in our studies. In a classroom study with Simmee Chung (Clandinin & Chung, 2009), funded by SSHRC (Clandinin et al., 2006), Jean and Simmee engaged with the children in the co-composing of photographs as a central kind of field text. We asked the eight- and nine-year-old children to take five photographs of their belonging places in the classroom, in the school, in their homes, and in their communities. We then worked alongside the children as they told stories of their photographs and then composed collages of their photos that became a way of co-composing their metaphors of belonging experiences. In another classroom study alongside children and a teacher (described in Chapters 6 and 7) Vera and the children took photographs as a kind of co-composed field text. They worked with these photographs, gave them captions, and then co-composed a book as a research text.

ONGOING TENSIONS IN CO-COMPOSING FIELD TEXTS

In this chapter we highlighted the range of possible field texts as well as the importance of co-composing field texts. The work of co-composing field texts is part of the relational commitments of narrative inquiry. As we have shown, there are multiple tensions as we engage in co-composing field texts with children and youth. We continually live within the tensions as we attend to who we are in relation with the children and youth, who we are within the institutions where our inquiries are situated, and who we are in the multiplicity of our lives as teachers, parents, family members, and so on. The intensity required by the continual need to stay awake to the lives and larger narratives that structure the layered landscapes around us is at times overwhelming. We return to these considerations of co-composing in Chapter 10 and show how they shape the processes of composing interim and final research texts.

CHAPTER 10

Moving to Interim Research Texts with Children and Youth

In this chapter we turn our attention toward the co-composition of interim research texts with children and youth. It remains important in these processes of co-composing interim research texts that we attend to who participants are and who narrative inquirers are and are becoming in the living out of narrative inquiries. As we engage in these processes of moving from field texts to interim research texts, it is important to continue to think with different kinds of field texts already shaped by processes of co-composing.

In Chapter 11 we share a narrative account, a key kind of interim research text that we co-compose with participants. As we co-compose and negotiate interim research texts, we also find ourselves returning to the co-composition of field texts, as negotiations call forth new experiences and new understandings might emerge. In Chapter 9 we saw how this iterative process of co-composing interim research texts sometimes creates moments where further field texts are co-composed. As Sean met with Cedar, his intention was to share an interim research text. The presence of Cedar's sister created a moment when the sharing of the interim research text created the possibilities of more co-composed field texts.

CALLING FORTH PAST EXPERIENCES

In the fall of 2008 Vera worked alongside Christian, a youth participant within the study of the experiences of youth who leave school early, a study introduced in earlier chapters. Christian's experiences reflected the processes by which he was pushed out of the public school system prior to graduation. Sean had introduced Christian to Vera. Vera and Christian met several times over some weeks that year to engage in conversations. They met in a small local Ukrainian food restaurant in the neighborhood in which Christian had grown up and where he still lives. From the view out the window at the restaurant Christian often pointed to particular landmarks that were connected to his experiences. The person in the restaurant always took his order with the same phrase, "the same thing?" expressing a sense of the familiar and the ordinary in unanticipated ways.

As described briefly in Chapter 9, on one occasion alongside Sean, Vera, Jean, and Truong, another participant, Christian, visited his former elementary and junior high urban school. Truong and Christian had known each other for a long time and had arranged, with Sean's help, the visit to the school. Vera and Jean both remember that visit as one akin to stepping into a huge memory box—each hallway they walked down, each stairway they climbed, each classroom they peered into, and each view from the windows called forth Truong and Christian's memories of experiences and led to new stories. Christian and Truong recounted stories of basketball, gangs, teachers, neighborhoods, friends, and families with such vividness, it was as if they had attended this school just yesterday. The photographs of the sports teams brought back stories of rivalry, delight, and their experiences on various sports teams, which seemed to be at the heart of their schooling experience. Stepping into the memory box provided a different insight into Christian's experiences, into what otherwise was filled with present events, unjust decisions, and hopes for what was yet to come. For Vera a beginning sense of who Christian was began to emerge from these conversations and events and the places in which they met.

Vera and Christian spent time together just before Vera was leaving for Germany to be with her family. Vera still remembers sitting in front of piles of field texts, which reflected tentative beginnings of a relationship that, with time, developed into a more profound connection. The more profound connection was linked for Vera to the conversations Christian and she had about the interim research texts, or narrative accounts. During Vera's time with her family she often thought about Christian and how she might begin the writing of his narrative account, drawing on all the co-composed field texts. As Christian was often on her mind at that time, Vera began to collect and write postcards to Christian to reflect what she had learned from him and who she saw them each being within the relationship. Vera never mailed these postcards to Christian, but they became the basis of the narrative account and a way to make sense of the experiences. In the midst of writing these postcards Vera also returned to her own narrative beginnings. That summer Vera revisited the high school she had left many years ago. She could be considered an early school leaver.

Vera wrote,

I remember leaving the school ground in silence. . . . when I left, my prin-cipal informed my mother that I cared too much for others, when school was more important, that I wasn't putting my intellectual abilities to the best use, and that missing school was not possible at his school. In many ways, he named the reasons for my leaving of school in far better ways then I ever could have at the time. . . . I recall many school events that cre-ated a sense of dis/ease and discomfort in my life; school was not a place I loved, or a place that I felt shared my values. . . . At that time in my life, people composed identities in, and with, schools as predominant plotlines, as obedient and good students, and somehow these were not my stories to live by. (Clandinin, Steeves, & Caine, 2013, p. 11-12)

Returning to the school that summer was a difficult process for Vera. Crossing the large concrete school lot to enter the school doors already brought with it an acute awareness for Vera of past experiences that continued to shape her life now. Opening the door and breathing the memories of a place that felt so profoundly miseducative in her life was challenging, to say the least. As Vera walked through the large entrance hall, she was mindful of not wanting to be recognized, of refusing to tell what had brought her back to the school that day. Watching the rats run alongside the concrete walls outside on the common ground, disap-pearing in the sewer lines, held an enormous symbolic power that day. The sense of surviving impoverished conditions, waste, and inequality resurfaced. The sense of deadlines thankfully was secondary to her sense of dis/ease.

The return for Vera to her narrative beginnings created a different sense and entry point for her into Christian's experiences. A sense of being alongside and the deep sense of injustice developed in new ways. The moment of physically returning to her narrative beginnings created a sense of urgency for Vera to return to the field texts and, in particular, to the importance of the memory box she had been privileged to step into alongside Christian. Although the postcards she wrote to Christian were not picked at random, the search for them now became more inten-tional. The images and texts become a way to make sense of experiences. What had seemed distant by time, geography, and context now seemed much closer.

When Vera returned to Canada, she went to see Christian to share the postcards, what she now saw as the beginning of a narrative account with him. As they sat together in the small restaurant, where Christian often ate his breakfast after his nightshift at the local casino, something had shifted profoundly for Vera. Vera had both been nerv-ous and excited to share this interim research text with him. As she had tried to imagine Christian's response to it, she was struck by the difficulty she had in thinking about what his response might be. She realized that although the shift had been profound for her, it might not be reflected in the relationship she had with Christian. Vera could hardly remember what she had told Christian about the interim research text, and she was not sure he would even remember the conversations. The postcards were bundled together with a blue ribbon, which created a sense of coherence for Vera, a sign that the narrative account hung together in some way.

As Vera shared the postcards with Christian, Christian's body posture changed, he focused on reading and looking at the images. He seemed less distracted and tired than Vera had remembered him being in previous conversations. His response to this interim research text was to pull out a book filled with drawings he had been creating for a long a time. In this moment new conversations emerged, focused on his gifts as an artist, as someone who dreamed of owning a tattoo studio, as one caring deeply for his family and needing to provide for them.

RETURNING TO RESEARCH PUZZLES AND JUSTIFICATIONS

Co-composing and negotiating interim research texts returns narrative inquirers to the research puzzles and to the personal, practical, and social/theoretical justifications around which the inquiry was initially threaded, puzzles and justifications that have also often shifted, grown, and become more complex through the living of the narrative inquiry. "It is in how we [continuously] live out our research puzzles alongside our participants that our ontological commitment becomes evident" (Caine, Estefan, & Clandinin, 2013, p. 576). In this way the narrative inquiry stays grounded in experience and relationships, and it is from within this grounding that "we begin to craft our always negotiated research texts. We see this commitment as extending beyond the immediacy of the research puzzle and have come to understand that narrative inquirers hold responsibilities and obligations for, and toward, the people whose stories are lived and told" (p. 576).

Staying attentive to "narrative coherence is one of the ways to open up how we think about methodological commitment" (p. 579). In the living out of narrative inquiries,

> as researchers we become part of participants' lives and are often drawn in to participants' ways of seeking narrative coherence. This way of researching is different to the practice of interrogating a research text such as a transcript—reaching into it as if it were life—and extracting "the story" that foregrounds experience and voice. (p. 579)

As in earlier chapters we draw on several studies to make visible processes we and others lived with children and youth in co-composing and negotiating interim research texts with participants. We make visible some of the complexities, considerations, and reconsiderations that shaped these processes. Vera's experience alongside Christian makes visible the iterative nature of the ongoing negotiations and shows the moves among field, interim, and final research texts, which are present in all narrative inquiries. Yet there are other considerations that are more specific to children and youth. As part of these considerations we include the narrative account Sean wrote in relation with Donovan, a participant in the narrative inquiry alongside youth and families of Aboriginal heritage. The narrative account is included in its entirety in Chapter 11. Chapter 11 ends with some further reflections on interim research texts.

RETURNING TO UNDERSTANDINGS OF NEGOTIATIONS

Sonia Houle (2012), who undertook her doctoral research alongside Jean at the Centre for Research for Teacher Education and Development, was interested in understanding the experiences of children who were not able to read by the time they completed grade 1 in a public school. Within her inquiry she wanted to listen to students, teachers, and parents' experiences and offer a multiperspectival understanding of experiences as children moved through grade 1 and into grade 2. The two child participants in the narrative inquiry selected the pseudonyms Tiny Tim and Matson. Sonia spent much time thinking about how she might compose narrative accounts with the participants. In the following we give a sense of her processes of co-composing narrative accounts with the young boys.

CO-COMPOSING AND NEGOTIATING NARRATIVE ACCOUNTS WITH MATSON AND TINY TIM

I went to Matson's house. . . . I showed him the copy of Voices in the Park *I bought for him. I told him I copied Anthony Browne's idea to write his book. I read* Matson's Story *to him. His mother, Marie, was present during our meeting. During the reading of the book, I felt Matson was comfortable with me. I told him the book was a draft and if there was anything he thought I should change in it, he should let me know. Matson liked the book and did not ask for any changes. He asked if I would give him a copy. I promised I would. He looked happy. (p. 50)*

We went to pick Tiny Tim up after school and took him home. He showed me his room and took me to the family room where we spent one hour reading and talking. I showed him Tiny Tim's Story, *the book I wrote about him, and told him we could change anything he felt we should change. He liked the book and made comments as we read it. He did not want any changes. (pp. 52–53)*

Voices in the Park (Browne, 1998) is a picture book that shows how four people, including two children, experience the same event, a trip to the park, in different ways. Drawing upon Browne's multiperspectival picture book, Houle (2012) found a way to compose interim research texts she felt were appropriate and respectful to Matson and Tiny Tim. The excerpts that show aspects of the negotiation of *Matson's Story* and *Tiny Tim's Story* happened some months after Sonia spent three days per week over approximately seven months in Matson's grades 1 and 2 classrooms.

As she entered into his home on the day she describes above, some months had passed since Matson and Sonia had seen one another. When she sensed Matson felt comfortable with her, Sonia shared with him the book *Voices in the Park*, which she had bought for him. Sharing *Voices in the Park* with Matson was a way for Sonia to describe to Matson how she had written *Matson's Story*. However, before Sonia read *Matson's Story* to him, she explained that it was just a draft and if he thought she should change anything, she would. When Sonia finished reading the entire story to Matson, he told her he liked the book. He also asked if she would give him a copy, which she did, some months later.

Sonia negotiated a similar process with Tiny Tim in relation with *Tiny Tim's Story*. Tiny Tim's family had moved to another Canadian province since he and Sonia had last seen one another in the fall of his grade 2 year. Sonia traveled to the province where Tiny Tim now lived to negotiate the interim research text with him. On the day when Sonia negotiated *Tiny Tim's Story* with him, she had the opportunity to drive with his mom to pick him up after school. They did not immediately begin to read *Tiny Tim's Story* when they returned to the family's home. First, Tiny Tim showed Sonia his room and around his new home. They then settled in the family room, where Sonia read *Tiny Tim's Story* to him. As she had in her negotiations with Matson, Sonia explained to Tiny Tim that the story was only a draft and that she wanted him to tell her about any changes he would like to make. Tiny Tim asked questions as Sonia read the story to him. When she finished reading, Tiny Tim told Sonia that he liked the story and did not want her to change anything.

Shaped through her earlier experiences alongside her daughter when, as a young child in grade 1, she did not begin to read, Sonia's two-year narrative inquiry was attentive to the experiences of children who do not learn to read in grade 1, their parents' experiences living alongside their children, and the experiences of the teachers who accompanied them at school. In the proposal she wrote prior to beginning the inquiry Sonia was already looking forward to negotiating research texts with the participants, including the children. She wrote in her proposal that her research texts would be constructed in collaboration with participants, with a constant concern for their psychological, emotional, and physical well-being. She noted that interim research texts would not be published without final approval or revision from the participants.

As she began her narrative inquiry alongside Matson, Tiny Tim, their mothers, and their grade 1 and grade 2 teachers, Sonia did so with no certain plan or final product in mind. What she imagined was the possibility of writing "narrative accounts of each child's experiences, interwoven by the experiences of their parents and teachers" (Houle, 2012, p. 44).

Entering into narrative inquiry alongside Matson and Tiny Tim in their school during the last two months of their grade 1 year and during the first six months of their grade 2 year, Sonia and the boys co-composed various kinds of field texts. These included weekly one-on-one tape-recorded lunch-time conversations held in a small, private room in the school, drawings that the boys made of what they were thinking and feeling in particular moments, as well as photographs the boys took of places in the school. During their grade 2 year Sonia engaged in research conversations with Matson and Tiny Tim in their homes. Although Sonia had by that time been in each boy's home as a result of her conversations with their mothers, this shift from being in the school to being with the boys in their homes helped Sonia come to understand more about who the boys were in places outside of school.

As Sonia began to work with the field texts co-composed with Matson and Tiny Tim, she also worked with the transcripts of tape-recorded conversations with their mothers and teachers. She had also collected relevant school documents, composed field notes of her participation in the classrooms, and also kept a research journal. Sonia eventually composed four narrative accounts, two narrative accounts of each boy's experiences, one for grade 1 and a second for grade 2, in which the voices of the boys, their mothers, and the teachers are interwoven.

As she completed full drafts of the first two narrative accounts, one for each boy in relation with grade 1, it was a question from Jean, Sonia's supervisor, that turned Sonia's attention toward imagining how she might co-compose and negotiate interim research texts with Matson and Tiny Tim.

Jean asked me how I planned to share the narrative accounts with the boys. Being that they would only be 8 years old, I could not share a long written text with them. It took me a few weeks to imagine how

> *I could share the narrative accounts with each boy. I remembered the*
> book Voices in the Park *by Anthony Browne (1998). The author wrote*
> *a story about people going for a walk at the park. What made his*
> *book interesting for me was its multiperspectival aspect; Browne wrote*
> *the story in four parts, from the perspectives of a mother, a father, a*
> *boy, and a girl. I found Browne's book concept inspiring, considering*
> *the multiple voices in my study. I decided that I would write a book*
> *for each boy, borrowing Browne's idea. One book I called Matson's*
> *Story and the other one Tiny Tim's Story. I picked parts from the nar-*
> *rative accounts I felt best represented the boys' stories of themselves*
> *and of school and the mothers' and teachers' stories of the boys in*
> *Grade 1. The different perspectives from which I wrote represented my*
> *understanding of the stories lived and told. I chose pictures to illustrate*
> *each page and left it to be completed after the writing of the Grade*
> *2 narrative accounts. I purchased copies of Browne's book to give to*
> *each teacher and family at the time I planned to negotiate the narrative*
> *accounts with them. (pp. 47–48)*

When she completed full drafts of the second set of narrative
accounts, one for each boy in relation with grade 2, Sonia added aspects
of these narrative accounts to *Matson's Story* and *Tiny Tim's Story*. As
she completed full drafts of each of the story books, Sonia returned
to her earlier thoughts about negotiating research texts with the boys.

> *It was important for me to show the narrative accounts to the boys before*
> *the other participants, as they were the focus of the research. . . . After I*
> *officially stopped having conversations with the participants in July 2010,*
> *I kept in touch with Marie [Matson's mother] through phone calls and*
> *email messages. I had not seen Matson for over a year. I hoped he would*
> *feel comfortable with me. I negotiated the narrative accounts with him*
> *first. . . . Tiny Tim and his family moved to another Canadian province*
> *in July 2010, after he finished Grade 2. I had once spoken with Morgan*
> *[Tiny Tim's mother] on the phone, exchanged email messages, and wrote*
> *to Tiny Tim twice by the time I visited them ... Morgan picked me up at*
> *the airport and took me to her house. (pp. 49 & 52)*

After negotiating *Matson's Story* and *Tiny Tim's Story* with each of
the boys, Sonia negotiated with each respective mother, the story book
and the grade 1 and grade 2 narrative accounts. Sonia then negotiated
Matson's Story, *Tiny Tim's Story*, and the grade 1 narrative accounts
with the grade 1 teacher and the grade 2 narrative accounts with the
grade 2 teacher.

Prior to negotiating the narrative accounts with the two teachers
Sonia experienced uncertainty about how they might respond to particular aspects of the mothers' perspectives of their son's experiences
alongside each teacher. Both teachers asked for particular aspects of the
narrative accounts to be changed.

The time I spent alongside Tiny Tim, Matson, their mothers, and the two teachers provided me with a window into their lives. Writing the narrative accounts required that I carefully piece together the stories they told me, and the stories we co-composed together. Those narrative accounts represent one version of their lives at those times; it is my version, and how I understood their lived experiences through their telling and retelling, their living, and through my participation in their lives. Even though I was the one who put the written words on the pages, I saw it as a co-composition. The words I was inspired to share, which appear on these pages, I picked meticulously, considering all participants. At times, though, their lives seemed at risk, as I felt that what I wrote from others' perspectives might hurt their feelings once they read them. I constantly reflected on the advantages and disadvantages of including specific fragments of stories, keeping in mind the participants' stories as well as our relationships. It is in that spirit that I chose the words for this dissertation. (p. 54)

We see this multiperspectivity as an important aspect in working with children and youth in narrative inquiries. Given that a recent review showed few narrative inquirers are engaging in inquiry with young children (Clandinin et al, 2015), the kind of careful tracing Sonia shows of her co-composing and negotiating of interim research texts with Matson and Tiny Tim is important. Sonia shows us the importance of being wakeful to co-composing interim research texts that are appropriate for negotiating with young children. As researchers, regardless of selected methodology, we know that in order for children to participate in research, the consent of a parent or legal guardian is required. As we noted earlier we ask children to sign assent forms for their participation in narrative inquiries. This is one way of honoring children's narrative authority; that is, it allows us to make visible that we understand children are composing their lives and can give accounts of their lives in the making. We realize that this crediting of children's knowledge of their life making may rub against other familial, social, cultural, or institutional narratives about who and how children should be.

LOOKING ACROSS OUR EXPERIENCES

As we look across these experiences, we can see that there are a number of key issues emerging. The processes of co-composing and negotiating interim research texts, such as narrative accounts, are complex and filled with many possibilities and tensions. The complexity is, in part, situated in the need to stay wakeful to how powerful these processes are in our lives, in the lives of participants, and in the relationships we have with participants. The power is embedded in the decisions we make and negotiate of what is told, what is left out, how a sense of coherence is achieved, and how we live through, sometimes needing to resist our own and others' perceptions of what is true.

In Chapter 11 we share the narrative account that Sean and Donovan co-composed. We include the entire account as it shows the complexity of the work involved as we move from field to field texts to interim and final research texts. At the conclusion of the narrative account we offer a reflective turn on the co-composing of the account.

CHAPTER 11

Meeting Donovan: A Narrative Account

GRADE 7-8 BEAVER HILLS HOUSE SCHOOL

Community

Cree Nation
Cultural and Familial Curriculum
"It is very important to me."
"I am losing family and gaining family."
"I have to be with my family."

Academics

"Art is my favorite class."
"I like physical education class."
"I get to be with my sisters at school."
"School gets tough as you go higher."
"I would want a school with two gyms."

Learning What Works Best

"When I am not distracted I learn best."
"I like to listen to my music."
"I was good in math last year."
"I like gym and math and activities."

School History

"I was at the reserve school-kindergarten."
"I then went to school in a small town."
"I went to two city schools."
"I then went to three more city schools."
"School tried holding me back, so I just skipped a grade."

Vision Board

"I want to be a police officer or a security officer someday."
"I want a good job."

"I want to help people."
"I want to stop people from doing bad stuff."

What Speaks to You as Being Important in Life?

"My mom is most important."
"My mom always encourages me."
"I want to do what my mom asks me to do."

Wise Words

"Be kind."
"I want to stay on a good path."
"I have good things in my life."
"I never used to listen. . . . I regret it now ... I listen to my Elders now."

Prologue

"Play that drum softly," she says. "Sean, this is what I was taught." These are the words of Elder Isabelle Kootenay, who has walked along-side me through the interwoven composing of my life in and out of schools, including this research process. Elder Isabelle Kootenay is a co-researcher. She knows many of the youth within the research project. When she spends time with them she often asks them to think of the medicine wheel as she teaches them gently about who they are and are becoming. Her words and her teachings weave their way through the stories of Donovan and help me see how the idea of gentle teaching and playing the drum softly as a way of teaching can help me think of Donovan and our shared stories over the past two years of coming alongside. "Play that drum softly," she says, is how I am thinking of this right now.

LEARNING TO LISTEN TO WHAT I COULD NOT HEAR

I first met Donovan at the art club, a Wednesday afternoon meeting space for two years in an urban junior high school. I remember him as young man who filled the room with his smile. His humor and laughter were gifts. He had a gentle presence. As I reflect on memories and read my field notes in the present, I see him in my mind as he flashes a smile, and I recall him sharing his stories of "taking care" of his newborn baby niece. I learned early on how important his family members were to him. He showed me many photographs as he let me into his world ... flipping through his phone, in another way telling me stories that he was a proud uncle, brother, grandson, and son.

As I write these words my memories flash backward and forward as I think of the stories and experiences we have shared over time. I think

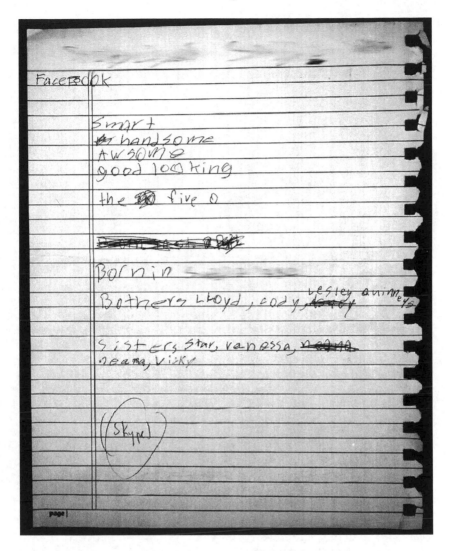

FaceBook

Smart
handsome
Awsome
good looking

the five o

Bornin

Bothers Lloyd, cody, Lesley auinneys

Sisters star, vanessa,
neama, Vicky

(Skype)

page 1

of Donovan and his drum, one that he created alongside an Elder, and how it is played with a certain rhythm in different places. I think of how the drum is played differently depending on how one is taught and in relation to the spaces the drum occupies. The drum is part of a process when I think of it in this way. It is animate and living. It is more than an instrument as it teaches in its own way, and it is meant to be taken care of in both a physical and metaphoric sense. I see Donovan through the memories of our early beginnings, and I fondly recall his presence, but I also see him as he is carrying songs and teachings through his drum.

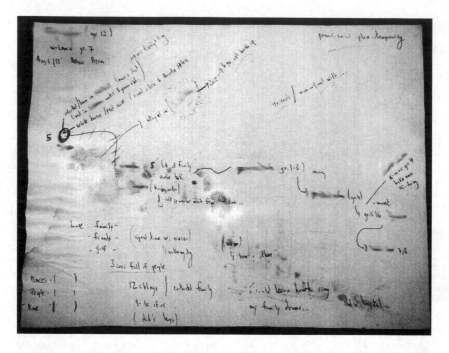

I slip back in time and recall being told by the other researchers that Donovan first came to the U of A art club, perhaps somewhat reluctantly, following closely behind his older sister. The stories that were shared were that Donovan was often led by his older sister and that she was always looking out for her little brother, like big sisters sometimes do. Stories of Donovan were often composed through those early interactions as a boy on the margins, on the periphery. It was as if he was connected but disconnected as he remained at a distance to many of us. I was uncertain, as I recall, where our relationship would take us, uncertain whether it would develop at all.

As I came to know Donovan we connected with brief verbal exchanges, a high five or a pat on the back that later led to a good meal and conversation. We met at the art club as we came to understand and trust one another with more certainty. Our relationship developed over careful time and through the symmetry between friends as I came to know Donovan through his friend Lane and Lane through his friend Donovan.

Long before I had these conversations with Donovan, Donovan would be accompanied alongside his best friend, Lane, at the U of A art club. It was Donovan who often encouraged Lane when Lane first came to the U of A art club to "stay just a little longer" until he finally did and found his own space within the group. As I look back at these *interactions it was Donovan who was leading in his own way and had recognized that the U of A art club was a space where he could enter feeling both comfortable and safe. It was safe enough that he first followed his sister, and through his experiences in the club, he began to lead others like Lane in his own way.*

These stories of early moments of relationship were stories Lane and Donovan later told me in our conversations as they described coming to know each other and the U of A art club. As they told their stories it was with fondness and a sense of a home place that they had found and created alongside each other. Through the sharing of earlier memories of the club and their evolving relationship they help me travel to my own memories of the U of A art club space. When I came to the club I noticed Donovan's sister and Lane, but I did not listen carefully enough to hear the gentle drumming, the beat that was present within Donovan.

I think of Donovan in the present as now I understand him differently. How, after the two years of research conversations I recognize more clearly who he was in that space and in the space between us. The gentle drumming is what I am reminded of when thinking of Donovan and how the way he moved and interacted was with quiet presence, a gentle rhythm or beat that would guide ... like that drum call Elder Isabelle Kootenay speaks of. It is a spirit or a way of living that is gentle and difficult to recognize if I am not listening carefully.

Now, as I turn and gaze backward to my notes and memories, I see it differently. Donovan's quiet leadership, leading in a gentle way, is how he moves in relation. In those early moments in the club space I didn't really recognize who was leading whom. I now see that the stories I first told were not the stories I came to know when I began to hear, for the first time, Donovan playing that drum ever so softly. The boys, Donovan and Lane, found each other, but what often seemed most evident during those first moments of observation is less clear to me now. I see the stories of a boy described as distant and quiet and as being led by others as miscast. I can see the lines more clearly when thinking of Donovan. No longer are they dotted representations of what I thought I knew; they are more pronounced with details and edges that provide more clarity when I am looking and trying to make sense of what I could not see and could not understand.

Lane, Donovan, and I began to build our relationships within the collective of the three of us meeting over suppertime conversations throughout the city. As I sit in the present I am transported back to those early moments of coming alongside in relationship. While I am trying to write of Donovan today, I know Lane is present. It was Lane who I was first encouraged to develop a research relationship alongside. Now I see that without Donovan, Lane may not have come to the U of A club. It was

Donovan who quietly remained present. I was "in the midst" (Clandinin & Connelly, 2000) of stories, and what has become the most important to me now was what I could not see and could not hear—Donovan gently playing his drum, calling to me in different ways. Donovan walked alongside Lane and me through meals and conversation ... his voice and stories always present, but I could not truly hear his stories until much later ... until he was ready to share in his own way, or perhaps he was waiting for me to listen more closely, to be more attentive. I see now that he was telling and living stories in his own way all along.

In our conversations outside the art club the three of us sipped tea, ate pizza, and laughed often over a two-year span, sharing stories of life and school. I see now that this separation between life and school seemed so pronounced, and I know now that their world in school was separate from their worlds outside school. Donovan's stories were often overshadowed at the beginning, lost in the spotlight of his good friend whose words were spoken eloquently and creatively on his behalf. I realize that his older sister also used to be the one who spoke as Donovan quietly entered in those shadow places behind her, behind Lane. He would remain quiet with words unspoken, not shared. Now, as I sit back, removed from the experiences and reading my notes, looking at the images and the artifacts, I realize he was sharing his story gently in many ways, but I was not always paying attention to the details and particularities that now became evident. It is only now that I begin to realize what I missed when I could not hear his drum ... the one he holds deep within himself playing so gently ... so softly.

AWAKENING TIME

At the U of A art club Donovan slowly began to let me into his worlds and to share stories with me of life in and out of school places (Clandinin et al., 2006). His laughter and his humor prevailed as he came up with little sayings and welcomed me with gentle barbs and jokes as we began to see each other more often outside the club space. He called out to restaurant owners, "Hey, Big Brother's buying today" or "My dad's got all the money—he better buy lunch today." In his stories he named me Big Brother or Dad, and he shared with me and with various restaurant owners, telling them and me with a smile on his face as he patted me on the back or tapped me on the arm in friendship.

Donovan and his friend Lane often took me home to my memories of early work, my early beginnings working alongside youth at the age of seventeen. Those moments in between were where I learned best, as the time spent after school and in the freedom of weekends was where youth taught me. It was rarely in schools that I would come to know the stories of young people. It was in the movement or improvisation where we would play sports and go on field trips and outings to see different things where the strongest relationships were created. The time spent alongside Donovan and his friend Lane in outside of school places created a space to share our stories in a safe way. The back and forth in our relationship was part of the rhythm we had co-composed together. Their loyalty and the strength in their actions and words continue to stay with me as I recall a memory of a time I was speaking at their school and they remained outside the room where I was presenting for over an hour just so they could say, "hi." I recall now, many months later, opening that door and them coming to greet me to my surprise, and all I could say is, "How are you boys? Why didn't you come in and see me speak?" Their simple reply: "We didn't want to bug you, so we just waited until you were done." In moments like these I recognized the relationship and the ethics (Clandinin & Connelly, 2000) in doing what I said I would do by coming alongside and honoring not only their words that they shared but also the consistency in being present. The stories of Donovan and Lane and the gift of sharing alongside each other over time is a thread that continues to shape who I am becoming, and it provides me the opportunity to think and remember the many times when the boys showed their ability to stay with it ... to stay with me ... to come alongside in relation, even if the past and their experience with this was not always a good story.

Relationships as a thread wove strongly throughout the stories Donovan shared with me. He is closely connected to his siblings, despite separate living arrangements within the city. Donovan lives with his aunt for the time being, but as he explained to me, this "changes depending on what is happening with my family." He told me about work and family and sometimes about space being scarce in his living arrangements. Through time I became more aware of the details of a life shared by a grade 7 boy from a reserve outside the city. He told of travels between these worlds of reserve life and urban life and the many places in between. Travel included different places, houses, and living arrangements, depending on what was happening within his family life. Homes and schools were places on his map without a real sense of permanence when he explained where he has been or where he might be going. Things remained temporary or for now when describing the people, the schools, his homes. Donovan sketched out moments of his life on a piece of paper when I asked him to create a timeline. He drew his timeline of the "important things," he said. He noted schools, his family members scattered throughout a province, and trips to different places ... even when those trips were the times spent between the reserve and the city.

The points on his memory map he could remember were based on events ... deaths, births, and celebrations mostly. Within those sketch book drawings gaps and silences were present that pointed to family members who were not a part of his life. He said, "My dad has never been there for me. I wish that he was. My mom is on the reserve. I see her sometimes. . . . just not now. My big brother, I can't see him now, but soon I will." And at these times we moved to another place in conversation, acknowledging the sadness and the feelings but looking together for the good things also present. I realize now as I write this that I am hearing Elder Isabelle Kootenay reminding me to move gently . . . move slowly as we compose a life together by sharing our stories, and sometimes those stories of relationships are difficult stories to share. It is through our sharing, through relationship, that ours would continue to shift.

Donovan and Lane: Co-Composing: Finding Their Songs Within

One sustaining relationship in Donovan's life in school was his relationship with his best friend, Lane. Another was his relationship with his older sister who lived in another home but attended the same school. Donovan explained his relationship with his friend to me: "If it wasn't for Lane, I would have a hard time going to school." When his friend Lane explained their relationship to me, he said, "Donovan looks out for me. He always helps me." They met each other in a gym. They tell the story in different ways . . . all I know as a researcher is that they found each other in the chaos of a grade 7 physical education class. In the pandemonium of a game of dodge ball, they managed to find time for a conversation and introduce themselves and form one of those grade 7 friendships that I too recall. It was one of those friendships that I hope sustains over the years as they learn to negotiate the tough places in school and life together . . . . with family and without family but trying to figure it out. They each said to me that the other was the reason they came to school.

From the time of meeting in school and developing a relationship outside of school that often involved time spent over the weekends, Donovan and Lane become almost inseparable. It would look different if one of them attended the U of A arts club without the other. They were closely connected. In school, at breaks, phoning each other, texting, and prompting each other to come to school was relational, not with the worry of missed assignments but with the longing for each other's company as they tried to make sense of their grade 7 school year together. As I look back at these moments and think about who they were in the midst of school, I begin to recognize how visible . . . how attentive they were to each other's stories. The stories of Donovan and Lane, their intricacies and the way they shared their gifts, the way they sang their songs, the way they found their rhythms in life in and out of school was so different yet connected. They were connected in the way that, despite the beauty and gifts in their stories, they remained largely invisible to the world of school that surrounded them. They were not known in their school for their songs, stories, or strength in both humor and friendship. They remained largely unknown in both the hallways and classroom spaces they occupied; they existed on the surface ... it was somewhat temporary. It was as if they could come and go, enter and leave, flicker on and off ... their footprints would be mostly unnoticed ... their voices would not be missed because the people within the school never really listened to who they were or heard what their gifts might be because no one knew where the sounds were coming from. I feel in this moment of clarity in writing that the boys became visible to each other, that they co-created a world for themselves. It seems so real when I imagine them meeting each other in the midst of chaos and noise in that physical education class. Like so much of what they do, they managed to find a space to share ... to connect ... and sustain that was different. They quite simply learned to play a different song within the place of school. Within that place of school they began to understand each other's lives by being alongside each other and co-composing a different rhythm ... a different beat ... a different song.

As I look back it becomes evident to me that they both understood each other in many ways, and perhaps part of becoming visible to each other was living in those places, traveling to each other's "worlds" (Lugones, 1987), and having a certain resonance when life got difficult. It was a part of the story that did not define the relationship. It was words left unsaid, an understanding that life at home involved complexities and that the lives they lived in other worlds involved many negotiations and rhythms familiar to each of them, visible to each of them in the world they were co-creating together. I wonder, when I reflect, whether the resonance in each other's stories helped them negotiate the relationship and open up the spaces where they could begin to share in different ways what sustained each other. In the places traveled together they learned to take care of each other's stories.

I have a photograph, a visual, an artifact, taken after one of our many conversations in those early moments of relationship. The boys' arms are stretched out around each other, they sit in a restaurant booth smiling, laughing, and I captured a moment in time ... a starting point for me as I try to tell the story of a young boy named Donovan and his friend Lane. It is through time and relation and the spaces in between that we negotiated that I am beginning to notice ... to see what I could not see at first. I find comfort in looking back at the pictures that the images of the boys, their stories, our stories, intertwined, are visible to me in so many new ways. The images of our time together encompass many of my thoughts and hopes for the future as I see them in my mind and imagine them in both school and life. The words begin to dance for me; they come alive when I think of their hopes and dreams. The boys' stories shone so bright when they shared them with me. Now those same stories become alive for me as I think of them and the "world"-travelling (Lugones, 1987, p. 68) that has gone on between us in those moments of telling, sharing, and listening to each other's stories. As we engaged in this relational work together, what once was not seen will ever remain visible within our stories.

Learning to Listen to Each Other, to Hear Our Stories

We met often over two years, many times weekly, even bi-weekly. Most of our recorded conversations were filled with laughter and sharing. Moments of seriousness, stories of loss and sadness were washed away in a hopefulness that was experienced through the sounds of laughter and "imagining otherwise" (Greene, 1995). It was at times individual laughter; other times it was a collective boom of emotion that filled not only my sound clips but also my memory markers that take me back to places at the edge of my memory—the soda pop fizzing, swishing as I heard Donovan taking sips, even when I play it back once again. We met in different places for our research conversations, paying attention to the shifting stories as we negotiated the constant movement and tensions of Donovan's grade 7 school year. When I go back over my field notes and listen to the audio clips, Donovan rarely spoke of school. He told stories of family, travel, culture, golf, adventures, his future. Our conversations at the beginning were on the surface as we learned together to build trust and share in different ways where school was not the dominant thread. The safe sharing with small stories stayed with us for many months, and it slowly shifted as Donovan let me understand more of his life in his multiple "worlds" (Lugones, 1987). He filled in gaps, and no longer were silences prolonged ... the awkwardness finally left, and we turned in a different way when the drums came calling one day.

The Drums Come Calling

In conversations Donovan expressed his desire to learn more about drum culture and protocol. He said, "I want to make a drum" when I asked what he wanted to do in the art club. I explained that we needed to think carefully about this because it wasn't "just about making a drum." Donovan and I would need to spend time with an Elder to learn more about Donovan's request. "It is just not about making a drum. It is a process that we need to go through," I said to him. He understood as he remembered back to his home community and his early beginnings what family members had taught him. "I just forgot some parts," he said. As we discussed the drum and what he wanted to do, our relationship once again started to shift.

We planned a visit to another school where an Elder worked. We had a relationship with Elder Francis Whiskeyjack, and when it was time to sit and visit with him, Trudy (another researcher) and I arranged a "field trip" for some teachings on drum protocols. My old friend—a sage and wisdom keeper—Elder Francis Whiskeyjack, teaches in gentle ways. I knew it was good to sit and visit with him ... where we could all learn in a safe way about the new journey we would be taking together. Elder Francis Whiskeyjack works with youth and has been instrumental in many lives, including my own. I felt good in my heart about bringing Lane and Donovan to ask questions and learn about drum protocol in a good way. Elder Francis Whiskeyjack takes care of youth's stories and helps them think deeply about what they are asking. We bought tobacco as a form of protocol and prepared to meet my friend Elder Francis Whiskeyjack. Donovan and I talked first about the questions he had and why we were bringing tobacco to ask Elder Francis Whiskeyjack for guidance with our questions. We talked about process and slowing down on this day and learning what this experience could teach us.

Donovan and Elder Francis Whiskeyjack shared the same community roots, despite not previously knowing each other. They were Cree brothers, tribal brothers ... an intergenerational narrative situated in place was possible.

My Friend Francis

I have been privileged to work alongside Elder Francis Whiskeyjack not only in school places but in the life moments of sharing time and laughter between cups of tea and the stories that accompany those places. We share a story of working with youth, coming alongside their school and life experiences ... not separated ... intricately woven. It is rare when laughter is not heard between us ... it is often our starting place as well as our middle and ending places. Our relationship has continued to grow and our friendship strengthened through the work we do together. Elder Francis Whiskeyjack's image remains strong in my mind and fills me with good feelings of a different place and a different time. I knew through relationship that Elder Francis Whiskeyjack would help us. He would help us understand the drum and teach us gently as I introduced him to both Donovan and Lane. The boys wanted to learn. They came into this situation with good intentions, and they were serious in their request for more teachings accompanied with protocol.

I had not seen the boys act so seriously as when they stepped out of the cab that brought them from their homes to the school where Elder Francis Whiskeyjack worked. I greeted them at the front doors of the school. I greeted Trudy, my fellow researcher, and thanked her for getting the boys organized as I prepared for our teachings with Elder Francis Whiskeyjack. I had made tea and sat with Elder Francis Whiskeyjack throughout the morning, giving him some background knowledge of the U of A art club and some of the stories of the boys and our relationship together. He looked forward to meeting them. In the school and community Elder Francis Whiskeyjack always welcomed others who came from great distances to hear his stories. I have been alongside many before this time and, through this process, have observed what possibilities might come out of it. With an open mind and an open heart I was hoping the boys might start the conversation.

We walked into the school, and Elder Francis Whiskeyjack welcomed the boys at the entrance with a smile and a feeling of openness. We walked together touring the school. Getting to know the place was important in coming to know each other. Elder Francis Whiskeyjack helped us to feel comfortable. He joked, created conversation with the boys, and smiled when Donovan told him where he was from. Elder Francis Whiskeyjack brought the boys to different classrooms and introduced them to other youth, teachers, and the administrators. It was as if the school belonged to them in this moment. It was an open space for learning by shifting how both the boys had previously understood schools. During our tour we walked into the principal's office for the first time. They walked in as welcomed and honored guests—not as youth to be disciplined or corrected but as people in relationship. We talked about this day long after and how this experience was different for them. Donovan smiled as he told the story of that day and how "he knew many kids from pow wows, community events, and sports who attended the school" and how "it felt good to be there for a visit."

We had now prepared to spend time and have a conversation with Elder Whiskeyjack about the drum and the importance of what drumming might mean. Elder Francis Whiskeyjack led us into his space, his cultural teaching room, where we entered with protocol and took off our shoes. The room was a former administrator's office and was intentionally changed into a space of teaching and healing.

No longer did the big oak desk fill the room nor did the wall hangings of degrees and awards granted dominate the space. There were no titles here, just relationships beginning. The big bookshelves with books of things removed from the realities of lives in a school had been dismantled to create this space. It was a purposeful response to shifting knowledge landscapes.

This space had become a healing space, a conversational space (Clandinin et al. 2006) in a school where people could connect in different ways. I watched the boys as they walked in the room and surveyed the area. They looked at the lack of seating, they looked at each other, they looked at me. There were no chairs here … just our little group together with the hides of various animals welcoming us, inviting us to sit on the floor, to sit on the hides and think about the living and who we were in relation on this day. It was different here.

It is with the ethics of relation on my mind that I tell some of the details of this story—not the process and the teachings but of what happened when we entered a space together in relation. Together we were trying to learn about thinking differently together. As we sat on the bear rugs and looked to the middle of the room where a buffalo skull rested with offerings surrounding it we were, in those moments, being invited to think alongside each other. It was a space where we could look at the four walls around us and see the colored prints connecting us to the variant directions.

We could now begin to think and feel in different ways alongside each other. The boys and I talked about this experience often and what they noticed and didn't notice … if it was what they expected. I always get the same resounding "NO." "We thought we were going to an office to talk about school." Soon after they entered the space the boys offered protocol and thanked Elder Francis Whiskeyjack for his time and for his teachings. We sat around the circle on this day long ago and entered a space that shifted all our stories as we became part of each other's stories, part of our memories in a place of shifting stories. We entered into that connecting space in schools that is so often miscast or not present in the time between school starting and ending. It is a space that disrupts our knowing by not knowing. We were unfamiliar with the space and the direction of the teachings. By dismissing how we had previously been taught, we were able to weave a new thread through the stories of beginning and coming alongside each other in relation through teachings. This conversational relationship with Elder Francis Whiskeyjack took us all to a place that was different and moved us in a direction that none of us quite expected. We sat together on that day for an hour sharing stories. Elder Francis Whiskeyjack told stories he had been told as a young man and shared his experiences over time and places, asking the boys to think alongside but never telling them. He was sharing with them gently. On that day he did not give the boys an answer to their question about drumming. That in itself was the best teaching. We did not get that checkbox answer of "yes, you can." However, what we did get was an invitation to come again. I could see by the smiles on the boys' faces that this was the best answer of all.

In-Between Time

Donovan shared with me how difficult it was to keep the commitments Elder Francis Whiskeyjack asked of him when learning about drumming. "It is hard, Sean," he said. He had been put in situations where fighting, alcohol, and drugs were prevalent. He said, "I feel pressure, but I will stay strong." Donovan was thinking in such different ways from the boy I first met who struggled to find who he was in those moments of grade 7 coming to know time ... this is the life he wanted to compose for himself. He wanted to learn about the drums, and he started a journey that resisted the fighting as he happily told me that he "walked away from a fight" or that he "didn't smoke" when asked. He recognized within himself the teachings being asked of him by Elder Francis Whiskeyjack. He often said, "I need to learn about respect for the drum." The teachings and the questions Elder Francis Whiskeyjack asked Donovan were creating a space within him to reflect on who he was becoming and what the process of building a drum involved. It was not about learning how to build a drum but learning how to take care of it once you built it alongside an Elder's teachings. Donovan was well aware of what was being asked. In those moments he remembered earlier teachings within his own community, within his own family stories of culture that are situated in place. The early teachings nested deep within him (Clandinin & Connelly, 2000) were becoming more alive and more present as he was thinking about what they meant.

More Teachings ...

Weeks later the invitation to come back and spend time with Elder Francis Whiskeyjack was too much to resist. The boys talked about their visit and shared stories with other youth. They eagerly awaited their opportunity to reconnect with their new friend for more teachings. The cab pulled up, and once again Donovan and Lane exited and greeted me at the door. "We have been here before," was the feeling I got from them ... a certain comfort was present within them. They were met with handshakes and a welcome from the school administrators. "It is great to see you again, boys," was all they needed. Around the corner Elder Francis Whiskeyjack appeared. He met them with his trademark smile, a handshake, and a hug. Silence came upon the conversation. He looked at the boys, smiled, and I remember his words: "Well, I guess you boys are ready to make a drum." I recognized that special feeling, and once again

a smile came across my face. In the present I am removed from this expe-
rience, but it stays with me ... deep within it reverberates, it sustains me
and casts an image of Donovan and Lane and Elder Francis Whiskeyjack
as we moved to a place within our stories that would always be different.
Thank you for teaching me my friends.

Donovan Meets Beaver Hill House School

During the summer between grades 7 and 8 Donovan decided that
because of travel and his older sister's determination to change schools
that he too must follow. As I reflect on it much later, I believe part of
the shift occurred during those first moments of meeting Elder Francis
Whiskeyjack, making his own drum, and developing relationships in a
space where he was welcomed. The shift to a new school that his older
sister was attending was with little hesitation as he knew more about the
new school because of our visits with Elder Francis Whiskeyjack. Through
conversation Donovan said, "It is only two buses" and "I know other
kids who go there." Changing schools did not concern him. It was what
he needed to do to be with his family. It was where he wanted to be to
continue to learn about the drum he had created. I wondered at this time
about "transition" and worried he would experience another change ...
another new beginning at a school. However, this transition concerned me
less than times past because I knew the teachers in the building, and they
would take care of not only Donovan but also his older sister. The idea,
the word transition, was also shifting for me at this time as I continued to
learn from Donovan that transition involved much more than changing
schools. Donovan taught me this with his stories of life and movement
between places. As I listened to Donovan explain his decision to change
schools I heard in his words how much he looked forward to learning
from Elder Francis Whiskeyjack, who helped him create his drum.

The drum was increasingly important to Donovan and to who he
was becoming. Through his travels during the summer his drum often
traveled with him. He was learning to "take care of his drum" like Elder
Francis Whiskeyjack had asked him through teachings. The songs that
were within him and the drum beat that was always present, nested
deeply within him, became more prominent as they emerged through-
out those summer months. I think of Elder Francis Whiskeyjack in this
moment as I write and think of what he might say. When I spend time
with him at celebrations, watching the young children dance to the beat
of the drums, when they hear the drums in the background and the songs
calling in a different way, they begin to move with freedom, with no hesi-
tation, he begins to smile. When he sees this he often says to me "Sean,
it is always in them ... it is their spirit moving to the beat of the drum.

It is in their hearts even when they are young." He has repeated these words to me often as we attended events together and as he reflected on moments of past teachings. I saw within Elder Francis Whiskeyjack how it moved his spirit to see this as he also used to dance. He used to be a champion pow wow dancer, and this can be seen in his movement as he often opens the grand entries and the celebrations we attend. His footwork is meticulous. His movement is effortless. He glides to the beat of the drums ... it is a poetic shuffle. He is also filled with spirit in these moments as he lets the sound of the drum take him on that journey with openness and good intentions. He travels backward and forward in those moments of experiences and teachings to the multiple worlds he lives within. I think of this image in my mind when I think of Donovan and who he was becoming, of how the creative processes of making a drum alongside Elder Francis Whiskeyjack had shifted who he was becoming. It was not just a "build a drum and then all is good" story; it was the process and the becoming visible within yourself by looking inward, by being alongside others and by letting that introspection eventually turn outward and take Donovan, Lane, Elder Francis Whiskeyjack, and me to unimagined places (Clandinin & Connelly, 2000). It is in this "world"- travelling" sense (Lugones, 1987) that we are always moving together. It was here that we had to become more attentive and more visible to the stories and the spirit we had inside us all along. Now the sounds became clearer, more pronounced. No longer faint and in the distance, the sounds became difficult to ignore because those songs, the drum beats, were shaping who we were becoming together.

Beaver Hills' House was a school with a cultural narrative. The dominant thread in this school was the life of the students who came from many communities. The curriculum lived out within the school created spaces for acknowledging the gifts within youth (Huber, Murphy, & Clandinin, 2011). It was a place where drumming, beading, language, and ceremony were present and welcomed. The smell of sweetgrass and sage linger in the air as I think of this place and how it gently greeted me each time I walked through the doors. It was different in that place. As I observed Donovan from a distance in this new school, I began to see shifts within him and his ideas of what school could be. I saw a smile on his face as he shared stories with me about what he did at school and who he was within it. Despite Donovan taking two buses each morning, he rarely missed a day of school, and when he did he contacted his teachers to let them know where he was. When I walked into the school I saw that he had a place to be a part of, where the acknowledgement of who he was becoming was alive. I could see it in the way he carried himself in relationship. He told me these same things when he said, "I even do sports now in this school ... I play basketball. I am part of a team."

I saw Donovan at Beaver Hills' House School, and there was a calmness within him as he had found a place where possibilities existed. The staff called him "Little Francis" in honor of the Elder he spent so much time with. They said, "We often see Donovan right beside Francis." This, to me, was special, and I saw it as I went for a visit to attend the morning song that took place each day at this school. Donovan, along with other students who work with Elder Francis Whiskeyjack, drummed alongside the staff in a morning song each day when they sang for all the creatures and the animate things in this world to wake up and be thanked as gifts of creation. It was a powerful part of the day that Donovan was involved in. He said, "It sets me up for the day. I just close my eyes and I know the words." It was his routine, a part of his rhythm, to start by singing with his heart and reflecting on all the good things. It was a shift that I was happy to observe as his drum played softly together with others and he finally had an opportunity to celebrate that voice that was always there; it had just not been as visible to me and perhaps even to Donovan in the art club space. A calm and introspective time comes over me when I reflect as I can not only hear the drum calling but also hear the distinct words and voices of a morning song taking me home to my own stories.

As I reflect on this shift and the relationship we developed over two years, it brings me happiness as I find it difficult to write without smiling because I know for now he is safe and in a good place of learning and living. The drum, a simple question—"Can I make one?"—a conversation, and relationship that has moved to places unexpected is what I feel has happened. I recently went for a visit to Beaver Hills' House School to see Donovan, and I also was able to spend time with Elder Francis Whiskeyjack. We walked together through the school, sharing stories and laughing about past experiences together. Elder Francis Whiskeyjack explained to me how well Donovan was doing and how committed he was to drumming and learning with him. Donovan simply told me, "I told you so."

Before I left to move to a different city, Donovan and I sat in a room at his new school, Beaver Hills' House. We shared stories with each other and talked about the experiences he was having in this new school place. "I hardly miss a day of school, Sean. I want to play solo for morning song," he told me. I recorded this conversation and reflect on an amazing gift that is difficult to capture with my written words. Our conversation moved to the words of the drum songs that he learned at Beaver Hills' House School and how he looks forward to his own songs one day. He shared, "When I close my eyes and I am singing beside Mr. Whiskeyjack, the words just come. I can remember them when I play my drum with him." With these words I asked Donovan if he could share with me "what this sounds like, what are the words that you are learning?" He began to sing quietly, softly, as he shared his songs with me, his stories. When I feel distance from his words and experiences shared over the course of two years, when I find it difficult to remember and transport myself back to those experiences, I put my headphones on and listen to our conversations and then listen to his song. It played for a brief moment as he closed his eyes and sang it on that day from within his heart. It helps me, in the present, to remember who he is, who he is becoming (Clandinin & Connelly, 2000). His words and his songs sustain me and help me stay connected to our shared stories. "Hey Haw Hey Haw Hey Haw Hey Haw," he chants gently, softly, and I can see him drumming in my mind, playing softly in his new school alongside Elder Francis Whiskeyjack. "Hey Haw Hey Haw Hey Haw Hey Haw," is what he is singing from deep within his heart ... no words to describe ... just that feeling of going to a different place in relationship that helps me to remember a young man who continues to teach me.

Kookum Muriel: "She Was an Elder to Everyone"

I grew through my relationship with Donovan, and this relationship we forged together continues to shift my stories. As I listen to our shared stories, certain stories speak to me, call to me in different ways. As we sat and had a meal together in the months before I left and started a new job in a new city, a sense of leaving lingered. I had within me a shifting tide of uncertainty that entered my mind ... it was unsettled, a transition and movement that is unknown to me. Perhaps it is more recognized in my co-researcher, Donovan, who told the most beautiful stories, and through his stories I recall my own knowing of this place. The space we shared opened up between us as we told stories filled with laughter and, at times, sadness as the thread of relationships and loss reverberated deeply between us. I can feel it in different ways as I listen to it in these moments spread over time and place. Perhaps the process of inquiring into the stories has kept me away from some of these more difficult conversations that live within me. The resonance in stories opens spaces and takes me on a storied journey that, at times, I am unprepared for because I did not know where the conversation would take us until time settled much later. I revisit these moments now with a different lens and a sense of what might have been happening as we wove our stories together. We were sharing in good ways between food and the laughter that helps even the most difficult of stories gently heal, even if for just a moment, with a grade 8 Cree boy who comes from a place that reminds me of places I have "world"-travelled (Lugones, 1987).

He wanted to tell me this story of his Kookum as I inquired into the places he had attended school as we looked back over time with our timeline art. We looked together at the sketching down of marks on a piece of paper and the places he had traveled in school and life. We visited about the people who were a part of his story. I would explain it as what mattered to him. Looking back at our timeline art and seeing where the waves and extensions on a piece of paper took us in a "world"- travelling" sense (Lugones, 1987) was most often our starting point in conversations. On this day he started to revisit his school on the reserve, and within that memory marker we both traveled down the road to his Kookum's house—to her stories, to the stories Donovan carried with him in the present.

During our conversation Donovan began to speak about his home community, his reserve. I asked him who he enjoyed visiting within this place. Donovan shared stories of his cousins and family members, and then he moved to silence. He said, "I used to always go visit my Kookum Muriel." After listening to his quiet words when sharing, I asked him "Has your Kookum passed?" With his head now looking down and the smile no longer present he shared with me part of her story.

> Yes, she was a good woman, she was kind to everyone, she was an Elder to everyone. She passed away in 2010. I still think of her. I went and visited my brother after when my Kookum died. I tried being strong ... but when I got to my brother's I just felt it ... and then I started to cry. She was my dad's mother. Muriel was her name. (Donovan, personal communication, December, 2012)

The conversation shifted rapidly as I recall. It was filled with silence on the voice recorder, and I am transported back to those moments of conversation within a restaurant. At that moment in conversation, as I say on the sound memo, "We don't have to talk about this Donovan ... it's okay," I can hear the silence and the difficulty in hearing him. His words struggle to come out shortly after, and I remember clearly. He started to tell me about walking a long distance to visit her. "Across the lake is where she lived" is how he said it. "She had a big house, and she made a farm so I would play with the animals—the chickens and the horses. I would go there by myself, just walking." I see him in my mind, walking down the rural roads of his community. That sense of taking care of the animals was what he enjoyed sharing with me at this time. The feeling of spending time that was free with his Kookum was what he helped me recall within my own stories. He continued his sharing moment, laughing as he told me his stories of "chasing chickens" and the time his horse "head butted" him. We both laughed at these stories, as I once again recalled the good moments of improvisation and playfulness of growing up on a farm. I asked Donovan ... "Favorite all-time memory of your Kookum." Donovan shared a story of the time his Kookum played chess

*with him and how she taught him board games. "She would speak to me
in Cree, teaching me all my numbers and the animals, but now I forget.
But the best memory of her is that she would just spend time with me."*

*His teaching words speak to me as a father, and I think of my family
in this moment of reflection time. Through these conversations I now
understand more deeply why the relationship between us moved to such
different places. I wondered about the times Donovan called me "Big
Brother" or "Dad" when we ordered a meal together. I wondered about
the shifting relationship and the importance of being there and showing
up consistently to share memories, stories, and laughter between us. I
thought of these moments when Donovan told me the most important
memories were "when she would just spend time with me." At moments
during those conversations it was difficult to articulate what was happening ... impossible in many ways because it happened through the
shared space of relationship over time. As I now reflect on the places we
have been and the people who have traveled with us in those places of
becoming, I can hear Donovan's voice more clearly, and it is a gift when
I can hear it. He reminded me of what was important when he said,
"When I close my eyes and I feel happy and wonder if Kookum Muriel
is looking out for me. I have had a lot of loss in my life." I can see the
ethics in relationship that runs deeply in the person he is becoming, in
what he carries with him as a grandson (Clandinin & Connelly, 2000).
It took almost two years for Donovan to share these stories with me. It
took longer for me to begin to understand who I was in relation to them.
It was because of his stories that I began to rethink and re-imagine some
of my own stories. Donovan said it best, though, and I thank him for
this: "She was kind to everyone ... she was an Elder to everyone."*

REMEMBERING SCHOOL

*Over the span of two years the conversations between Donovan and I
shifted rapidly. At the beginning in the place of his grade 7 junior high we
shared stories on the surface, never really going to those deeper places,
or simply covering them over with humor and laughter (Clandinin et al.,
2006). I listened and relistened to the audio clips of our conversations,
and I was reminded of places we had been and the stories we had shared.
During our last meal together, before I left for a new city, we had a moving conversation when we reviewed the timeline he had created and I
asked him to share memories from the places of schools he has attended.*

*As I looked at his starting place of school on the reserve and noticed
the movement and then a gap, he once again told me he "skipped grade
2." I asked him to explain this to me in more detail. When revisiting this, I
thought it may have been a result of the numerous transitions taking place*

in his life. He had always explained this gap in his school story as "moving around because of jobs." Today he spoke more about his early beginnings in school. "The reason why I skipped grade 2 is because I failed grade 1. I didn't know plus and minus, what the hell that is." As he explained to me I understood more clearly the jumping between grades. I asked him if he could tell me about this experience in school. Donovan explained,

> *I felt bad ... I like being usually happy in school, but I remember being so scared to tell my mom that I failed. It sucked because I had friends. It was difficult. I remember telling my mom I failed and she said ... it's okay, you will do better. (December 2012)*

On his timeline Donovan showed me how during the next school year he had moved numerous times between the reserve and the city with his family. He explained, "My mom helped me in school because she told the city school that I was ready for grade 3, and so when that school started I was in grade 3, and that is how I skipped grade 2." I looked at him during this conversation. We both began to laugh, and I told him how smart he was ... and how smart his mom was, and that it made much more sense for me to understand how a person could skip a grade. His mom always knew what was best for Donovan.

When Donovan and I looked at his timeline together he brought to light many more details as he let me walk in his "worlds" with him (Lugones, 1987). He had distinct memories from the schools he attended, sometimes "three schools in one year," he said, and essentially a new school every year was what he experienced. I asked him what he thought the main reason was for going to different schools, and he said "My mom . . . . she needs jobs and there was nine of us kids sometimes, so we would go where we live by. I like where I am going to school now. There are people who look out for me ... my last school, it's like they gave up on me." The calm within him was evident as he shared, and I thought about his life within Beaver Hills' House School. It was a great place for him to be for now. Donovan learned over time to keep certain stories to himself. They were silent within him because they were stories of experiences that had caused pain and that he remembered vividly. The school story of failing and being scared to tell an adult was difficult, and the relief he had when he was able to tell his mom resonated with me. Her words of wisdom brought a smile to my face: "It's okay. You will do better." "It's okay. You will do better."

The Spirit of the People

The Spirit of the People is a blanket gifted to me on my last day of school at Beaver Hills' House with a school board where I worked as a teacher for ten years. It was an unexpected gift, one I will continue to treasure. It is a memory marker for me going forward. An eagle feather and a blanket gifted by Elder Francis Whiskeyjack, Donovan, and students I had come to know in this place were part of my next journey. Elder Francis Whiskeyjack explaining "The Spirit of the People" at Beaver Hills' House School evoked strong feelings within me. I thought of the Spirit of the People and what that might mean in the moments of relation. Coming from Elder Francis Whiskeyjack and Donovan, it felt fitting to be honored with these words to live by that represented how I felt about them and how they continued to shape me (Clandinin et al., 2006).

That spirit, that song within that sometimes plays softly, sometimes calls loudly, depending on how I am listening for it or what might be going on in those moments of a life, is what I think about when I think of the Spirit of the People. The stillness, the pause, the reflection are important as I slow down in this writing and try to understand that Spirit of the People within my own words and experiences.

I felt the warmth as the blanket surrounded me. It captured my emotions as I was embraced with friendship on that day. The drums were on my mind, and the images were clearly present within. I can still feel that good blanket wrapped around me with my friends on each side and Elder Francis Whiskeyjack explaining his teachings. The Spirit of the People is a feeling I will not forget, that I will continue to look for within my own stories. It is comfort time, taking me home time, wrapping me with the reds and yellows. And in the solace of good words and good feelings in relation, it is the spirit between us that gives me strength in the present, when I meet special people like Donovan and Elder Francis Whiskeyjack, who I had the privilege to walk alongside. The small moments defined by time cannot measure the feeling or the teachings I have received through the relationships and the stories we have shared. It is the Spirit of the People that reminds me of how I want to live when I gaze backward to those moments. The stories of the people, the songs, the Spirit of the People will continue to guide me as I learn to take care of the stories that Donovan, Elder Francis Whiskeyjack, and I have shared.

As I write these words, I have now been in a new city for two months and can carefully reflect on two years of relationship with Donovan. I am at the start, the beginning of a new journey, as Elder Francis Whiskeyjack would say. I find myself at a prairie university as a professor working with aspiring teachers, and these stories that are removed by distance are present in the gifts I have received. I see them in the blanket I have brought with me to my new office and carefully display. It carries stories that sustain me. It is that same Spirit of the People that Elder Francis

Whiskeyjack spoke about that I try to carry into this new place that I am living within. The gifts—the blanket, the eagle feather, the stories of the lives—stir my emotions in the present. I often think of Donovan as I try to compose a life being away and looking back over the experiences we have shared together. I have Donovan and Elder Francis Whiskeyjack to thank as they teach me what Spirit of the People actually means. It is through their way of living that I am continuing to learn as they helped shape the day when I was honored by the people, the students, and the school that I was a part of for a small moment in time in my life. Their way of gently walking, drumming softly, just living is the Spirit of the People that I think of and the meaning that is held within the blanket gifted to me on that special day.

I can still hear that drum when I close my eyes and look back, as they wrapped that blanket around me on that last day. It is as Donovan teaches me "Hey Haw Hey Haw Hey Haw Hey Haw." "Hey Haw Hey Haw Hey Haw Hey Haw." The best gift is seeing through the sound of those songs playing gently, playing softly on my mind in the present. It is what I would call the Spirit of the People.

When You Hear the First Thunder

"When I hear the rain, I know what that means. It reminds me of my name. Sometimes I forget what it means just for a little bit. My name is First Thunder. I was named in a ceremony on the reserve when I was little." These words echo throughout as I listened to them closely on my voice audio today. Recorded months earlier, I have thought about these words often, these wonderful words that dance through my mind and fill my heart with happiness. I heard them again—his words, his voice—and I let them take me to those faraway places in my mind. I let the words rest within me. I let them teach me and carry me, thinking of who I am in relation to the stories shared through the silence that comes when walking in the outdoor spaces. Donovan and his stories resonate with me and help me travel home in my mind, even though some of those places remain difficult places to travel to.

Finally the sun was shining again today in this cold prairie winter setting. A touch of seasons changing time was in the air. I could feel it. The sun was casting its rays beautifully, filling the air with expression as I walked through the downtown corridor. The softness of snow falling added to the majesty around me. The words of First Thunder I played over on my phone... walking ... enjoying the pureness in simplicity. I was thinking with the words. I was letting them come to life in the outdoor spaces that help me think ... clearing my mind with openness and possibility. Donovan let me into his "world" (Lugones, 1987) gently in this conversation where we co-created a space for sharing shortly before I moved away to my new life in a new city. He let me know who he was in a different way. He taught me. First Thunder told me about recalling the story of getting his "Indian name" and what it meant to him. It underscored the narrative thread of relationships and a family story that guided his life making. It was a story that shaped who he was becoming, and with that becoming he was guiding me along the way in my own life negotiation.

Donovan explained to me "When I hear the rain fall" that "I should think about him." Those words stop me. "I know I will," was my recorded response. "I know when I hear the rain fall I will think of you," and now in the present retelling that good sadness overcomes me. When thinking about a life and the young person a research project brought me to, I feel overwhelmed and gifted. It was a gift when he said, "When I hear the rain fall" to me. I have an image in my mind of a young boy and how he thought with those words and his connection to his family and the places he moved within, both geographically and metaphorically. He said to me with quiet strength, "I was told that when I hear the rain and the first thunder I should take some food and tobacco and bury it beside a tree to give back and remember my name." First Thunder told me his story with a small whisper of words and intermittent silences and the pause that slowed down the conversation allowing time for reflection as he thought when he told me. This young man left me with such gifts and shared with me why, in that moment, he believed he was honored with the name First Thunder. He spoke of his older sister. . . . and the stories told of her:

> *She would have been the tenth. We would have had ten of us in our family, but she passed away when she was two days old. It makes me sad when I think of her—she would be the third oldest. I know about her because my mom always tells me about her. Her name was Brittany. I really wanted to meet her ... my mom always tells me stories about her. That is why I have the name First Thunder.*
> *I am the youngest.*
> *They want me to remember.*

IN RESPONSE TO STORIES

First Thunder, I thank you for your stories. I thank you for teaching me gently along the way and letting me walk alongside these stories over time. As I sit with these stories, far removed from the first place where we shared these good stories together, I can hardly wait until the seasons change and the winter begins to rest for another year. I can hardly wait until the sun celebrates again with the warmth that shifts the skies. It is

the place where the sun stirs the clouds and conjures up the sweeping
wind that I will be looking for. It is the springtime clarity. I will be wait-
ing "to hear the rain fall" once again. In that moment of cleansing time
I will be looking up and waiting to hear your voice tell me those good
stories again. I will be listening for the First Thunder, and with that I will
be reminded of those words you told me not so long ago. Your stories
stay with me and connect me to the elements in ways I have not thought
of before. Keep telling those good stories of healing, of celebration, of
hope, and I will be waiting "to hear that rain fall" once again.

THINKING WITH THE NARRATIVE ACCOUNT

As part of composing this book we spent many days writing together at
the same table. Sean traveled from his new place to be with Janice, Jean,
and Vera in Edmonton on a regular basis. On one of those days, before
Sean joined us, he visited with Donovan at Donovan's school. It has
been almost five years now since Jean, Vera, and Sean met Donovan, and
much has changed. When Sean entered Donovan's school that day he
smiled as Donovan has grown into a tall young man who soon will finish
high school. Drumming is still central to Donovan's life. Donovan did
not hesitate to talk with Sean and to pick up where they had left off in
their conversations. As part of these conversations there was talk about
family members, community members, and the places on the reserve
Sean knew mattered to Donovan.

As Sean talked with Vera, Jean, and Janice, we were reminded that
life continues to unfold in many ways. We are always in the midst.
In thinking with Donovan's account we see just how much care was
taken in the co-composing of this interim research text. We see that the
co-composing of the narrative account involved response groups and
multiple conversations so that it could be written in ways that shows
it is tentative and does not reduce a life to a page. Sean was mindful
about how Donovan's narrative account held the potential to shape a
life. Thinking about the relation between the written text and a life in
the midst, Janice and Vera wondered about the report cards their own
children had recently received and how those report cards were shaping
their children's lives and their family lives.

Sean and Donovan worked on the narrative account together. It was
evident that their journey alongside each other did not have a sense of
ending; perhaps our journeys alongside participants do not end. In the
writing and negotiation of narrative accounts we are all changed—as
researchers, as participants, as people. Although this holds true for our
work alongside diverse participants, it is important to stay particularly
wakeful to this in the lives of children and youth. Children and youth are

not often seen as having the power to engage in negotiations or as having the power to make decisions about their life stories. Sean, in paying close attention, found ways alongside Donovan to create a relationship where Donovan does hold agency.

While being mindful of the agency necessary for Donovan to make decisions, Sean was always aware that he, too, was negotiating his work with Donovan's family members, in this case, Donovan's mother. Alongside both Donovan and his mother, Sean attended closely to the long-term impact and consequences of the narrative account. Family stories were made visible within Donovan's stories, stories of death and the celebration of the life of his older sister. Perhaps these stories were not Donovan's to tell. As the narrative account was negotiated, Donovan and his mother learned new things from each other, things that had not known about each other. Reading the accounts became a powerful process of recognition and learning.

In the moments of reading narrative accounts with participants, we also have the opportunity to engage further in the co-composition of the accounts and in understandings in relation to the research puzzles. It is in these moments when we realized how important it is to stay with notions of research puzzles, as there are many ways to write narrative accounts and what is pulled forward in the co-composition. It is important to note that in these moments we are not raising questions about what is true but rather what is possible, what could reflect participants' told and lived stories and our stories in relation with them. These wonders stay with us as we consider the issues around representing the narrative inquiries with children and youth.

CHAPTER 12

Representations in Final Research Texts: Moral and Ethical Considerations

In this chapter we take up issues around how we represent narrative inquiries when we are working with children and youth, populations that are often considered inherently vulnerable because of their age. This concern for their vulnerability sometimes means we do not ask them of their experiences. Sometimes the concern about their vulnerability is rooted in the sense that someone else needs to speak for them, that they cannot be seen as research participants who are able to co-compose, inquire into their experiences, or make decisions. Sometimes, implicitly or explicitly, we address the perceived dangers due to their vulnerability by not allowing them to speak, by co-opting their stories of experience, by writing over their stories, or by unintentionally minimizing the complexity of their experiences. In narrative inquiry with children and youth we take up the concerns around vulnerability to show how we find ways, alongside children and youth, to make them visible in the research and, consequently, to make their stories matter in the research literature and policy documents. We do this through maintaining a relational ethical stance throughout all aspects of each inquiry. In this chapter we turn our attention more directly to issues of representation.

For example, drawing on the narrative inquiry with youth in the study of experiences of leaving school early, participants often shared memories of looking back to the institutional landscapes of their elementary, junior high schools, and senior high schools. Engaging in the telling of their stories was sometimes challenging, as some of their experiences were difficult ones to make visible for several reasons. As we shaped spaces where the youth were called to recollect hard-to-tell stories, we were attentive to the youth shifting backward in time from present situations, where they were composing their lives, to more difficult times and places. We see something of this in Sean's stories of coming alongside Leanne.

As our conversation came to a close I brought out of my book bag a small narrative account I had written about Leanne prior to our meeting. I wrote the narrative to help me remember, to help me form a clearer picture in my mind. I read the account of my memories of her as a basketball player and student at the high school. I wrote what I remembered about her and told her how happy I was that I could share some stories with her and reconnect after such a long period of time. After I read my story there was silence and quiet thoughts about times past, the present, and the uncertainties of the future. I told her that as we continued to have conversations the stories will change and we will develop it together, co-construct school and life stories. At this time we both packed up our belongings and walked to the entrance of the coffee shop. Symbolic of our first meeting, we decided it was best to go separate ways. After all, I do realize the social stigma of walking in the mall with your old teacher [Sean was previously her high school teacher]—it's still not cool.

Sean continues to write,

Her response helps me to understand as I move forward as an educator. She said, "Lessard, even you, we just talked about the sports. You never asked me too much about the other things—everybody had a business attitude." I looked at her and responded with a simple "I know" and "I am sorry." I told her how I looked at the story from one point of view, that I only ever saw her in the hallway, and that one day we were talking and the next day she was gone. "I had no way to track you down or ask whether I could help". We talked about this moment, reflecting on that school year. I told her how I felt about the situation and that I was shocked she "dropped out," and she corrected me: "I didn't drop out. I took a break, dropping out is negative. It's different." We talked for a long period of time about her high school story, and she explained to me the importance of having someone to talk to in all parts of life. I wonder about the stories we have shared and how the many avenues in her life had expectations and composed who she was or who she was expected to be. I wonder whether her decision to take a break from school is a response to the numerous voices telling her who we wanted her to be.

As we listened to the stories of their experiences in these earlier times and places, we were in the midst of shifting research relationships that required us to consider what Thomas King (2003) described as taking care of one's stories, an idea we introduced in Chapter 5. As they told stories that allowed us to enter their lives, we wondered whether we—and they—were interrupting their life composing as we asked them to pause, to recollect moments that may be difficult to tell. As we came alongside, we dwelt with them in storied memories, coming alongside them to retell stories that may have been smoothed over. We learned that for some youth, when leaving happened over time, talking with us in research conversations was the first time they had made sense of the connections between and among their experiences.

Many of the youth told us that they did not tell themselves stories of being dropouts; rather, they were not in school for now but had plans to return to school when they could. This was visible in Leanne's resistance to Sean naming her as a dropout. Many youth were telling themselves forward-looking stories in which they imagined new ways into the future that included school for them and schooling for their siblings and for their own children. We knew the importance of attending to them in all of their complex vulnerability rather than allowing the research focus to be on achievement and completion, a focus that would allow policymakers to write over their stories of experience in ways that frame them as deficit.

CONTEMPLATING VULNERABILITY

We are mindful that vulnerability is a fluid concept and that it can be understood in multiple ways. When the concept of vulnerability emerges in discussions around narrative inquiries with children and youth, we need to ask: What are children and/or youth vulnerable to (Tronto, 2014)? Do these vulnerabilities lead us to consider different obligations and responsibilities, and if so, what are these obligations and responsibilities? These questions are important because when these obligations and responsibilities call forth elements of care, there is a danger of pathogenic vulnerability, a vulnerability that arises from oppression or injustice, from a place of not respecting the choices of children and youth (Mackenzie, Rogers, & Dodds, 2013). In these moments we need to pause to carefully consider the connections between power and research, both in the research processes and also between participants and researchers. In this pause, what Hannah Arendt (1958) might call a stop and think, we question: Who is responsible for dealing with vulnerabilities in children and youth's lives? Inherent vulnerability, a vulnerability intrinsic to the human condition, can neither be equated with a situational or contextual vulnerability nor be seen to be a reason to call forth a sense of oppression or further victimization.

As we contemplate the unfolding of this chapter we recall experiences of imagined vulnerabilities, where we or others imagined what might happen. In these moments we risk calling forth a protectionist attitude, one in which we imagine possible horrors that could happen, triggering surveillance and/or care that is based on perceived needs rather than the experiences of participants, experiences that are grounded in the midst of their lives. It is important to differentiate this kind of care from what we do as narrative inquirers, as traditional notions of care are different from the relational ethics of care we enact as narrative inquirers.

LIVING ALONGSIDE: CONSIDERATIONS FOR WHAT DOES AND CAN BECOME VISIBLE

In this chapter we first look backward to create a context from within which we can show how final research texts evolve and how issues of representation are shaped along the way. We return to the arts club in which our study alongside Aboriginal youth is embedded. Vera considers her relationship with Chris and how many of the conversations with Chris were shaped by talking about his father and mother, his siblings and cousins, and his friends. Vera recalls the first times she came to know Chris in the arts club. Chris always came to the arts club with Val, Lane, Donovan, or Annie. It seemed he never came alone. Vera thought about how Chris surrounded himself with people, and she recollected that Chris spoke very little. Vera remembers a conversation with his mother as Vera was seeking her consent for Chris's participation in the study. Vera recalls her laughter and look, as, his mother said, this means he has to talk. Even after knowing him for three years, Chris still does not talk much in the ways Vera thinks his mother imagined was necessary for a research participant. Instead, Chris has always invited Vera into the living, to be alongside him and alongside those to whom he was closest. As Vera continues to live alongside him, there are brief moments, moments that are often profound. Vera writes,

> It is in these moments when I learn about his father's death, his nephew's apprehension of social services, his cousin's suicide many years ago, and also his joy of being an uncle, his deep love for his mother, and his worry about her. It is in these moments when I realize how significant my living alongside Chris has been.
>
> About two years into our research relationship Chris talked about his challenges of living with his mother and her boyfriend and how he was contemplating ways to find a new place to live. He struggled to make sense of this decision yet was firm that, in this moment, it was best to find a new place to live—I remember him saying, "Maybe things will change later." Given the complexities of social services involvement, we tried to find ways to think about this and ways for Chris to be heard. Amidst the conversations with Chris I was reminded of my stories and began to see not only how much my story shaped my responses to him but also how much his experience had begun to shape my retelling of my stories of experience.
>
> As Chris talked about leaving home, vivid memories come back of me having run away from home when I was thirteen. Unlike Chris, I ran away because of a deep sense of wanting to resist the ordinary, the complacency, the social rules, the lack of imagination—it was perhaps a resistance

to what I would metaphorically call "falling asleep" to what I felt was important in the world, my world. Chris's wish to find a new place was a way to resist the impact of his mother on his daily life, his inability to see her in situations that he felt were jeopardizing her health. What I saw was a deep love for his mother. As he talked about his mother, I both felt and saw his deep love and admiration for her. I wondered how much of that was visible in my youth. Did others see that despite the act of running away, I never lost my deep love for my mother? And as I asked this question, I wondered whether Chris's mother knew how much he loved her.

This return to my experience and the months of living alongside Chris helped me ask different questions alongside Chris. Alongside him, I wondered whether he had talked with his mother about his love for her. Were there ways in which he had shared these experiences with her? Had he made visible to her his worries and his sense of who he was in relation to her? Had he made visible how much he continues to miss his father and his father's ability to make his mother smile and sing? As I wrote and recollected these moments I realized that two things were important: one was that both Chris and I had become comfortable in living alongside each other over an extended period of time as well as the possibility to find ways to not have to answer questions, no matter how directly they had been asked.

As Vera thinks about her experiences in relation to her work alongside Chris and to engaging in narrative inquiry with children and youth more generally, her childhood experiences and her experiences as a parent often intermingle. Vera began to think about what has shaped her understanding of stories both in and outside of schools. There are moments that stand out, moments that continue to be filled with tensions, but she also experiences a renewed sense of agency and resistance as she composes forward-looking stories. The ways in which Clandinin, Murphy, Huber, and Murray Orr (2010) understand tensions is resonant with her. Using this view of tensions allows us to "understand tensions in a more relational way, that is, tensions that live between people, events, or things, and are a way of creating a between space, a space which can exist in educative ways" (p. 82). These are the spaces that are opened in the living alongside research participants. As Vera continues to think with the experiences of being alongside Chris, she wonders about the ways in which final research texts might hold open the possibilities of continuing to live alongside that exist in the actual living.

SILENCES IN THE LIVING AND IN THE RESEARCH TEXTS

Thinking with the experiences of living alongside Chris, Jean reminds Vera of how Vera's early life was also shaped by silences—silences that were profound. Some of these silences become visible in Chapter 3. In the etymological dictionary *silence* has its roots in being still and being quiet; the roots of the word point us to more complex notions than the absence of sound. Prochnik (2011) reminds us that

> Among the word's antecedents is the Gothic verb anasilan, a word that denotes the wind dying down, and the Latin desinere, a word meaning "stop." Both of these etymologies suggest the way that silence is bound up with the idea of interrupted action. The pursuit of silence, likewise, is dissimilar from most other pursuits in that it generally begins with a surrender of the chase, the abandonment of efforts to impose our will and vision on the world. Not only is it about standing still; with rare exceptions, the pursuit of silence seems initially to involve a step backward from the tussle of life. . . . It's as though, as a culture, we've learned to 'mind the gaps' so well that they've all but disappeared. We live in an age of incessancy, under the banner of the already heard and forgotten. (p. 12–13)

Perhaps in this way silences in the living and in the representation in final research texts are invitations to think with participants' diverse and unfamiliar experiences.

As Jean continues to talk about the ways that silence is in Vera's living as well as Chris's, Vera wonders whether she is drawn to and into Chris's life in part because they each have and continue to live in and with particular silences. Memories come back of driving in the car with Chris one day.

> That day the rain was pouring heavily, the gutters were swelling, the lanes on the roads were becoming less visible, and the windshield wipers could not move quickly enough. As Vera focused on driving, Chris turned to her and spoke only two words: "my dad." There was silence in the car, both before, after, and in between the words spoken. The silence in the car was palpable and intense. In the moments that followed, the moments of long silence, Vera slid into her own childhood memories—a Sunday afternoon, her dad driving, her mother in the front seat, and Vera with her brother, a newborn, and her sister, just three years old, in the backseat. They were on their way to Vera's aunt's house in the next town, just a few kilometers away. It was another rainy day, almost like the day now, the day Chris whispered the words "my dad." Reaching the end of town, the twisted road with two sharp bends was before them. They barely reached the first bend, and the screams in the air still ring in Vera's ears—screams so loud, at least in memory so loud, that they could not be forgotten. Vera's dad turned off the car and told everyone not too look or leave the car, brief instructions in a tone that made any opposition impossible. The screams of a young girl continued. Only much later, in between fragments of a storyline, Vera noticed the blood on her father's clothes and the tears in his eyes and his slumped over and wet body. It was then she came to know of someone dying, of children left without parents ... nothing more was said. Vera has no memory of how much time passed, how long they sat in the car, how long her dad was out of the car. A silence engulfed them, a silence that could not erase the loud scream. As a girl no more than six years old, the scene is etched in Vera's mind. Chris, only a few years older,

lost his father in a car accident—tragic, unexpected, never to be erased. "My dad."

As Jean continues to speak, Vera wonders not only about how these profound silences can become visible in research texts but also what it was that resonated across the silences. What are the ways in which we can make them visible in the final research texts, texts that are public, silences that may or may not be shared with readers? Knowing that Vera could not take her eyes off the road on that rainy day, Vera's response to Chris was silence. Vera knew she neither could nor wanted to fill the silence, replace the memories, sooth the devastation. In this chapter we want to hold open these questions of how we hold on to these experiences, for these are the experiences that allow us to contemplate what it means to move toward final research texts from interim research texts and, equally importantly, from the experiences that are shaped by living alongside research participants.

From Interim Research Texts to Final Research Texts

Moving from interim to final research texts is not a linear task. There is a back-and-forth movement that involves both extensive writing and also a return to the field and to co-composing more field texts in order to be able to write interim and final research texts that are attentive to participants' experiences. We saw some of this in Chapter 9 as Sean met with Cedar, with a plan to negotiate an interim research text but found himself once again immersed in co-composing more field texts. It is in these movements back and forth from field to field texts to interim and final research texts that tensions become visible as well as tangible. It is, as we struggle alongside participants with what to include in final research texts, that we face questions once again of what and how we show to larger public audiences.

Questions of audience are with us throughout an inquiry, but it seems they become more pressing as we consider writing research texts. Although we at times may have a sense of who audiences are because of the journals, publishers, conferences, and/or funding agencies, we are wise to stay awake to the uncertainties that exist around who the audiences are for our work and how our research texts will be situated. We wonder, for example, will those unfamiliar and distant from our work be able to "world"-travel in the ways Lugones (1987) suggests, so that their reading comes with loving perceptions? Calling on Frye, Lugones explains, "the loving eye is 'the eye of one who knows that to know the seen, one must consult something other than one's own will and interests and fears and imagination'" (p. 85). We cannot know this with any certainty, and we must stay wakeful to the multiplicity of ways that our research texts can be read and positioned. It is at these points that response communities can be helpful, as readers within those groups can provide insights that come embedded within loving perception as well as within arrogant perception.

As researchers on present-day academic landscapes, we are positioned frequently within different disciplinary knowledge systems that are built around theoretical ideas, ideas that are shaped by knowledge systems that often do not reflect the pragmatist groundings of narrative inquiry. The pragmatist groundings of narrative inquiry keep us close to experience and to the living of experiences. As we live within landscapes shaped by different disciplinary knowledge systems, we experience tensions, places where our ontological and epistemological assumptions bump with other assumptions. Although we experience this tension throughout the inquiry, it is important to recognize that

> The research self is not separable from the lived self. Who we are and what we can be, what we can study, and how we can write about what we study are all tied to how a knowledge system disciplines its members and claims authority over knowledge. Needed are concrete practices through which we can construct ourselves as ethical subjects engaged in ethical research, even if that means challenging the authority of a discipline's cherished modes of representation. (Richardson, 2003, p. 197)

As narrative inquirers, we agree with Richardson that we need to develop concrete practices that allow us to step outside of a discipline's cherished modes of representation, yet this is demanding work for us as researchers. There are constant reminders of disciplinary boundaries, of what is and is not acceptable. However, as narrative inquirers, our task is even more complex, for we must continually attend in at least two ways. We cannot only attend to the disciplinary modes. Although these challenges are reiterated in the venues in which we present our research texts, at the same time, we are challenged with the obligations and responsibilities to stay close to particular lives and experiences in ways that do not turn knowledge into abstract ideas and theories. We must maintain a relational ethical stance with participants and with ourselves.

Vera and Chris have struggled with writing both interim and final research texts, as their silences, abbreviated talks and experiences are difficult to represent in words. They struggle with notions of vulnerability that are placed on them. These assigned vulnerabilities lead to potential misinterpretation, and they both fear that the interpretations made with arrogant perceptions could create experiences of judgment. As they struggle with how to create modes of representation, they have turned to arts-based practices and find themselves in a printmaking studio. When Chris first came to the arts club he was drawn immediately to print making, and he continued to create prints during many hours in the arts club. Vera, too, has also been drawn to print making for many years, and together they are now exploring modes of representation that may allow them to disrupt what is known and to create what might be acceptable as a research text. Both Chris and Vera have a strong sense that they engaged in this research because they want to make their experiences visible, to shift understandings of who Aboriginal youth are and are becoming in a complex world that will not "erase their Indianness."

RETURNING AGAIN TO RESEARCH PUZZLES

Situating Vera and Chris's experience within the larger narrative inquiry into the experiences of urban Aboriginal youth returns our attention to the research puzzles that we wrote as the team of researchers imagined the study. We return also to the considerations of the contexts, places, and times within which we shaped the research puzzles. These returns also bring us back to our narrative beginnings.

However, even as we compose research texts with attention to considerations of puzzles and narrative beginnings, we also need to turn toward considerations of how our puzzles and we, as inquirers, have shifted throughout the inquiry. New puzzles, intentions, and purposes may have emerged in the living alongside and in the ongoing negotiations of purposes and intentions. These ongoing shifts reflect what we have come to know about participants and the ways in which participants helped us see that our initial puzzles may not have reflected who they are and are becoming. We learned something of this in the narrative inquiry into the experiences of early school leaving when we first created posters that named potential participants as people who had dropped out of school. We learned from the youth that they saw themselves as not in school for now rather than as school dropouts.

These ongoing shifts also show how, over time, new experiences unfolded, experiences that we could not have anticipated or even imagined. Cindy Swanson, who worked closely with a research participant in the study with the youth and families of Aboriginal heritage, found herself alongside a participant, Craig, and his mother. Craig, who attended the art club, did not appear to want to enter into an intensive research relationship with any of the researchers. His intentions were only to attend the art club. However, his mother approached Sean and asked whether Craig could be in conversation with a researcher. When Craig's mother met Cindy, she shared pages and pages of assessments and letters and asked whether Cindy could help to intervene in how various schools had positioned her son and her in the schools. In these moments we needed to widen our understanding of how advocacy efforts for Aboriginal youth might be shaped or bump against dominant narratives of Aboriginal students as deficit or as less than. Although Craig's mother wanted her advocacy efforts and the school response to be a primary focus of the inquiry, we were less certain that this was also Craig's intention. Although we are open to the possibilities of these negotiations, we know that we also hold responsibilities to funding bodies, academic institutions, community partners, and research participants.

Connelly and Clandinin (1990) remind us "that narrative inquiry [is] driven by a sense of the whole and it is this sense which needs to drive the writing (and reading) of narrative. Narratives are not adequately written according to a model of cause and effect but according to the explanations gleaned from the overall narrative" (p. 7). In this way, through negotiations, we needed to both enlarge our understanding of the research puzzle as well as be mindful that we not only understood Craig's life through his ongoing struggles to be heard in school. Craig's stories of who he is and is becoming are more complex and need to be understood with attention to the layers of his experiences both in and out of school.

As each study calls forth the place and time of composing final research texts we, too, anticipate that we will continue to inquire into our narrative autobiographical beginnings. This is important because, as "narrative inquirers, we study the lives of participants as we come alongside them and become part of their lives and they part of ours. Therefore, our lives and who we are and are becoming on their and our landscapes is also under study" (Clandinin, Murphy, Huber & Murray Orr, 2010, p. 82). The sense of temporality, as lives composed over time and place, needs to include the ways we are shaped as we live alongside participants.

Significance of Narrative Inquiries: So What?

As we consider the significance of narrative inquiries, the question of "So what?" that always lives within our studies becomes more overt again. We showed something of this in Chapter 2 as we wrote of designing narrative inquiries. When we return to the question of "So what?" as we begin to compose research texts, this question sharpens our focus on what is important, what we may want to share with diverse audiences, and the ways in which we can do this.

Most often we think of our narrative inquiries as holding personal, practical, and social significance. In many ways what we offer as final research texts is meant to disrupt common understandings, perceptions, and practices. It is these disruptions that are intentionally part of the research texts we write. As we have shown throughout the book, it is important to recognize that "we are not merely objective inquirers ... people who study a world we did not help create. On the contrary, we are complicit in the world we study. Being in this world, we need to remake ourselves as well as offer up research understandings that could lead to a better world" (Clandinin & Connelly, 2000, p. 61).

FURTHER ISSUES IN REPRESENTATION

In what follows we open up questions around what we see as eight inter-related issues in representation that are not unique to narrative inquiry with children and youth but do seem particularly salient in such studies.

The first challenge in representing narrative inquiries is the need to go back and forth between the whole and the detail within lives (Connelly & Clandinin, 1990). We do this shifting back and forth in order to not lose sight of or privilege one understanding. We need both a sense of the particularities of a life and the whole of a life. By looking too closely at the particularities, we may no longer see participants in their entirety. It would be too easy to see Chris only as a youth who has been affected by trauma, including the death of his father, without seeing the ways he connects to the world around him as well as how he composes who he is and is becoming within his larger family. This ability to shift focus from the particularities of a life to the wholeness of a life in the making amidst the larger cultural, social, institutional, and familial narratives is difficult when there is often a push to focus only on a particular facet or aspect of a phenomenon. Sean, in his narrative account of Donovan (see Chapter 11), begins in a way that attempts to foreground features of Donovan's life in places and relationships.

A second related challenge in representing narrative inquiries is the need to consider how we first introduce participants. What do we intro-duce to the reader first? In narrative inquiry we are often asked to write a brief précis or summary of each participant as a way to introduce partici-pants. In this moment we need to be wakeful, as how we shape the sum-mary provides a kind of frame that sets readers up to focus on what we initially highlighted. We see in Sean's narrative account with Donovan how he offers multiple ways to see Donovan in the opening pages of the account. He offers a version of short sentence fragments about commu-nity, academics, learning what works best, school history, vision board, "What speaks to you as being important in life?," and wise words fol-lowed by Donovan's sketches of who he is and the more complex life annal. This multiple telling of who Donovan is provides a way of show-ing the complexities of his life as he begins to make his experiences vis-ible to Sean. This framing of participants is a particular challenge in the work with children and youth, whose lives are frequently in such fluid composition. For example, in the work with Tara, as she tried on different ways of expressing who she was in her life-making through her early teen years, she moved from experimenting with wearing beautiful clothing to cheering to becoming part of a wrestling team. Her clothing and physical appearance altered as she moved through those years. Related to this challenge is how we ourselves, as narrative inquirers, choose to represent ourselves in the research texts. We see Sean opening up questions of who he is in relation to Donovan in the narrative account, trying to show the multiplicity of who he is in the account and without fixing himself as only researcher, as only male, as only Aboriginal, and so on, but rather opening up his multiplicity in the living and the telling.

A third challenge relates to the importance of representing children and youth in ways that the children and youth want to be introduced in our representations. As Elbaz reminds us (2010), "one important task is finding ways of rendering the experience of children, whose voices are easily overridden by the controlling voices of researchers. It is easy to distort or marginalize children's voices because we fail to understand them or because we hear them through the filter of our own nostalgia" (p. 272). As Jean and Jason worked together in representing who he is (see Chapter 13), Jason rejected Jean's way of beginning his narrative account, noting that in his story he saw his experiences of school in simpler, more overarching ways. This concern about seeing children and youth only through our researcher gazes is a continuing concern as we compose research texts.

A fourth challenge is one that is present in all representations or renderings of a life. That relates to the ever-present question of what to leave in and what to leave out. And here we can draw on Dillard and others. Dillard (1987) notes that "the best memoirs, I think, forge their own forms. The writer of any work, and particularly any nonfiction work, must decide two crucial points: what to put in and what to leave out" (p. 288). What to leave in and what to leave out must be considered with an understanding that life is in the midst, that lives and experiences are evolving and are always partial in their representation; it is in these moments that we need to imagine what is yet to come.

A fifth related challenge in representing narrative inquiries is the importance of disrupting and working against ways of telling that fix participants in particular ways or in chronological events. As writers, we need to "remember that readers may freeze the narrative with the result that the restorying life quality intended by the writer may become fixed as a print portrait by the reader" (Connelly & Clandinin, 1990, p. 9). We need to find ways to show that lives are always unfolding, are always in the midst, and that the tellings we create are "for now" tellings. We see the possibilities of leaving openings in research texts that invite readers into our relationships with participants. We do this in order to create openings where readers can imagine future possibilities of lives unfolding and becoming rather than holding a fixed story. We too draw the reader in so that their own lives and experiences may be shaped by what they come to know about the participants and themselves. This becomes particularly important in our representations of narrative inquiries with children and youth where, too often, readers want to be able to predict what will happen if programs or interventions are provided.

A sixth challenge relates to the concerns around how these narrative accounts can have shaping influences on the children and youth as they work alongside narrative inquirers to co-compose the field texts and interim research texts. They may choose to stay with a story or begin to see themselves in one way, and they themselves might foreclose the possibilities of seeing themselves otherwise, as seeing themselves as becoming. This is perhaps most concerning when youth have been storied as vulnerable, as needing services, as deficit. There are times when participants begin to tell their stories in this way.

A seventh challenge in representing narrative inquiries comes when readers or editors or supervisory committees ask us to consider or reconsider theoretical notions. Academics often frame the experiences of others with reference to scholarly norms. As Clandinin and Connelly (2000) write, this is, in part, a question of starting point; that is, do we start with attention to theoretical ideas or do we start with attention to experience, to lives? We know that this is too simple a dichotomy. However, it draws our attention to how we might proceed as we represent narrative inquiries. We know that "theory is tremendously helpful when it generates new questions and is utterly constraining when it predetermines answers" (Cruikshank, 1998, p. 165). Narrative inquiries are grounded in the stories lived and told, in the relationships of living alongside. Sarris (1993) points out that what is too often missing from scholarly studies are interruptions and risks. In narrative inquiries our work is grounded in the living alongside, in interactive situations, where we are exposed and vulnerable, where the norms of research are interrupted and challenged. Without being situated in the living alongside, "we can never recognize the limitations of our own descriptions" (Cruikshank, 1998, p. 165).

An eighth challenge raises the issues around the need to consider questions of the personal in what becomes public and what stays private. In a society where so much is freely shared on social media, sometimes without enough consideration of the short- and long-term implications, perhaps readers of narrative texts are becoming accustomed to wanting to know more, to know it all, to know the exotic, the sensational of lives.

As we leave readers with somewhat foreclosed representations that allow participants and researchers to draw boundaries around the private, there may be a call to "say more," to remove the boundaries we inscribe around our representations of the lives of participants, ourselves, and shared experiences. This is an ongoing challenge, something we work against in composing and co-composing interim and final research texts.

There may well be more than these eight challenges to representation. What we have presented so far are the ones we most frequently bump against in our work as narrative inquirers. What we know is important is that we attend to the complexity of experiences, that we attend to issues of place, context, and time—the three dimensions of any narrative inquiry.

RETURNING TO THE THREE-DIMENSIONAL NARRATIVE INQUIRY SPACE

We continue to attend to the three-dimensional narrative inquiry space throughout narrative inquiries, including when we write final research texts. Within the three-dimensional narrative inquiry space, with its dimensions of temporality, sociality and place, we can show the ways that experiences are always in the living, always situated in time, place, and relationships.

As Sean writes alongside Donovan and Lane, he recalls,

> I come from a place surrounded by trees and water. My life is connected to the land, a place where there is meaning in the trees. There is a knowledge that is situated in place, where the fish and the food are taken care of differently. There is knowledge rooted in experience and within the experience. I think of the stories I have come to know, in particular places and how I move within a place. There is a knowledge in knowing that I am home. This knowing brings me back to the question: What does it mean to be Woodland Cree? What does it mean in this place?
>
> When I think of my mother, my family, my grandfather, I cannot help but think about the stories that are intergenerational. I know where my family has walked and where they have moved in different ways. I begin to slowly understand the rhythm and how it plays out differently in my home place.
>
> The fondness in looking for meaning in the seasons and thinking about the water, the frozen ponds and the stories. It is in these places where I get more rooted in place; it is when I am removed from them that they call me in deeper and meaningful ways—of wanting to come home and creating a space for my own girls to come home and to come to know home.
>
> Our ancestral home and our territory is connected to the way in which they think with the fish. To go home to the rapids that are forever, an ancestral gathering place filled with meaning. These places I must listen

carefully to, as many experiences will not be animate or visible to me if I do not pay attention, if I do not walk slowly. The land and its markings, the movement of the fish, the depth of the water, and the way it flows and moves are shifting and identity making. The way in which I come to understand the place is to listen to it—to pay attention to it by visiting and walking—softly and gently with a mindset that opens space for wakefulness.

The ways in which Sean attends to place in the above fragment reminds us that this is also the way we need to attend to participants, both as we live alongside them and as we write research texts. It is important to be mindful that the places, times, and relationships are particular and carry forward knowledge and knowing about participants' and our lives. Attending and knowing in this way calls forth close attention to both empirical and philosophical work. As Cruickshank (1998) reflects on her work over years alongside Elders from the Yukon, she writes,

One of the many things I learned from working with Mrs. Ned [one of the Elders she worked with] and her contemporaries is that their extensive knowledge is not amenable to direct questions, nor can it be easily formulated as a set of rules. It must be demonstrated so that others can see how it is used in practice. Such knowledge is a relational connect, more like a verb than a noun, more process than product, and it cannot easily be constructed as a written, formally encoded, reified product. Once it is, and once it becomes authorized in this way, it begins to accumulate different meanings. (p. 70)

Perhaps we have come to understand, like others, that the "boundary between their [social science researchers'] empirical and philosophical work [is] increasingly hard to distinguish" (Rosiek & Pratt, 2013, p. 578). In attending to the three-dimensional inquiry space, we also see the dimensions as always unfolding and always filled with possibilities for holding new meanings.

In Chapter 4 we highlight that understanding the meaning of our names and participants' names within different landscapes is important, particularly as we share experiences through research texts with wider audiences. Each text needs to be grounded in the particularities of the places and times. Heilbrun (1988) wrote,

what matters is that lives do not serve as models; only stories do that. And it is a hard thing to make up stories to live by. We can only retell and live by the stories we have read or heard. We live our lives through texts. They may be read, or chanted, or experienced electronically, or come to us, like the murmurings of our mothers, telling us what conventions demand. Whatever their form or medium, these stories have formed us all; they are what we must use to make new fictions, new narratives. (p. 37)

Keeping the possibility of making new narratives, as we compose research texts that attend to lives in the making, allows us to keep living alongside participants as writers and readers of final research texts.

CHAPTER 13

Issues of Quality: Touchstones of Narrative Inquiry with Children and Youth

I wake early and carefully choose my clothing, more carefully than usual. I discard the jeans as too casual, the two-piece suit too formal. I finally settle on slacks and a plain sweater with a parka as my outerwear. Figuring out what to wear is difficult, as today I am meeting Jason's mom for the first time, a 2 p.m. meeting at their house. Jason will still be at school. I wonder whether I would feel more comfortable if he were going to be there, to somehow create a space to tell his mom that he trusts me. And then I recall the nervousness that always comes with me when I am meeting a new research participant and I feel a bit calmer.

Even though Jason and I have been talking for several months now, he has only recently given me his mom's phone number and said I could call her. I had called her and she agreed to meet. She knew, of course, that Jason and I had been talking. She asked me to their house for the conversation. It has taken a long time for Jason to begin to trust me, to trust me enough to talk to his mom, to visit his house.

I'm thinking of Jason as I drive to their house. I drive carefully off the freeway and along a major route in our city. I am used to turning right off this major road, as some friends and colleagues live in that direction. Looking at Jason's address, I see I need to turn left and that his address is close to the main road. I know that the more expensive homes are to the right. I drive slowly down the road until I see the address on a small bungalow duplex. The snow-covered front yard is tidy, no fence, little landscaping.

I park in front of his house and sit for a minute to gather my thoughts. Memories of all the home visits I have made as a teacher, counselor, and psychologist crowd in, and I wonder how Jason's mom will see me. Will I be seen as a psychologist talking assessment? Will I be seen as a teacher, someone who can address learning issues? Will I be seen as someone who knows Jason from school? I wonder how he has storied me to her. I notice a young child looking out the window and realize that my arrival has been noticed; I need to go in—no more delaying.

As I get out of the car I gather my purse, the file folder containing consent forms, and the digital recorder. I am hopeful we can begin to record the conversation after his mom, Sheri, signs the consent form to be a participant. I realize I may look a bit like a social worker or psychologist with the file folder. But then I also gather up the box containing the small doughnuts, Timbits, which many people like as a snack with coffee.

I had spent some time considering what to bring. As a school psychologist or social worker, I would not have brought snacks, but somehow it seemed like the right thing to do. I always brought food when Jason and I met at school. I also brought food when I visited friends and neighbors as I had learned from my family so many years ago. My mother taught me to always bring something when I visited, and I lived that story out in how I lived my life. I bought lots of these small doughnuts, as I knew that Jason would be hungry when he arrived home from school in an hour and a half. What to bring was a careful set of considerations.

I walk up the walk, climb the three steps, and ring the doorbell. Sheri opens the door almost immediately, and I walk in, saying, "Hello, I'm Jean. I'm so glad to meet you." As I speak I hand over the box containing the doughnuts, and Sheri's face freezes. She says, "We don't need any food."

I feel the room change, and I am instantly awake to the intergenerational social and cultural narratives in which I am embedded and that Sheri makes visible by her statement. Quickly, carefully, I respond with a smile and "I just picked these up as I know Jason likes them. He'll be hungry when he gets home from school. He's always hungry when we meet." Sheri smiles then as she realizes I know her son well enough to know what he likes to eat and that he is hungry after school. She takes the box, saying, "Would you like coffee?" and invites me to a stool at the high kitchen table. "I'd love one," I say, as I sit. We begin. (Interim research text, April 2014)

We begin with this brief story fragment of a moment in the midst of the narrative inquiry with youth and families of Aboriginal heritage. We draw on our (Clandinin & Caine, 2013) work around the touchstones or quality markers of narrative inquiry to show how the study fulfills the quality markers of a narrative inquiry and illustrates the ways to engage with narrative inquiry and, more particularly, to engage in narrative inquiry with children and youth. In some ways this chapter allows us to return to some of the key concepts and ideas we have developed in the book. The return, though, allows us a way to judge the quality of each narrative inquiry, asking us as researchers to try to assess the strength of a narrative inquiry.

As is evident throughout this book, narrative inquiry, working from a particular ontological and epistemological stance, is a way of understanding and inquiring into experience. Narrative inquiry is always with and within stories, the stories of participants, the stories of inquirers, the social, cultural, institutional, familial, linguistic narratives within which all stories are lived and told and inquired into. As narrative inquirers, we do not try to get outside of stories. We linger in the complex layers of the intertwined and interwoven stories. We return again to the opening fragment of an interim research text and spin outward to some of the stories within which the fragment is nested and attend to the experiences of Jason and his mother as participants in the research, to Jean's experiences as an inquirer, and to the social, cultural, institutional, and familial narratives within which all of our stories are lived, told, and retold—that is, inquired into.

The research puzzle for the study with Jason is the three-year narrative inquiry into the schooling and educational experiences of urban Aboriginal youth and their families. This study is woven throughout the book. The research team is large and diverse and includes Vera, Sean, Jean, Florence Glanfield, Cindy Swanson, Simmee Chung, Shauna Bruno, Trudy Cardinal, and Elders Isabelle Kootenay, Francis Whiskeyjack, and Mary Cardinal Collins. Funding was provided from the Social Sciences and Humanities Research Council of Canada and the Alberta Centre for Child, Family and Community Research (Caine et al, 2010a, 2010b).

We do not work from a belief that schooling and education are the same. Education is a more expansive concept that explores all of one's life-making experiences. The overall goal of our inquiry is to understand the educational and schooling experiences of urban Aboriginal youths and their families. By narratively inquiring with the youth and their families, our overall intent is two-fold: to offer perspectives of Aboriginal peoples to school systems and to help non-Aboriginal peoples who dominate provincially funded school systems to appreciate Aboriginal knowledge and knowledge systems.

TOUCHSTONES OF NARRATIVE INQUIRY

As we noted at the outset, we draw on Vera and Jean's writing around the touchstones of narrative inquiry (Clandinin & Caine, 2013). One touchstone highlighted the **relational responsibilities of narrative inquirers, the ethical responsibilities that live at the heart of narrative inquiries.** In narrative inquiry we are attentive to what it means to live as researchers in relationships, to live in collaborative ways in the inquiry processes. Narrative inquiry spaces are spaces of belonging for both researchers and participants, spaces marked by ethics and attitudes of openness, mutual vulnerability, reciprocity, and care. Although narrative inquiry also opens up a relational knowing and understanding of experience, each relationship between researcher and participant opens up a relational world, a world co-composed in the spaces between researcher and participant.

> As I prepared to meet Jason's mother I felt my relational responsibilities to Jason first and foremost but also to the other research participants and researchers. I also felt my relational responsibilities to the intergenerational stories that lived in that moment of meeting Jason's mother. These stories of Jason, his mother, and me reach back to and are nested within larger narratives: a narrative of colonization, where the nations of France

and England arrived to the land now known as Canada, although named by the first residents as Turtle Island. Within a narrative of colonization, England claimed the land and began to negotiate treaties with the Aboriginal peoples they encountered. These treaties were ones in which the land was claimed by England as colonizing power, and in negotiations Aboriginal groups were forced to move to reservation land. There are many other aspects of these treaties, but it is clear that the narratives at work around land and ownership and power were situated in the narratives of the colonizing powers. It is also clear that there were conflicting narratives at work in how treaties would shape lives. For example, although it was clear that education was part of the treaties, the stories that people lived within the colonizing narratives included stories of assimilation, stories in which children of Aboriginal heritage were forcibly taken from their families and communities and taken to live in distant residential schools. These residential schools operated for more than a hundred years. I cannot imagine what it would be like to have my child taken forcibly from me. I also cannot imagine what a community would be like when all the children were taken. Within these colonizing narratives the intergenerational reverberations in the lives of people of Aboriginal heritage are profound. In this talk I do not detail the stories shaped by the dismal statistics, but they are often repeated by policymakers, educators, sociologists and others. Stories of Aboriginal peoples as "addicted, violent, not responsible for caring for children, lazy, and bad parents disinterested in their children's schooling" reverberate in present-day stories of school.

With a sense of these larger narratives, I realize how much was at work in that moment when I entered Sheri's house, in the meeting of two women. A white woman with an expensive car arrived at a small duplex to meet a woman of Aboriginal heritage. The white woman brings food, perhaps part of the larger narrative that assumes that food is required, as poverty would mean that children were not cared for. Had Sheri experienced that before? As I entered I knew that I was trying to begin a relationship between two women shaped by different sets of social and cultural narratives, me as a white settler, Sheri as an Aboriginal woman.

As Jean entered, she realized she was entering **in the midst,** a second touchstone. Narrative inquirers enter into research relationships in the midst: in the midst of researchers' own ongoing lives, both personal and professional; in the midst of researchers' lives enacted within particular institutional narratives such as funded projects, graduate student research, and personally compelling studies; in the midst of institutional narratives; and, as is evident in the story fragment, in the midst of social, political, and cultural narratives. Participants are also always in the midst of their lives, and their lives too are shaped by attending to past, present, and unfolding social, cultural, institutional, linguistic, and familial narratives. The narrative inquiry was well underway before the day Jean met Sheri, Jason's mom.

A third touchstone is **negotiating entry to the field.** In narrative inquiry we negotiate with participants an ongoing relational inquiry space. This relational space is what we most commonly call the field. There are two starting points for narrative inquiry: listening to individuals tell their stories and living alongside participants as they live and tell their stories (Connelly & Clandinin, 2006). The starting point for the inquiry was coming alongside the youth in order to come to know them slowly, over time, in a local grades 7 to 9 school. Our research design was to first develop relationships with youth, with the hopeful intention they would take us home to their families and communities, places where we could come to know more of their educational experiences. We negotiated a time and place within an urban junior high school that was outside school hours—that is, in the time allotted for school club meetings' after-school hours—and in a largely unused classroom place. We did not enter relationships with the teachers who taught the youth before they came to the art club. In living in the art club, we were intentional in trying to come to know the youth and to not be constrained by the stories of school that shaped the youths' lives.

Living in a classroom place called forth the stories that each researcher lived by, shaping who we were in the place and with the youth. Embodied stories to live by were evoked. As a person who knew schools, school policies, and usual school practices, Jean felt at ease around drawing attention to possible difficulties the youth might face. When other teachers came to the classroom, they often sought her out as someone who knew schools.

This wide awakeness to who we are and are becoming as researchers draws attention to a fourth touchstone, the importance of engaging in **narrative beginnings.** Because narrative inquiry is an ongoing reflexive and reflective methodology, narrative inquirers need to continually inquire into their experiences before, during, and after each inquiry.

In writing and inquiring into our narrative beginnings as researchers, we attend through the three-dimensional narrative inquiry space to our own experiences. This may mean that we reach as far back as our childhoods to understand and, at times, to name our research puzzle; it also means that we attend to the places in which our stories have unfolded and make evident the social and political contexts that shaped our understandings. In Chapter 3 Jean wove in her stories to live by of bringing food to friends and neighbors when she visits, a story shaped by growing up on a small farm in the 1950s in western Canada. Other autobiographical narrative inquiries made visible how her parents taught her to be attentive to others as well as to the land and to animals who lived on the land. These stories to live by were planted in her early, as Ben Okri (1997) noted, or shaped on early landscapes, as Maxine Greene (1995) wrote. As Jean began work with the youth in the arts club she also engaged in telling stories of growing up in a small rural community not too distant from a reservation and of attending a high school where at least one of her classmates was of Aboriginal heritage. She awakened to the social, institutional, and cultural narratives of people of Aboriginal heritage as "other," narratives in which they were seen as deficient, as less than. Her told and retold stories allowed her to position herself in the research and to become more wakeful to the ways children and youth of Aboriginal heritage are often positioned in institutional narratives such as stories of school.

It has been through engaging in autobiographical narrative inquiries as we each write narrative beginnings that we have awakened to these stories that live in, that are embodied within, us. In the art club Jean awakened to other stories she lives by, such as stories of completing projects and working until there is a finished product. These stories to live by were threaded around not only her stories as a child but also her stories as a teacher who knew the need to complete schoolwork for assessment purposes. As she engaged with the youth, these embodied stories were often called forth and became visible in the inquiry.

It was almost time for the youth to be released from their classrooms and to come join us in the art club. I had carefully pulled out the paintings started last week, searching for names of the youth who had begun them. This one is Skye's, that one is Tara's. "Who remembers who was working on this one?" I asked. I looked forward to the youth coming in and settling down where they had left off a week earlier. The youth began to trickle in and headed for the food table. They always came in hungry and were always keen to eat. I stood back, amazed at the quantity of food they ate. We learned early that snacks were not what they wanted; they wanted more substantial food like grilled cheese sandwiches and hot dogs as well as juice and fruit. Part of the process of eating was reconnecting with the other youth whose classrooms they were not in. Perhaps, I thought, they had not seen the other youth since they were in the art club a week ago.

I watched as they headed for new activities, different activities from the ones they had been working on last week. Skye picked up the camera and began taking photographs. Gently I pointed her to the painting. She smiled but kept the camera and continued with photography. "Hmmm," I wondered.

Later, as a research team, we talked as we put away supplies for another week. I mentioned how projects were not completed. I talked about how I wondered why. And then, gradually, I came to recognize that it was my stories to live by that were shaping my intention that projects need to be finished. In the living the youth had shown me that they did not see finished art projects as part of living in the art club place. I bumped into myself and saw that it was my stories to live by that were called forth in the place that seemed much like school, where work completion was part of my stories of school.

In multiple moments such as these Jean awakened to the multiplicity of who she was and was becoming in relation with the youth. She was awake to how the place of the school, hallways, and classrooms called forth her stories to live by that were part of who she was as a teacher. The youth resisted the press to be congruent with the stories of school she was evoking.

Learning to live alongside the youth draws attention to a fifth touch-stone—that is, **the negotiation of relationships.** Entering the field begins with negotiation of relationships and the research puzzles to be explored.

In the work with youth in the art club there were multiple layers of negotiation. Initially we negotiated time and place in a school with administrators. We then advertised the art club as part of the research and negotiated participation with the youth who came to the club. We negotiated assent with each youth and asked them to have a responsible adult caregiver give consent for them to come to the club. As we came to know the youth, we began the negotiation of the one-to-one research relationships with the youth and the families. We awakened to how we, as researchers, are only part of the negotiation; the youth also choose to work with us.

As we look across past studies we see that there is not one way to negotiate relationships with participants. No one entry is like another; each time we are aware that we enter into a new context, a new geographic place, and into the midst of ongoing lives. What echoes across studies is that each entry is marked with anticipation, an eagerness to form new relationships, yet also a sense of uncertainty, of not knowing how the inquiry will unfold. Particularly when we enter into relationships alongside children and youth we are mindful that we, too, enter, intentionally or unintentionally, the lives of their families, their parents and/or guardians, and their friends and peers.

In the narrative inquiry design we realized that although we wrote of going wherever participants would take us, we were not always awake to what that would mean. In living alongside participants we enter places important to participants, and in this way we, too, enter the multiple social milieux of which they are part.

Part of the negotiation of relationships involves watching and waiting with feelings of uncertainty, of not knowing what will happen next. We are awake to the need for improvising ways forward that allow us, as narrative inquirers, to be open to responding to the multiple alternatives that may open up. There is a certainty that something will happen, that one moment leads to other moments. What is uncertain is what, out of a range of possibilities—some imagined, some not imagined—will happen. What is certain is that if it is to open into a relational inquiry space, it is not all on our terms as narrative inquirers.

"Hold my phone," Jason says as he enters the art club and heads to the table where the snacks are laid out. I take his phone, put it in my pocket, and wonder what this moment means. I begin to watch.

It was not that I did not know who Jason was. He had been a partici-
pant in the arts club for several weeks before he handed me his phone to
hold in safekeeping. I had, however, kept him in my peripheral vision;
that is, I had attended but not attended to him, to who he was. I was busy
watching other youth, thinking about who I would invite to participate
into the study to work more intensely with me. I carefully watched many
youth, trying to imaginatively story myself into a relationship with each of
them, a relationship in which we would tell stories, spend time together,
be taken "home" so I could spend time with their family members. Jason
was not one of them.

The next week Jason again handed me his treasured phone for safe-
keeping while he ate the snacks, talked with his friends, and occasionally
engaged in some rough play with the others. I began to awaken to who
he was and for the first time noticed his humor, his wry sense of drawing
attention to what did not fit. I watched as he crawled into a locker as he
worked to make the others laugh, as he stuffed extra food into his jacket,
as he crawled under a table to have a different vantage point on what was
happening, as he played with the materials. I also noticed that he did not
engage with the art materials for any period of time, not like many of the
others. He kept away from them.

As the weeks passed and the research team began to select research par-
ticipants, I made visible that perhaps Jason had chosen me for conversa-
tions and had signaled his interest in working with me through his requests
that I hold his phone for safekeeping. I wondered then—and now—about
the negotiation of participation. I wonder about how long he had watched
me, watched my expressions, watched who I was in the art club. Did
he watch how I cared for his phone? Did he watch and see that I rarely
worked with the art materials? Did he sense resonances with me? Now, as
I write these words, I wonder about his attentiveness and mine, of how I
only came to attend to him when he signaled that he had noticed me.

In narrative inquiry it is moments such as this that shape what we see
as beginning to create spaces to come alongside children and youth in
narrative inquiries. We began to see how the selection of participants is
not a one-way selection process. Although we may have criteria for participants, we are not solely in charge of the negotiation of research relationships. Participants are choosing us, choosing how much and what
they will tell us, choosing whether or not they want to participate; their
intentions for joining the research also shapes the research processes.

As we engage in negotiating research relationships this wide awakeness to the mutuality of each relationship is heightened in work with
children and youth. Their intentions for participating are part of the
watching process: them watching us to see how we fit into their unfolding stories, and us watching them to see how the processes might unfold.
And the deliciousness of the surprise when the unexpected happens, as in
the moment when Jason said, "Hold my phone," and I knew just enough
in that moment to honor his request.

Jean and Vera describe a sixth touchstone as attending to **moving from field to field texts.** As we co-compose the relational three-dimensional narrative inquiry space with participants, we begin to compose or co-compose field texts. In the narrative inquiry with Jason there are multiple forms of field texts, including photographs and artifacts from the art club, transcripts of one-on-one conversations with Jason at lunchtime in school places, transcripts of conversations with Sheri, and personal messages on Facebook. We also engaged in photographic work with the youth, at times giving them cameras to take photographs in out of school places. We also gave them cameras and asked them to take photographs of places in the school and art club. The photographs Jason asked others to take of him were of him squeezing himself into lockers, hiding in the art club room, and sitting in places that allowed him unusual vantage points. We also engaged in some work around timelines, what we call annals, that provided a sense of the times, places, and schools that shaped their lives. As a research team, we also kept records of ongoing e-mail conversations among team members after each Wednesday art club time and wrote field notes made during several day-long and weekend sessions of reading field texts.

In the work with the youth we found ourselves surprised by the many moves the youth made as they moved from school to school, from homes in different places and with different people who were their families. We began to write field notes about the many moves from school to school, from home place to other home places, from urban center to different family reserves.

> Jason told me we could get together in the summer when he was back in the city. He left right after school was out at the end of June, heading to his mother's reservation in another province. "I'm not looking forward to playing hockey on the team, but I'll have to. . . . I'll be back for the [July celebration] in the city. We can go out then." I send a personal message on Facebook early in July. He writes back, "I can't come." No further explanation. I am disappointed, as I had been looking forward to getting together and seeing a movie. Jason has such a sense of humor, I enjoy trying to understand what sense he makes of popular culture.
>
> Later, when we met again in the fall, he told me that he was on his mother's reservation for a month in the summer: "Yeah, it's pretty boring there. I'd just sleep, but I'd wake up at five and then I'd just watch TV and go to my cousins' and play games there, and go back to my house and just sleep again. I just do it all the time. I was at my kookum's. She was always at work. My auntie lives there."

The **move from field texts to interim and final research texts** is a seventh touchstone. Moving from field texts to interim and final research texts is a complicated and iterative process, full of twists and turns. As part of the move from field texts to interim research texts, we continue to live within the three-dimensional narrative inquiry space. Field texts are read and reread, looked at and relooked at, and attention is paid simultaneously to temporality, sociality, and place.

When Jean initially began the move to an interim research text, a narrative account, she began with drawing on field notes and transcript segments that gave a sense of Jason's experience in school. Her tentative account, in part, read something like this:

> In the field texts composed when Jason was part of the arts club there is this one photo of Jason. I am not sure who took it, but it lives in my mind. He is both in the locker and not in the locker, part of him hidden but visible through the door. But of course he is not hidden. He is very much visible, and yet there is a sense that Jason keeps so much of himself hidden while he is in school.
> I love to cook.
> In foods class I wrote down all the recipes.
> I made lists of what I needed.
> Mostly I did not cook, but I love to cook.
> My favorite is KD with wieners cut up really small.
> My auntie is a good cook.
> It is all about the spices that you use.
> I love to cook.
> In these few words I saw enthusiasm in Jason's face as he talked about school. There was not much that he said about school that showed such enthusiasm.

When Jean began to share the account with Jason, many pages were filled with field notes of his stories of experiences in school. He responded with a comment: "Jean, this is too complicated. Just write across each page, *School Sucks*, like this," he said, taking the pencil and writing the words across the first page. His words stay with Jean as she sees that, for him, his school experiences did not speak to who he was and who he was becoming in the wholeness of his life.

Although interim research texts are the beginning place of attending to our research puzzles, a place to begin to make meaning of our field texts, we eventually need to move to final research texts. Even as we make this move from field texts to interim and final research texts, we remind ourselves there will never be a final story. "Attending to uncertainty and to the ongoingness of lives lived and told over time brings researcher commitment to understanding lives in motion, a commitment to seeing and representing lives as always in the making (Greene, 1995), to the forefront" (Clandinin, 2013, p. 204).

It is by this continual return to the ontological commitments of a relational methodology that we can begin to imagine the processes of moving to interim and final research texts.

And another fragment of the interim narrative account with Jason:

And yet this story of cooking showed the links between the familial curric-
ulum-making world at home with his family who loves him so much and
his school curriculum-making world where he feels like he is unable to do
the work, so much so that it has had complications for his physical health.
> *I take drugs now.*
> *He laughs.*
> *But he does and it bothers him,*
> *I can see as he tells me,*
> *Taking quick side looks at B.*
> *I asked if they helped him do the work.*
> *No, but it is easier to pay attention.*
> *I wonder.*

Final research texts are often difficult to write, in part because researchers and participants now need to turn their attention to public audiences, audiences they may not know and who may be far removed from the lived and told experiences of participants.

This attention to composing research texts draws our attention to an eighth touchstone—that is, the need to **represent narratives of experience in ways that show temporality, sociality and place.** By making all three dimensions of the inquiry space visible to public audiences, the complexity of storied lives also become visible. In this way we avoid presenting smooth or cover stories (Clandinin & Connelly, 1995). Avoiding cover stories and layering the complexity of the inquiry also helps to draw readers into the stories, to lay their own experiences alongside the inquiry, to wonder alongside participants and researchers who were part of the inquiry.

It is often when we attend to all of the dimensions that we begin to see disruptions, fragmentations, or silences in participants' and our own lives. Final research texts are never meant to have final answers; they are intended to engage audiences in rethinking, retelling, and inquiring into experiences in collaborative and ethical ways, to look at the ways in which they practice and the ways in which they relate to others.

Attending to the texts we create draws attention to a ninth touchstone, **relational response communities.** In the study with Jason and his mother we invited three Elders to come alongside. They attended some of the art club activities and often met with our research team to ask questions and to wonder about what sense we were making of the experiences of the youth and their families. As a research team, we also shaped a response community, talking and e-mailing each other after each experience in the art club and as we wrote narrative accounts and shared them with youth.

Working within relational response communities over the time of a narrative inquiry reminds us to frame and to continue to return to a tenth touchstone—that is, the importance of **three kinds of justifications: the personal, practical, and social justifications** of a narrative inquiry. As narrative inquirers, we share with all social science researchers the need to be able to justify our research through responding to the questions of "So what?" and "Who cares?"

Attending to the "So what?" and "Who cares?" questions that arise from considerations of the personal, practical, and social/theoretical justifications of our narrative inquiries draws attention to an eleventh touchstone—that is, the importance of being **attentive to audience.** Narrative inquiries are always filled with rich, temporally unfolding narrative accounts as they represent the lived and told experiences of participants and researchers.

In one article that is part of this study we (Lessard, Caine, & Clandinin, 2014) wrote that

> the forward looking story ... asks those of us who work with children and youth in school curriculum-making worlds to acknowledge, to name, other curriculum-making worlds that families engage in with their children ... As we moved alongside the youth into their worlds of home and community, we heard stories of their lives as dancers, grandchildren, siblings, and those who attend to, or are cared for by, others. (p. 219)

Although in the article we highlight work that Sean engaged in with Donovan and Lane, two youth from the study, we know that Jason kept many of his stories of experience silent in his school curriculum-making world. He did not tell stories of leaving school each day promptly when the bell rang to come home to care for a younger sibling. He did not tell stories of waking before dawn to deliver thousands of advertising flyers to homes in order to save money for a cell phone, which allowed him access to technology.

From our article again,

> We came to know not only diverse stories the youth tell of themselves and/or their families, but also of stories they leave behind because there is no safe place to tell them, share them, or celebrate them. . . . Those of us who work in school curriculum-making worlds often do not understand how the experiences of youth in their familial curriculum-making worlds sustain them in schools.
>
> We [also] awakened to how important and difficult it is to continuously resist the stereotypical story of being Aboriginal, to resist categorizations and single stories. (p. 211)

Jean and Vera noted a twelfth touchstone as a **commitment to understanding lives in motion.** As narrative inquirers, we bring a commitment to understanding lives in motion, a commitment to seeing and representing lives always in the making (Greene, 1995). It means that there is no final telling, no final story, and no one singular story we can tell. Although this is troubling to researchers who rely on the truth or accuracy and verifiability of data, it is opening the possibility for narrative inquirers to continuously inquire into the social fabric of experience and to not lose sight that people are always becoming.

As we enter into the work with children and youth in narrative inquiries we realize that we are becoming, in some ways at least, part of their lives. We meet them in school classrooms, in and out of school places, and in other institutional places. It makes a difference as to who we are in our complex lives, which are always at work in the relational spaces. Attending carefully to who we are as we engage in the relational work of narrative inquiry is an ongoing and always negotiated process across the multiplicity of places in which we engage with children and youth. We need to be attentive to who we are as we live alongside the children and youth over months and, perhaps, years, knowing that we are changing not only our own life-making but also the life-making of children and youth.

CHAPTER 14

The Relational Ethics of Narrative Inquiry

In each chapter we attended closely to ethical issues in narrative inquiry—that is, to issues about what it means to live alongside, as we engage in relational research with participants. We adopt a particular ethical stance in narrative inquiry, a stance we refer to as relational ethics (Clandinin & Connelly, 2000). Relational ethics live at the heart of narrative inquiry, and we consider all of what we do in narrative inquiry as guided and shaped by relational ethics. This ongoing attention to ethics is central from the outset of planning a narrative inquiry and extending long after a study ends through our ongoing long-term relational commitments. Throughout the research we need to negotiate "a narrative way of presenting our research so that it foregrounds relationships while maintaining research rigor with which others can identify" (Craig & Huber, 2007, p. 272). In this final chapter we pay close attention to relational ethics at work throughout our narrative inquiries alongside children and youth.

RELATIONAL ETHICAL COMMITMENTS AT THE HEART OF NARRATIVE INQUIRIES

Although our focus in this chapter is on relational ethics and the ways relational ethics shape our inquiries with children and youth, we want to acknowledge the complexities of working with human ethics review boards, a topic we have discussed in several earlier chapters. Elsewhere (Clandinin, Caine, & Huber, accepted) we made visible how the work of ethics review boards has evolved over time and noted that a relational ethical stance sometimes bumps against the stance adopted by these boards. We acknowledge the importance of ethical review boards, yet we also want to make clear that relational ethics demands more from us as researchers and as people in relation. As we wrote (Clandinin, Caine, & Huber, accepted), "Thinking narratively with people's experiences involves a relational ontology, which calls forth obligations and commitments. It is in how we live out our research puzzles alongside participants that commitments become evident. These relational commitments move us beyond research puzzles to long-term responsibilities, as well as ethical questions of care" (p. 1).

In this chapter we highlight the importance of holding our relational ethical commitments at the heart of our work. Although we imagine at the outset of each inquiry what our responsibilities and obligations to and with participants might be, we do not always know what all of these will be at the outset of an inquiry. Janice remembers being asked questions about whether it was possible to engage in narrative inquiry with children during her master's research. As a teacher, Janice had a strong sense of the importance of listening to, of being guided by, and of valuing children. This sense of valuing children as active participants in research helped Janice hold firm to her commitments that it was important to engage in research alongside children. She knew, as she proceeded with the study, that she would engage in ethical ways, but she had not imagined that one of her obligations to a child participant would be to honor the child's request to have her "real" name included in the research text (See Chapter 3).

In narrative inquiries with children and youth there are similarities to engaging in narrative inquiries with adults, as our understanding of relational ethics does not change. What does change, however, is how we live these commitments with children and youth. We know that we need to engage with a greater attentiveness to the nestedness of children and youth's ongoing lives within their familial contexts and within their multiple communities. In our study alongside Aboriginal youth and in our study alongside youth who left school early, we paid close attention to who we, the children and youth, and others defined as family and also as community were and were becoming. We were mindful of the importance of attending to the children and youth as we included them in discussions and decision making around who their families and communities were. Sometimes families were composed of aunts and uncles, cousins, and peers rather than biological families. We saw this careful attention to the nestedness of children and youth's lives in Sean's account of coming alongside Skye and her family.

Attention to the nestedness of children and youth's ongoing lives challenges us to consider what we privilege, such as notions about how families are composed, of whether or not schools are good places, and about what is educative. As we think about what we privilege in relation to commitments to hear and attend to children and youth, we see that these are questions about the ethics of our work.

As we think with our ongoing learning about what we privilege and how this shapes our understanding of relational ethics, Janice recollects a long-ago memory. On a long weekend in October 1990 while she was engaged in her master's program, Janice returned to her family's home. With her was Dewey's book *Experience and Education* (1938). Her dad noticed the book and read parts of it. His emotions were evident when he asked Janice about the book: Who was John Dewey? Why was Janice reading this book? What was the person like who encouraged her to read such a book? Janice's dad then told stories of how his life was shaped because he was seen as "lacking an education"; with tears in his eyes he encouraged Janice to remember that school learning was only one kind of education and that the learning he, she, and others carried because of their privilege of living where and how they did—with the land, with the animals, with the water, and with the people with whom they interacted—was not less important.

LINGERING IN RELATIONAL RESPONSIBILITIES

While we return many times to experiences in our early landscapes to help us understand what has shaped and continues to shape our responsibilities and obligations, we also see the importance of lingering in these relational responsibilities at the end of our studies. At the end of his doctoral work (Lessard, 2013) Sean returned to thinking about his experiences alongside the participants.

I have Donovan, Lane, and Cedar on my mind.

I took a walk out on Elder Bob Cardinal's land today; it is a place where we spend time together. It is a teaching and knowledge place that he shares with me. The trees surrounding and the wild grasses blowing, they were dancing in the wind, and one might consider them the teachers within this place. If I listen to the sounds on the landscape and pay careful attention, I can understand differently with what it is I am hearing. The rocks ... the water ... the details of the landscape can also be considered subject matter when I think of them in this way, within this place. As I walked outside today the animate and living was all around me, as I could hear when I let myself go to the silent places of reflection and turning inward. It is in this place within myself that I begin to also notice the possibilities and richness in this type of milieu. The teachers to me, in this place I enjoy, are the wind calling and the birds communicating. I sit in this place, and time is no longer a consideration as I let the sun fill my spirit and give me energy as it shines its way down and lifts me up. It is beautiful to think of the stories situated in the places where I need to continue to listen to and listen for. Listening and observing, paying attention to the details of the landscape is what I so often am missing.

As I continue to write, I think about the experiences in different places alongside the youth and families I have come to know. I can see Donovan walking down the gravel road to remember the stories his Kookum [grandmother] taught him ... these stories keep him going; they sustain him as he continues to bring them alive through his drum and the songs he is learning. I have a vision of Cedar as she moves alongside her family; the intergenerational stories are alive as the women within the family are all dancing alongside one another through the multiplicity of the worlds they travel. From place to place ... beyond geography ... these stories they have come to know are shared through the movement and creative forces nested deeply within.

Finally in this moment of thinking and reflection time I look up to the trees surrounding and watch the leaves move, pushing back and forth through the hush of the wind. I can imagine Lane as he is on the road again. I understand through his stories something of the landscapes of his youth and the imagery etched within him. He has stories of places in memory where the water and the rocks combine ... white waters moving ... splashing on rock faces. It is the images of places he has traveled in and between that sustain his stories and continue to remind him of what is important in his life. These stories hold his memories. They are his teachers. He is taking care of the stories with kindness and not forgetting about these early moments of experience where the water flows and fills the landscape in different ways from what I have known. (Lessard, 2013, pp. 292–294)

As we reread Sean's doctoral work, we are reminded that care lingers, that it grows even when we, as researchers and participants, are no longer in each other's physical presence. The relationships are there even when we are no longer physically present to one another. We, as narrative inquirers, carry a responsibility to have learned from the stories told and the experiences shared. In Chapter 1 we turned to Robert Coles (1989), and we return to his words now. "Their story, yours, mine—it's what we all carry with us on this trip we take, and owe it to each other to respect our stories and learn from them" (Coles, 1989, p. 30). In this way our obligations and responsibilities are never ending; they call us to act differently and, as Sean reminds us, to reflect on what happened and what is becoming within a life we have come to know.

Huber, Clandinin, and Huber (2006) wrote of long-term relational responsibilities when they met Ryley, a former child research participant, years later when Ryley was experiencing difficulties in his junior high school. In the narrative inquiry with youth who left school before graduating, Kevlar, a youth participant, contacted Pam Steeves, the researcher who had engaged with him. More than a year after the study ended Kevlar sent a message to let Pam know what was happening in his life. In many of the research relationships we develop, participants continue to stay in touch. They sometimes call or write to ask how we are or how our work is going. Sometimes they ask us for something we are in a position to help them with, such as letters of reference and so on. Sometimes they ask us to return, to show us that their lives have changed or to find ways to contemplate alongside each other again or to engage in a new study, as in the ongoing relationship with Vera and Tammy. Sometimes participants we have worked with as children call us when they become adults. These are fascinating moments, as participants stay in our minds. There are lingering memories of what we learned alongside them when they allowed us into their worlds so that we could inquire into research puzzles. When we hear from participants after the studies are over, their messages and voices bring back memories of what we learned alongside them. It is akin to hearing from friends after a long period of time. Caine and Estefan (2011) write about these long-term relational responsibilities that extend well beyond the time of actual fieldwork; they puzzled over relational ethics as they waited for participants' responses to their ongoing work.

GROUNDING OUR RELATIONAL WORK WITHIN ETHICAL THEORIES

Bergum and Dosseter's relational ethics: Although our work as narrative inquirers has been significantly shaped in the living of relational ethics in numerous studies, we also draw on several ethical theorists who offer us ways to think about relational ethics, about how we are called to live alongside participants, and about how we leave the field and the immediacy of relationships. When we think about ethics, we situate our thinking and knowing amidst relationships, relationships that call us to action. Keith Basso (1996) was one of the first who drew our attention to the relational. Sometime later Bergum and Dossetor (2005) named what we were considering as relational ethics. They write,

> We may, in the end, see our work as that of nurturing the space that can hold the dialectical tension between principles and care, between scientific and experiential knowledge, between what we should do and what we can do, and even between what is good and what is not good. A relational space may be a place where there is a flow between rationality and embodiment, between the challenges of the thinking mind and the realities of the feeling body. A relational space is found both between people as well as within each person. (p. xvii)

Bergum and Dosseter's (2005) words remind us of Sean's words as he shows us how he navigated this relational space. He also shows us how he enlarged this relational space by including people who were important to him, people like Elder Bob. He also names geography as part of this relational space, as part of the ethics of narrative inquiry. The ethical space for us as narrative inquirers extends across time, place, and relationships.

The relational space for engagement is enlarged as we invite families and others with whom children and youth's lives are nested. The relational space for engagement is also enlarged, as we do not see the children and youth as only research participants; we see them as people composing lives in particular times and places, embedded within particular social, cultural, institutional, and familial narratives. We wonder about what experiences have shaped their further experiences and how their experiences alongside us will continue to shape their lives, even after we leave.

As we continue to learn with our experiences we see that the "attention to the relational-space offer[s] us an opportunity to consider the importance of this space for ethical action, not only at the bedside, but within the world surrounding individual relations of two or more persons [... and] the need to respect relational space as an ethical responsibility" (Bergum & Dossetor, 2005, p. 221).

Amidst these relational spaces and the ongoing ethical responsibilities we live are often lingering questions, questions such as "What happened?" "What are you going through?" "How do you want me to act?" and/or "Who am I alongside you?" These questions exhaust us when we ask them, as they call us into the ways in which we live out our ethical questions (Bergum & Dossetor, 2005, p. 221).

As each relationship is different, so too are the ways in which we live ethically in the field. Most important is to consider that

> The call to relationship is a call to dialogue. . . . Listening, hearing, giving, and receiving is ongoing. With an ethic of relationship, our task is to search for understanding, for the middle ground, and to avoid entrenchment into ideology. Only then can we create space for new results—results opened by the imagination to foster growth and reduce suffering. There is no map or script in relational ethics to fall back on. (Bergum & Dossetor, 2005, p. 220)

It is important not only to attend to ethics in this way but also to show how narrative inquirers live ethically in the field. As we noted in earlier chapters, it is important to think of co-composing places and field texts alongside participants, attending to them and to us and to the spaces where our lives touch. Thinking ethically is also, as we have shown in earlier chapters, important as we move to interim and final research texts. This requires us to make both our thinking and actions visible in the interim research texts, narrative accounts, and final research texts we write. It matters that Sean spends time with Elder Bob and that he shows us throughout his research text who he was alongside participants and how his multiple worlds intertwined and embraced what Cedar, Donovan, and Lane were teaching him. When we see and gain a sense of the living, we can begin to "consider what we can do to give renewed attention to the development of deep respect for each other, to foster tolerance and compassion, based on recognition that we all live together" (Bergum & Dossetor, 2005, p. 220).

Noddings's ethic of care: Early on in the development of narrative inquiry Clandinin and Connelly (2000) pulled forward Noddings's theory and understanding of an ethics of care. Noddings's (1984) work remains important to us, as it situates ethics outside the Kantian ideal of values and rights and stays close to life. For Noddings, relatedness and receptiveness between people is at play in the ethics of care.

> In contrast "ethical" caring does have to be summoned. The "I ought" arises but encounters conflict: An inner voice grumbles, "I ought but I don't want to," or "Why should I respond?" or "This guy deserves to suffer, so why should I help?" On these occasions we need not turn to a principle; more effectively we turn to our memories of caring and being cared for and a picture or ideal of ourselves as carers. . . . Ethical caring's great contribution is to guide action long enough for natural caring to be restored and for people once again to interact with mutual and spontaneous regard. (Noddings, 1998, p. 187)

Noddings brings us back to what matters and to knowing that we cannot turn away as narrative inquirers. Noddings's ethics of care reminds us that we need to continue to attend with our whole lives within the research relationship. As Kathleen Casey (1993) noted many years ago, we need to answer with our lives in narrative inquiry.

When Sean worked alongside Lane, Lane called him to act when he was unable to engage with his family or social services. He asked Sean to come and be alongside him as he negotiated what would happen in his life after he left home at a far too young age. Lane, in this moment, held Sean accountable to an ethics of care.

> The key, central to care theory, is this: caring-about (or, perhaps a sense of justice) must be seen as instrumental in establishing the conditions under which caring-for can flourish. Although the preferred form of caring is caring-for, caring-about can help in establishing, maintaining, and enhancing it. Those who care about others in the justice sense must keep in mind that the objective is to ensure that caring actually occurs. Caring-about is empty if it does not culminate in caring relations. (Noddings, 2002, pp. 23–24)

Sean attended to Lane from this place of care. As Sean answered Lane's call, Sean remembered his own life on a farm, as he traveled daily between his worlds of school, home, and community. As he turned inward to his memories of traveling, it was possible to see that the

> Ethical life is not separate from and alien to the physical world. Because we human beings are in the world, not mere spectators watching from outside

it, our social instincts and the reflective elaboration of them are also in the world. Pragmatists and care theorists agree on this. The ought—better, the "I ought"—arises directly in lived experience. "Oughtness," one might say, is part of our "isness." (Noddings, 1998, p. 187)

As we engage with children and youth we need to recall our own experiences as children and youth. Furthermore, we need to recall our childhood and youth experiences within the places of our childhood, such as schools. We do this at the outset in our autobiographical narrative inquiries and as we revisit our experiences throughout each narrative inquiry. This is often very difficult work, as we begin to understand what has shaped our social instincts and our ability to act and be alongside children and youth. We return to Sean's experience alongside Lane, as Lane is not at school.

> *My day started off with the best of intentions. I stopped by the school, the place of our research, to set a formal time to meet and connect with Lane. We had planned to work together on the research project that day, and I was filled with that good, nervous anticipation that comes with new conversations. I was looking forward to moving to a different place in our conversational relationship (Clandinin et al., 2006), inquiring further into some of the stories we shared over the previous months. My anticipated conversation was sidetracked as I quickly found out that the "boys" (Lane and two friends) were skipping school. At first disappointed, my response to them missing school was immediate as I texted one student who texted another student, who pointed me in the direction of the local mall and a favorite place of many youth—the arcade.*
>
> *Without hesitation I drove to meet Lane, Donovan, and one of their friends. As I drove to the mall I thought of these boys who had developed a connection through similar interests and their shared age and grade. It was grade 7 and, it seemed to me at that moment, they were trying to figure school out; it was a day-to-day negotiation. Sometimes they said they hated school, their classes, the teachers, whereas at other times they accepted it, but rarely if ever had I heard this group of boys speak as if they loved it. School, their time spent in it and with it, seemed to be an afterthought. School was a physical place where the boys could connect with each other. It was a mechanism that provided a space for them in a different way.*
>
> *I decided the best way to approach this scenario was to have a simple conversation, as I worried about their trend of skipping school at such a young age and being so intentional about it. I texted Lane and asked, "What are you doing ... shouldn't you be in school?" The simple response was, "I am trying to set a high score." A smile crossed my face, and it certainly appeared that he was not worried about missing school or what his parents or guardians might say. Remembering my own experiences in grade 7, I could not imagine skipping, as I would have been scared of what my parents might say or do. Shifting forward, I thought of my own daughters and imagined them in grade 7. I thought of the long conversation that would ensue if I found out they were skipping school to "set a high score"*

at the local arcade. I reminded myself as I walked through these scenarios in my mind that I was a researcher in this moment and that it was difficult to separate the many identities I lived out in each moment. I reminded myself that the worlds I was currently composing in my life were very different from the worlds of the youth I was coming to know. It was not new to me that young people found other ways of being together besides school and that schools were not always the best places to be. It was with worry that I thought through scenarios and sometimes got lost in the fear of seeing young people start to lose their way in schools so early. This was how I was feeling that day.

In Sean's words we can see the possibilities of who he is alongside Lane, possibilities that speak to living with and within an ethics of care. It also speaks of the importance of staying wakeful to these tensions and how they shape our experience, the experiences of participants, and the experiences we share: "Because we are attending to, inquiring into, and representing participants' and our experiences with careful focus on what we can learn from tensions, we are increasingly awake to the importance of ethical relational practice" (Clandinin, Murphy, Huber, & Murray Orr, 2010, p. 88).

PRACTICING WAKEFULNESS

To engage with the relational ethics of narrative inquiry, we must learn to live with wakefulness. Wakefulness is not something we can live in the abstract; it is a way of living that must be grounded in experience. Wakefulness is a way of living that is congruent with the ontological and epistemological commitments of narrative inquiry, commitments that are coherent with the theoretical work of Dewey and other pragmatist philosophers.

> When the pragmatists critically attacked absolutes, when they sought to expose the quest for certainty, when they argued for an open universe in which chance and contingency are irreducible, they were not concerned exclusively with abstract metaphysical and epistemological issues. They were addressing ethics, politics, and practical questions that ordinary people confront in their ordinary lives. (Bernstein, 2005, p. 23)

Linking our concept of wakefulness, a sense of diligence that life matters in all of its details, we see that the relational ethics we practice in narrative inquiry are linked to the ordinary, to ordinary life. Charon and Montello (2002) helped us see that "the ethics in question are the ethics of ordinary life: how to fulfill life goals, to honor obligations, and to make sense of events in ways that make it possible to go on. These ethical issues ... are also the ethics of life" (p. xi). The ordinary holds everyday experiences and also links these experiences to both ethical and political issues.

In thinking with Sean's experiences we return to a field text in which he tells of his experience with Elder Bob Cardinal:

> As I think about the stories I shared with Elder Bob Cardinal on various theories I was learning at the university, I recall that he asked me questions about school, and I excitedly responded. One day, as we worked together on his land preparing for a sweat lodge ceremony, he said, "That is good what you are learning ... but don't forget about my granddaughter when you teach her at the school." My thoughts were, "How could I forget her? I see her all the time." While I wondered what he meant by this and why he said it in the way he did, he slowly, carefully, gently started to tell me a story. He began his teaching with questions, like he so often does, his way of getting me to think in a different way. "Sean, when you speak, you talk up and down, how people go from one level to another in their lives. . . . Well, what if I teach her in a circle? The way I teach my granddaughter is by starting in the south ... where the grandmothers are. It is where wisdom is." He took his hand and, with his finger, began to draw in the air. He painted an imaginary line moving to the west and said, "Sean, in the west, it is where bear and knowledge live ... that is my four directions teachings ... that is how I teach my granddaughter each day."
>
> Elder Bob then brought his hand from the point in the west and drew the next part of his circle in the sky, as he moved slowly with his finger to the north. "Sean, in the north, in the north, that is where buffalo and responsibility reside ... that is my four directions teachings ... that is how I teach my granddaughter each day." His hand now moved in a gentle way, in a soft way; slowly and purposefully, he brought his finger down, forming that familiar circle shape. "Sean, in the east, in the east, that is where eagle and wisdom lives. . . . and that is maybe someday where I will go ... that is how I teach my granddaughter each day ... that is my four directions teachings." At this time he slowly closed the circle ... moving his hand down ... his finger moved to another place on the skyline painting that he was creating in his teaching.
>
> "Sean, in the south, in the south we always go back home to the grandmothers ... that is how I teach my granddaughter each day ... it is my four directions teachings ... it is how I think about her identity. It is how I teach her. Now don't forget about her in school." ... "Don't forget about her in school now" he said as he smiled and looked at me. I think about that story often, and I share it when I can because it stays with me as I think about the lives of people, their stories and my stories in relation to them.

Sean's words cause us to pause, and we can see the ordinary at play in his and Elder Bob Cardinal's words. We are called to not forget people and places in our endeavors of learning and understanding and research. In Chapter 2 we drew on Greene's (1995) ideas of seeing small and seeing big. In the stories Elder Bob Cardinal shares with Sean we can see him drawing "seeing big" in the circle teachings. As Greene wrote, it is important to see "from the point of view of the participant in the midst of what is happening if one is to be privy to the plans people make, the initiatives they take, the uncertainties they face" (p. 10). We cannot see only from the detached and distanced view of seeing small. As Elder Bob Cardinal shared his teachings with Sean he drew Sean's attention to his granddaughter, a particular youth in the school where Sean taught. Sean brings Elder Bob Cardinal's teachings to our work as narrative inquirers.

As we worked in multiple places and contexts with children and youth we have come to both hear and to also experience some of the uncertainties they face. We can see how often Lane and Donovan told stories of feeling less than, of living at the margins, of not finding places in which their voices mattered. We experienced that alongside the youth at the school when we too felt the uncertainties they faced. Yet we also saw and became part of stories of resistance. We were part of the stories when they snuck through the school's back door into the arts club after skipping school all day because, for them, at that time in their lives, school was not an educative place. We were part of the stories of protecting their parents through their willingness to show their love and affection. In these moments we learned how important it is to recognize that "the prospect of reconfiguring our actual practices of ethical deliberation and ultimately deliberate conduct, even in its more entangled communal forms, in such a way that imagination becomes critical and critique, efficacious" (Colapietro, 2011, p. 162). And we can see that it is significant to imagine new stories to live by, to imagine alongside children and youth, their families and communities, in loving ways.

Lingering in the Relational Tensions

We need to learn to linger in the relational tensions shaped by our ethical stance. We need, as we have shown throughout the book, to attend to the ethical shaping of our research puzzles and our unfolding work and, in so doing, to not turn away from ethical tensions, challenges, or responsibilities. Relational ethics are lived and informed by the messiness of lives and living and the tensions this calls forth.

These tensions we experience in the living of relational ethics call forth complex processes that often require us to engage with the participants, their families, and communities as well as with our response communities. As Bergum and Dossetor (2005) point out, relational spaces also live within us, and the tensions we experience often challenge our own ethical spaces. By attending to these tensions we learn from them, even when there is no intention to resolve them; rather, our intentions are to learn and live in ways that make visible our commitments.

Vera remembers her work alongside Ben, one of the youth in the early school leavers study. As part of the study Vera only met face-to-face with Ben once. Vera tried to reconnect with Ben, who lived in a different city, several times. After multiple attempts and two conversations with his sister and mother, Ben talked with Vera. In their conversation Ben was very clear in his reasons to participate in the study—he felt his story was important and that it provided a unique vantage point on early school leaving. As Vera and Ben talked, Ben also mentioned that he felt he had told his story and that he did not want to offer any other insights. He stated, "I told you my story and I want you to use this." Although Ben's directions were unequivocal, it caused several tensions for Vera. Most of all she felt unsure about how her writing of Ben's narrative account without Ben's willingness to negotiate and co-compose this could indeed adequately reflect his experience of leaving school. Did Ben trust Vera to make visible his experiences in ways that honor who he was and was becoming?

Vera remembers how she has experienced tensions within her ongoing work alongside children and youth, where a single participant's experiences are often dismissed and rigor is seen to be equated with large numbers of participants, where inferences and commonalities are emphasized, or negative cases that disrupt commonalities need to be identified. The tension is when rigor is seen from this detached point of view that we can no longer view participants in their integrity and particularity (Greene, 1995). Working from a relational ethics within narrative inquiry, we see the particularity of each life in the making.

TELLING DIFFERENT STORIES: CONSIDERING THE IMPACTS OF NARRATIVE INQUIRIES

As part of our ethical responsibilities and obligations, Lopez (1990) reminds us that "the stories people tell have a way of taking care of them. If stories come to you, care for them. And learn to give them away when they are needed. Sometimes a person needs a story more than food to stay alive. That is why we put these stories in each other's memory. This is how people care for themselves" (p. 48).

We have written throughout the book of the ways that engaging in narrative inquiry shifts lives. We have written that no one leaves a narrative inquiry unchanged. We have learned the importance of Lopez's words through Sean's work alongside Skye.

> As I looked back at my master's research and recall the sharing of the interim and final research texts and the narratives co-composed, I thought of Skye Song Maker. I wrote and rewrote and shared the stories, negotiat-

ing along the way, paying attention to the family stories, their wishes that her name not be changed within the narrative because her name comes from a place of ceremony. Her name was gifted to her when she was born; it holds meaning ... it has a story. I learned in the process to stay awake to what is important and to listen to what is important to a family, to the stories I shared, recognizing that stories can be shared in many ways once they go out in the world (King, 2003). I remember sitting and eating with Skye's family and starting to read what we had created together. As I shared they watched me. Skye's mother spoke, "This is a good story of our family, Sean ... this is a real good story ... not a bad story and we thank you for that" (Personal communication, 2010). Skye Song Maker and her family continue to help me in the present to stay awake and not take for granted the experiences shared in the relational processes of narrative inquiry. It is through their shared stories that they stay with me and continue to weave their way into how I listen and honor the stories of youth and families in my doctoral research. I thank them for that.

In Sean's reflections on his work with Skye Song Maker we see the reverberations in the experiences of Skye and her family. And this is part of the impact of narrative inquiries that we think about as we engage in relational ethics. In Sean's words we also hear how he has been shifted and changed. He too has felt the impact of the inquiry on who he is and is becoming. So have we all felt the changes in who we are and are becoming.

As we worked together in writing this book, gathered again around the table in the Centre for Research for Teacher Education and Development, we look backward across our work alongside children, youth, and families. Even now we are *still*—where *still* takes us back to "even then, even now, yet" (Online Etymological Dictionary, accessed 2015).

Sean talks often about how much he has changed because of his involvement in the narrative inquiries, including the early school leavers study and the study alongside Aboriginal youth and families. His sense of change comes from a way in which relational ethics calls him to listen sideways.

Sideways teachings are those that some Elders that I am in relation with refer to as the conversations that are indirect and the teachings and conversations that become more alive through working alongside each other. The conversations that occur when we are engaged in activities like cooking or preparing a meal together. In this narrative it was through the creative and intimate work involved in making a drum, where the conversational relationship continued to shift between all of us.

The Elders that I am in relation with encourage me to pay attention, reflect deeply, and try to look past what I might initially hear or see. Looking-listening sideways to the stories means to try to see beyond what might be noticed and look for the lessons from what might not be aware in the present (i.e., the silences can tell a story or the teachings that come at a later time when you reflect; it is not a direct answer to my query).

As I listened to a recording of a conversation with Lane and Donovan, a short conversation filled with text, words, and sentences that took me in many directions, I wrote out each word, did my best to recall the activity, paid attention to the details. The drum, the indirect activity, and the "sideways conversations" are sometimes the most powerful where the conversation flows through the activity and takes the conversational relationship to unexpected places. I watched as the two boys worked through lunch on something that was important to them; they were creating a drum and thinking about the teachings that an Elder had taught them about what it means to carry this responsibility. The bell rang, and it was time to put the drums down and go to class, to other subjects, different activities. I wondered what might happen if a class like this was available to them, where they could continue to hone their new skills, refine their craft, and think alongside the activity ... reflecting on the process they were involved in. It was powerful to observe ... the boys carefully placed their drums on top of a cupboard, tucked away from view ... they walked out the door with a wave heading to the next class.

This notion of listening sideways remains important to Sean, as it shapes how he understands relational ethics, an understanding marked by obligations and responsibilities to tell a good story. Learning to listen sideways remains challenging, and without careful attention and wide awakeness, it is easy to return to the questions, to lose sight of the profound and mysterious ways in which we lose ourselves in the lives of children, youth, and families.

And perhaps part of listening sideways is embedded in the way we are ourselves situated within narrative inquiry studies, studies that often begin with a sense of commitment over time. For Vera this sense of commitment over time has shifted her.

staying with you
over time
slowly counting the years of having known you
 i still can see the house,
 the blanket, that was your mother's, covering the window
 you took me in and wondered aloud why i stayed
 stayed alongside you and the children born and yet to be conceived
shifting our attention from who you are and are becoming as a women
to your children and as you began to compose your experiences as a mother
 profound in their ease
 yet, complex in their profoundness
i could not have imagined the joy you would bring into my life
how you and i and our children shifted by knowing each other in playful
and sustaining ways
and as you stayed
i was able to begin new adventures

of juice boxes flying, and paper set on fire too close to school doors
the chorus of discipline and order deafening
yet defeated at last
only to find ourselves on new landscapes
where we stayed alongside each other
over time
slowly counting the years of having known you
to disrupt my knowing of you and perhaps yours

Questions of who she was and was becoming as a teacher alongside children and who children were and were becoming as they interacted with Janice as a teacher carried Janice into a master's program. It was her parents who were her response community when she was a young teacher. They sat at their old worn kitchen table and listened late into the night as Janice returned home on Friday evenings and told stories of her many tensions with teaching. They were and were not shocked by Janice's stories of how children were treated. The racism toward the children of First Nations ancestry, who were bused to the small town school, the strapping of children as a way to educate them, the deficit ways in which rural and/or parents and families who were struggling to survive were often positioned, were aspects of life in schools that were not new to them. In these conversations some of the silences that shaped Janice's life as a child and youth in and outside of school were broken as her parents told stories of experiences they said they hoped she might have forgotten. Janice draws forth these stories as she reflects upon her experiences as a narrative inquirer alongside children and families.

For Jean, it has been a sense of learning to imagine otherwise, to stay with people and experience, to stay with the possibilities present in all lives. As she recollects walking alongside her father in the fields where she grew up, she learned of patience, of stillness, of waiting, and of imagining otherwise. These ways of living can be part of what counts as research if we attend to all of the lives in the making, to the silences and to the sounds. She now knows that if we listen carefully, if we attend closely to who we are alongside children and youth, we can disrupt the taken for granted, we can learn to live differently in what counts as research. No one leaves a narrative inquiry unchanged. And if we can honor the stories of children and youth, we can begin to shift the stories that count in policies and practices.

And as we come close to the end of this chapter and end the book for now, we can see how important the notion of disruption is as we contemplate our understanding of relational ethics. Perhaps it is these memories that sustain us in our journeys as narrative inquirers.

References

Arendt, H. (1958). *The human condition.* Chicago: University of Chicago Press.

Basso, K. (1996). *Wisdom sits in places: Landscape and language among the western Apache.* Albuquerque, NM: University of New Mexico Press.

Bateson, M. C. (1989). *Composing a life.* New York: HarperCollins.

Bateson, M. C. (1994). *Peripheral visions: Learning along the way.* New York: HarperCollins.

Bergum, V., & Dossetor, J. (2005). *Relational ethics: The full meaning of respect.* Hagerstown, ML: University Publishing Group.

Bernstein, R. J. (2005). *The abuse of evil: The corruption of politics and religion since 9/11.* Cambridge: Polity.

Browne, A. (1998). *Voices in the park.* New York: DK Pub.

Bruner, J. (1986). *Actual minds, possible worlds.* Cambridge: Harvard University Press.

Caine, V. (2010). Visualizing community: Understanding narrative inquiry as action research. *Educational Action Research, 18*(4), 481–496.

Caine, V., Clandinin, D. J., Glanfield, F., Donald, D., Baydala, L., Ebbers, M., Dellaire, P., & Whiskeyjack, C. (2010a). *A narrative inquiry into the educational experiences of Aboriginal youth.* Funding proposal submitted to the Social Sciences and Humanities Research Council (SSHRC).

Caine, V., Clandinin, D.J., Glanfield, F., Donald, D., Baydala, L., Ebbers, M., Dellaire, P., & Whiskeyjack, C. (2010b). *A narrative inquiry into the schooling experiences of Aboriginal youth and their families.* Funding proposal submitted to Alberta Centre for Child, Family, and Community Research (ACCFCR).

Caine, V., & Estefan, A. (2011). The experience of waiting: Inquiry into the long-term relational responsibilities in narrative inquiry. *Qualitative Inquiry, 17*(10), 965–971.

Caine, V., Estefan, A., & Clandinin, D. J. (2013). A return to methodological commitment: Reflections on narrative inquiry. *Scandinavian Journal of Educational Research, 57*(6), 574–586.

Carr, D. (1986). *Time, narrative, and history.* Bloomington: Indiana University Press.

Casey, K. (1993). *I answer with my life: Life histories of women teachers working for social change.* New York: Routledge.

Charon, R., & Montello, M. (Eds.). (2002). *Stories matter: The role of narrative in medical ethics.* New York: Routledge.

Clandinin, D. J. (2006). Narrative inquiry: A methodology for studying lived experience. *Research Studies in Music Education, 27,* 44–54.

Clandinin, D. J. (2010). Potentials and possibilities for narrative inquiry. In M. Campbell & L. Thompson (Eds.), *Issues of identity in music education: Narratives and practices* (pp. 1–11). Charlotte, NC: Information Age Publishing.

Clandinin, D. J. (2013). *Engaging in narrative inquiry.* Walnut Creek, CA: Left Coast Press.

Clandinin, D. J., & Caine, V. (2013). Narrative inquiry. In A. Trainor & E. Graue (Eds.), *Reviewing qualitative research in the social sciences.* New York: Taylor and Francis/ Routledge.

Clandinin, D. J., Caine, V., & Huber, J. (accepted). Ethical considerations entailed by a relational ontology in narrative inquiry. In I. Goodson, A. Antikainen, M. Andrews, & P. Sikes (Eds.). *The Routledge international handbook on narrative and life history.* New York: Routledge.

Clandinin, D. J. & Chung, S. (2009). The interwoven stories of teachers, families, and children in curriculum making. In M. Miller Marsh & T. Turner-Vorbeck (Eds.), *(Mis) understanding families: Learning from real families in our schools* (pp. 179–195). New York: Teachers College Press.

Clandinin, D. J., & Connelly, F. M. (1995). *Teachers' professional knowledge landscapes.* New York: Teachers College Press.

Clandinin, D. J., & Connelly, F. M. (2000). *Narrative inquiry: Experience and story in qualitative research.* San Francisco: Jossey-Bass.

Clandinin, D. J., and Connelly, F. M. (2001). *School landscapes in transition: Negotiating diverse narratives of experience.* A proposal to the Social Sciences and Humanities Research Council of Canada.

Clandinin, D. J., & Huber, J. (2010). Narrative inquiry. In B. Peterson, E. Baker, & B. McGaw (Eds.), *International encyclopedia of education*, Vol. 6 (pp. 436–441). Oxford: Elsevier.

Clandinin, D. J., Huber, J., Murray Orr, A. & Murphy, M. S. (2006). *A Narrative inquiry into children's and teachers curriculum making experiences.* A proposal to the Social Sciences and Humanities Research Council of Canada.

Clandinin, D. J., Huber, J., Huber, M., Murphy, M. S., Murray Orr, A., Pearce, M., & Steeves, P. (2006). *Composing diverse identities: Narrative inquiries into the interwoven lives of children and teachers.* New York: Routledge.

Clandinin, D. J., Huber, J., Menon, J., Murphy, M. S., & Swanson, C. (2015). Narrative inquiry: Conducting research in early childhood. In A. Farrell, S. Kagan, & K. Tisdall (Eds.), *Handbook of early childhood research* (pp. 240–254). Thousand Oaks, CA: Sage.

Clandinin, D. J., Lessard, S., & Caine, V. (2013). Reverberations of narrative inquiry: How resonant echoes of an inquiry with early school leavers shaped further inquiries. *Educação, Sociedade and Culturas, 36,* 7–24.

Clandinin, D. J., Murphy, M. S., Huber, J., & Murray Orr, A. (2010). Negotiating narrative inquiries: Living in a tension-filled midst. *Journal of Educational Research, 103*(2), 81–90.

Clandinin, D. J., & Rosiek, J. (2007). Mapping a landscape of narrative inquiry: Borderland spaces and tensions. In D. J. Clandinin (Ed.), *Handbook of narrative inquiry: Mapping a methodology* (pp. 35–75). Thousand Oaks, CA: Sage.

Clandinin, D. J., Schaefer, L., & Downey, A. (2014). *Narrative conceptions of knowledge: Towards understanding teacher attrition.* London: Emerald.

Clandinin, D. J., Steeves, P., & Caine, V. (Eds.) (2013). *Composing lives in transition: A narrative inquiry into the experiences of early school leavers.* London: Emerald.

Colapietro, V. (2011). Customary reflection and innovative habits. *Journal of Speculative Philosophy, 25*(2), 161–173.

Coles, R. (1989). *The call of stories: Teaching and the moral imagination.* Boston: Houghton Mifflin.

Connelly, F. M., & Clandinin, D. J. (1988). *Teachers as curriculum planners: Narratives of experience.* New York, NY: Teachers College Press.

Connelly, F. M., & Clandinin, D. J. (1990). Stories of experience and narrative inquiry. *Educational Researcher, 19*(5), 2–14.

Connelly, F. M., & Clandinin, D. J. (1999). *Shaping a professional identity: Stories of educational practice.* New York: Teachers College Press.

Connelly, F. M., & Clandinin, D. J. (2006). Narrative inquiry. In J. Green, G. Camili, & P. Elmore (Eds.), *Handbook of complementary methods in education research* (pp. 477–487). Mahwah, NJ: Lawrence Erlbaum.

Craig, C., & Huber, J. (2007). Relational reverberations: Shaping and reshaping narrative inquiries in the midst of storied lives and contexts. In D. J. Clandinin (Ed.), *Handbook of narrative inquiry: Mapping a methodological landscape* (pp. 251–279). New York: Sage.

Crites, S. (1971). The narrative quality of experience. *American Academy of Religion, 39*, 291–311.

Cruikshank, J. (1998). *The social life of stories: Narratives and knowledge in the Yukon Territory.* Lincoln: University of Nebraska Press.

Dewey, J. (1938). *Experience and education.* New York: Collier.

Dewey, J. (1981). *The later works, 1925–1953: Vol. 4. The quest for certainty: A study of the relation of knowledge and action* (J. A. Boydston, Ed.). Carbondale: Southern Illinois University Press.

Dillard, A. (1987). *An American childhood.* New York: Harper Perennial.

Downey, C. A., & Clandinin, D. J. (2010). Narrative inquiry as reflective practice: Tensions and possibilities. In N. Lyons (Ed.), *Handbook of reflection and reflective inquiry: Mapping a way of knowing for professional reflective inquiry* (pp. 383–397). New York: Springer.

Elbaz Luwisch, F. (2010). Narrative inquiry: Wakeful engagement with educational experience: An essay review of Narrative Inquiry: Experience and Story in Qualitative Research (Clandinin, D. J., & Connelly, F. M.). *Curriculum Inquiry, 40*(2), 263–280.

Frye, M. (1983). *The politics of reality: Essays in feminist theory.* Trumansburg, NY: Crossing Press.

Greene, M. (1995). *Releasing the imagination: Essays on education, the arts, and social change.* San Francisco: Jossey-Bass.

Greene, M. (2001). Flunking retirement: A chat with Maxine Greene. Accessed September 12, 2015 at www.tc.columbia.edu/news.htm?articleId=2931

Heilbrun, C. G. (1988). *Writing a woman's life.* New York: Ballantine Books.

Houle, S. T. (2012). A narrative inquiry into the lived curriculum of grade 1 children identified as struggling readers: Experiences of children, parents, and teachers. Unpublished doctoral dissertation, University of Alberta, Edmonton, Alberta, Canada.

Huber, J. (1992). Narratives of experience: Voice as evaluation. Unpublished master's thesis, University of Alberta, Edmonton, Alberta, Canada.

Huber, J., Murphy, M. S., & Clandinin, D. J. (2011). *Places of curriculum making: Narrative inquiries into children's lives in motion* (Advances in Research on Teaching, Vol. 14). Bingley, UK: Emerald.

Huber, M., Clandinin, D. J., & Huber, J. (2006). Relational responsibilities as narrative inquirers. *Curriculum and Teaching Dialogue, 8*(1 & 2), 209–223.

Kerby, A. P. (1991). *Narrative and the self: Studies in continental thought.* Bloomington: Indiana University Press.

King, T. (2003). *The truth about stories: A native narrative.* Toronto, ON: House of Anansi Press.

Lessard, S. (2013). Red worn runners: A narrative inquiry into the stories of Aboriginal youth and families in urban settings. Unpublished doctoral dissertation, University of Alberta, Edmonton, Alberta, Canada.

Lessard, S., Caine, V., & Clandinin, D. J. (2014). A narrative inquiry into familial and school curriculum making: Attending to multiple worlds of Aboriginal youth and families. *Journal of Youth Studies, 18* (2), 197–214.

Lewin, K. (1946). Action research and minority problems. *Journal of Social Issues, 2*(4), 34–46.

Lindemann Nelson, H. (1995). Resistance and insubordination. *Hypatia, 10*(2), 23–43.

Lopez, B. (1990). *Crow and weasel.* New York: Strauss and Giroux.

Lugones, M. (1987). Playfulness, "world"-travelling, and loving perception. *Hypatia, 2*(2), 3–19.

Mackenzie, C., Rogers, W., & Dodds, S. (2013). *Vulnerability: New essays in ethics and feminist philosophy.* New York: Oxford University Press.

Marmon Silko, L. (1996). *Yellow woman and a beauty of the spirit: Essays on Native American life today.* New York: Touchstone.

Morris, D. B. (2002). Narrative, ethics, and pain: Thinking with stories. In R. Charon & M. Montello (Eds.), *Stories matter: The role of narrative in medical ethics* (pp. 196–218). New York: Routledge.

Neumann, A. (1997). Ways without words: Learning from silence and story in post-Holocaust lives. In A. Neumann & P. L. Peterson (Eds.), *Learning from our lives: Women, research, and autobiography in education* (pp. 91–120). New York: Teachers College Press.

Neumann, A. (1998). On experience, memory, and knowing: A post-Holocaust (auto) biography. *Curriculum Inquiry, 28*(4), 425–442.

Noddings, N. (1984). *Caring: A feminine approach to ethics and moral education.* Berkeley: University of California Press.

Noddings, N. (1998). *Philosophy of education.* Boulder, CO: Westview Press.

Noddings, N. (2002). *Starting at home. Caring and social policy.* Berkeley: University of California Press.

Okri, B. (1997). *A way of being free.* London, UK: Phoenix House.

Online Etymology Dictionary. Accessible at www.etymonline.com, retrieved October 24, 2014.

Prochnik, G. (2011). *In pursuit of silence: Listening for meaning in a world of noise.* New York: Anchor Books.

Richardson, L. (2000). Writing: A method of inquiry. In N. K. Denzin & Y. S. Lincoln (Eds.), *The Sage handbook of qualitative research* (2nd ed.) (pp. 923–949). Thousand Oaks, CA: Sage.

Richardson, L. (2003). Poetic representation of interviews. In J. F. Gubrium & J. A. Holstein (Eds.), *Postmodern interviewing* (pp. 187–202). Thousand Oaks, CA: Sage.

Rosiek, J. L. (2013). Pragmatism and post-qualitative futures. *International Journal of Qualitative Studies in Education, 26*(6), 692–705.

Rosiek, J. L., & Pratt, S. (2013). Jane Addams as a resource for developing a reflexively realist social science practice. *Qualitative Inquiry, 19*(8), 578–588.

Sarris, G. (1993). *Keeping slug woman alive: A holistic approach to American Indian texts* (pp. 1–13). Los Angeles: University of California Press.

Sewall, I. (1996, October). Blessed be the spirit that carries us from day to day. Paper presented at the Centre for Research for Teacher Education and Development, University of Alberta, Edmonton, Alberta, Canada.

Sweetland, W., Huber, J., & Keats Whelan, K. (2004). Narrative inter-lappings: Recognizing difference across tension. *Reflective Practice: International and Multidisciplinary Perspectives, 5*(1), 45–74.

Tronto, J. C. (2014). Book Review. *Notre Dame Philosophical Reviews.*

Young, M. (2005). *Pimatisiwin: Walking in a good way: A narrative inquiry into language as identity.* Winnipeg, MB: Pemmican.

Appendix 1: Examples of Consent and Assent Forms

This Appendix contains the following documents:

1. General Information Letter
2. Parent/Guardian Consent for Youth Participation
3. Assent Form for Youth
4. Parent/Guardian Consent
5. Use of Real Name

FACULTY OF
NURSING
UNIVERSITY OF ALBERTA

A Narrative Inquiry into the Schooling Experiences of Aboriginal Youths and Families

Information Letter

What is this Research Study?

We would like to invite you to participate in our research study. We want to understand the experiences of Aboriginal youths and their families in urban schools. We want to listen to your stories of school. Your participation will help us understand the impact of schools on your life.

Who are the Researchers?

We have several team members. These include: Aboriginal community organizations (Bent Arrow Traditional Healing Society, Ben Calf Robe Society); Traditional Knowledge Holders (Elders: Isabelle and Mary) who will work as mentors and guide our team; Edmonton Public School (Margaretha Ebbers); Aboriginal students (Trudy Cardinal, Sean Lessard) and non-Aboriginal student (Simmee Chung); and professors from the University of Alberta (Vera Caine, Lola Baydala, Florence Glanfield, and D. Jean Clandinin).

What is Narrative Inquiry?

We think people's lives and stories are important. We will listen to, learn from, and reflect on how your stories will teach us and others abut schools. We know your stories will help to make positive changes in school practice and policies for Aboriginal students and their families.

How do I participate?

If you agree to participate in this study then you will be given more information. Our study will take place in an afterschool club, in your home, or in places around the community. You or your family may also be interviewed by a researcher.

What about my privacy?

Your privacy and your schools privacy will be respected. We will not share real names or the school's name in our writing. What you tell us during our personal conversations will be kept private and only be tape recorded if you agree with this. Whenever we have group conversations, we will remind everyone of the importance of having respect for each other and the stories shared in these spaces. We will follow the guidance of the elders. If you later decide to share your real name in exhibitions, conferences, or publications to display the work that you created in the afterschool program, you will have to sign another consent form.

All members of the research team will comply with the University of Alberta Standards for Protection of Human Research Participants. We will keep all the information you tell or give us private. Only the research team at the University of Alberta will have access to the field texts (data). Your real name is not on any files. We will destroy any personal information given when we finish the final report.

How long will this study be?
YEAR ONE: We will work closely with youths in an afterschool club. We will collect data. What we mean by data are things such as: one-on one or group conversations, projects or work created in the club(s), notes on events and activities.
YEAR 2 &3: Our research team hopes to stay connected with you. In some cases, the youth participants and researcher may wish to continue on a special project or club. During this time we will also connect with your family to learn more about their school experiences.
Building your trust and maintaining our relationship over time is important to us.

Our research team wants you to know …
We are excited for you to be a part of our study. We believe that we have a lot to learn from you and with you. Your voice is important!

FACULTY OF
NURSING
UNIVERSITY OF ALBERTA

Family Letter of Consent for Participant in School

I am the parent/guardian of _____.

(name of youth)

I have been told about the research study entitled, *"A Narrative Inquiry into the Schooling Experiences of Aboriginal Youths and Families."* The study is funded by the Social Sciences and Humanities Research Council of Canada and the Alberta Centre for Child, Family and Community Research. I have been given a copy of the information letter and I understand that this research will be carried out by Vera Caine from the University of Alberta and members of the research team.

I have been informed that members of the research team will be working with my child in an after school program. I know that they will have conversations with my child. I know that they will write about what they will see, learn, and wonder from working with my child. I know that the research team will write field notes of their participation. I know that the information that my child shares with the researchers will only be shared with me if my child wishes to.

I am aware that the data collection of my child's participation may include: photography or visual arts work, memory box, sharing of artifacts (items of importance), field notes on events or activities to which researchers are invited, researcher journals, writing and work samples, art work, work created from projects or clubs, one-on-one or group conversations. One-on-one conversations may be tape-recorded and typed.

I know that the members of the research team will write papers and go to local, national, and international conferences to share what they are learning from the work with my child. I know that the work that my child creates in the afterschool program ((i.e. photography, collages, artwork, poetry, etc.) may also be shared in exhibitions, conferences, or publications. I know that when they share data collected in the afterschool program (i.e. artwork, photography, collages, etc.) or talk about my child, they will not tell their real name or the school's name. I know that my child's privacy will be respected at all times. If my child decides to share their real name or choose a pseudonym in exhibitions, conferences or publications to display their work created in the afterschool program, I know we will need to sign another consent form.

I know that I can ask questions and share my concerns about this study. I know that I can stop my child's participation in the research at any time.

I know that if we choose to stop participating in the study, all data about my child will be taken out. I feel comfortable in talking with a member of the research team to talk about this possibility if we choose to stop. My signature below shows that I agree to have the research team work with my child.

_____

Print Name

_____

Signature

_____

Date

For further information concerning the completion of this form or this study, please contact Vera Caine at the University of Alberta, 780-492-7770.

The plan for this study has been reviewed so it follows ethical guidelines and is approved by the Faculties of Education, Extension, Augustana and Campus Saint Jean Research Ethics Board (EEASJ REB) at the University of Alberta. For questions regarding your rights and ethical conduct of research, you can contact the Chair of the EEASJ at (780) 492-3751.

FACULTY OF
NURSING
UNIVERSITY OF ALBERTA

Informed Consent—Youth Participants

My name is _____. I agree to participate in the research study entitled, *"A Narrative Inquiry into the Schooling Experiences of Aboriginal Youths and Families."* The study is funded by the Social Sciences and Humanities Research Council of Canada and the Alberta Centre for Child, Family and Community Research. I have been given a copy of the information letter and I understand that this research will be carried out by Vera Caine from the University of Alberta and members of the research team.

I know that members of the research team will work with me in an after school program. I know that we can decide on special projects together. I know that they will write about what they will see, learn, and wonder from working with me. I know that they and I will talk about my experiences in school and out of school.

I know that the data collection of my participation may include: photography or visual arts work, memory box, sharing of artifacts (items that are important to me), researchers' notes on events or activities, journals, work samples, art work, work created from my projects or in a club, group conversations, one-on-one conversations. One-on-one conversations may be tape recorded and typed.

I am aware that the members of the research team may write papers and go to local, national, and international conferences to share what they are learning from our work together. I know that the work that I create in the afterschool program (i.e. photography, collages, artwork, poetry, etc.) may also be shared in exhibitions, conferences, or publications. I know that when they share data collected in the afterschool program, talk, or write about me, they will not tell my real names or the school's name. I know that my privacy will be respected at all times. I know that if I decide to share my real name or choose my own pseudonym in exhibitions, conferences, or publications to display the work that I created in the afterschool program, my family and I will sign another consent form. One of the members of the research team has talked with me about this research. My questions have been answered. I know that I can stop participating in the research at any time. I know that if I choose to stop participating in the study, all data about me will be taken out. I just have to tell one of the researchers. My signature below shows that I agree to participate in this study.

_____

Print Name

For further information concerning the completion of this form or this study, please contact Vera Caine at the University of Alberta, 780-492-7770.

_____

Signature

_____

Date

The plan for this study has been reviewed so it follows ethical guidelines and is approved by the Faculties of Education, Extension, Augustana and Campus Saint Jean Research Ethics Board (EEASJ REB) at the University of Alberta. For questions regarding your rights and ethical conduct of research, you can contact the Chair of the EEASJ at (780) 492-3751.

Informed Consent of Parent Participant

My name is _____, I agree to participate in the research study entitled, *"A Narrative Inquiry into the Schooling Experiences of Aboriginal Youths and Families."* The study is funded by the Social Sciences and Humanities Research Council of Canada and the Alberta Centre for Child, Family and Community Research. I have been given a copy of the research information letter and I understand that this research will be carried out by Vera Caine from the University of Alberta and the members of the research team.

I have been informed that the research team will write field notes of their participation with me. We will have tape-recorded conversations. These conversations will later be typed. The research team will share our observations, reflections on, and understandings of my experiences. All researchers will comply with the University of Alberta Standards for Protection of Human Research Participants.

I am aware that the data collection may include: sharing of artifacts (items that are important to me) or memory boxes, researcher journals, participant journals, one on one or family conversations that will be tape-recorded. I am aware that the writing based on this study will be submitted for publication in journals and those presentations will be made at local, national, and international conferences. I have been informed that my privacy as well as the privacy of others, and the school, will be respected. All materials collected will be kept safe to ensure confidentiality and my privacy.

I have been given the opportunity to ask questions and to share any concerns about this study. I know that I can withdraw from the research at any time. I know that if I choose to stop participating in the study, all data about me will be taken out. I feel comfortable in talking with a member of the research team to talk about this possibility if I should choose not to participate.

_____

Print Name

For further information concerning the completion of this form or this study, please contact Vera Caine at the University of Alberta, 780-492-7770.

_____

Signature

_____

Date

The plan for this study has been reviewed so it follows ethical guidelines and is approved by the Faculties of Education, Extension, Augustana and Campus Saint Jean Research Ethics Board (EEASJ REB) at the University of Alberta. For questions regarding your rights and ethical conduct of research, you can contact the Chair of the EEASJ at (780) 492-3751.

Informed Consent for Exhibition, Conferences & Publications
(Use of Real Name or Pseudonym)

I am a participant in the research study entitled, *"A Narrative Inquiry into the Schooling Experiences of Aboriginal Youths and Families."* The study is funded by the Social Sciences and Humanities Research Council of Canada and the Alberta Centre for Child, Family and Community Research. I have signed a consent form.

I, _____ **would like to share my real name or choose my own pseudonym (fake name) in an exhibition, conference, or publication where we will display the data that I created in the after-school program (i.e. photography, collages, artwork, poetry, etc.). In this form, my parent/guardian will also sign to give their permission for me to share my real name or for me to choose a pseudonym.**

One of the members of the research team has talked with me about using my real name or choosing my own pseudonym. I know I have the choice and that my privacy is respected at all times. I know that I can choose and change to use a pseudonym whenever it feels more comfortable to me. I just have to tell one of the researchers. My questions have been answered. I know that I can stop participating in the research at any time. I know that if I choose to stop participating in the study, all data about me will be taken out.

My signature below shows that my family and I want to use my **real name** or for me **to choose a pseudonym** when we share some of the images/artwork that we created in the afterschool program in exhibitions, conferences, or publications. We want to use the name _____
_____.

_____
Print Name (Youth Participant)

For further information concerning the completion of this form or this study, please contact Vera Caine at the University of Alberta, 780-492-7770.

_____
Signature of Youth

_____
Print Name (Parent/Guardian)

_____   _____
Signature of Parent/Guardian   Date

The plan for this study has been reviewed so it follows ethical guidelines and is approved by the Faculties of Education, Extension, Augustana and Campus Saint Jean Research Ethics Board (EEASJ REB) at the University of Alberta. For questions regarding your rights and ethical conduct of research, you can contact the Chair of the EEASJ at (780) 492-3751.

Index

A

Addams, Jane, 36
Arendt, Hannah, 171
arrogant perception, 99–100
attention, example of, 40
attentiveness, 106, 196
audience, questions of, 175
autobiographical narrative inquiries,
    26, 35–37, 55–58, 87–88,
    189–191
awakeness, 94

B

Basso, Keith, 203
Bateson, M. C., 12, 40, 44
Beaver Hill School, 157–160
Bergum, V., 203, 209
Bruner, J., 12–13

C

Caine, V., 57, 203
Cardinal, Bob, 61, 208
Casey, Kathleen, 205
Charon, R., 207
Clandinin, D. J., 12–13, 16–18,
    22–23, 29–30, 33, 36, 57,
    91–92, 178, 181, 202
co-composing field texts
    alongside Aboriginal youth and
        families, 120–121
    at art club, 121–123
    back and forth relationship in, 149
    example of, 125–128
    one-on-one conversations, 124
    with photography, 124, 131
    process of, 119–120
    with video camera equipment, 124
    willingness to accompany youth to
        different places, 130
    with youth who left school early,
        129–131

co-composing narrative accounts,
    137–141
Coles, R., 12, 118, 202
coming alongside
    difficulties in, 117
    within institutional contexts, 72
    multiplicity of lives, 56
    within nested familial contexts, 117
    reciprocal ethical obligations, 37
    response communities, 31–32, 195
    shaping lives, 118
    in world travelling, 128
    youth, 23
commitment to understanding lives in
    motion, 196–197
communities of inquiry, 36, 57
community, understanding of,
    102–103
Connelly, F. M., 12, 16, 22–23,
    29–30, 36, 178, 181
conversational spaces, 52, 155
Cree First Nations, 19
criterion of interaction, 15
Crites, S., 12
Cruickshank, J., 183

D

data. *see* field texts
detached researcher, 97
Dewey, J., 13, 15–16, 38, 201
Dewey's conception of experience,
    15–16, 33, 37
Dewey's notion of situation, 15–16
Dillard, A., 180
dimension of temporality, 16
Donovan, narrative account of
    at the art club, 144–150
    awakening time, 148–150
    Beaver Hill School, 157–160
    co-composing field texts, 150–152
    conversational spaces, 154–155
    drum culture, 152–153
    as First Thunder, 165–166

Donovan, narrative account of
  (continued)
  Francis and, 153–155
  Kookum Muriel and, 160–162
  Lane and, 146–147, 150–152
  prologue, 144
  remembering school, 162–163
  skipping grade 2, 162–163
  in-between time, 156
  world travelling, 158
Dossetor, J., 203, 209
Downey, C. A., 33
drum culture, 152–153

E

early school leavers/leaving, 129, 134,
  177, 211
early school leaving study, 87, 93–95,
  210–211
Elbaz, Luwisch F., 180
Estefan, A., 203
ethics. *see also* relational ethics
  co-composing field texts, 149
  in health care settings, 72
  Nodding's ethic of care, 205–207
  relational theories, 203–207
  research ethics boards, 71–73, 80
  review boards, 199
  university ethics boards, 73
ethics of care, 205–207
experience
  Dewey's theory of, 15–16, 33
  as narrative composition, 12–13
  narrative conceptualization of, 22
  as a storied phenomenon, 11–14
Experience and Education (Dewey),
  201

F

field notes, 131
field texts
  co-composing methods, 119
  from field to, 24–25, 31–33,
    175–177
  interim to final, 193–195
  photographs as, 131
  types of, 139
final research texts, 32–33, 175–177,
  193–195

finding participants outside of
  institutional contexts, 73–78
First Thunder, 165–166

G

Greene, Maxine, 28, 38, 189,
  208–209
Greene's way of seeing narratively,
  28–29, 208–209

H

healing space, 155
Heilbrun, C. G., 183–184
Houle, Sonia, 137, 138
Huber, J., 52, 91–92, 202
Huber, M., 202

I

identity and place, relationship with,
  49
imaginative thinking, 24
institutional narratives, 56
intergenerational narrative
  reverberations, 49–50, 114–116
interim research texts, 32–33,
  133–136, 175–177, 193–195

J

Jackson, Margot, 83
"just get an Elder," 67–69

K

Keats Whelan, K., 52
King, T., 11, 94
King, Thomas, 170
knowledge generation, temporality of,
  17–18
Kookum Muriel, 115–116, 160–162
Kootenay, Isabelle, 67–68, 144

L

landscapes. *see* layered landscapes
layered landscapes
  attending to, 65–69
  living within, 59

multiple, 62–63, 69–70
shaped within, 62
stratified, 59–60
unfamiliar, 63–65
wide awakeness to, 69–70
leaving school early, 169–170
Lessard, S., 57
life, definition, 110
liminality, 122
listen sideways, 211–212
the lived self, 176
lives in motion, 196–197
living alongside
aspects of, 110
becoming visible, 172–173
in the Field, 110
within nested familial contexts,
110–113
silences in, 173–175
understanding of, 109–110
living and learning, 40–41
living stories, 22–23
Lopez, B., 210
the loving eye, 175–176
loving perception, 99, 101–102, 107
Lugones, Maria, 32, 99–100, 175

M

Marmon Silko, Leslie, 49, 59, 114
methodological commitment,
136–137
methodological reflexivity, 36–37
Montello, M., 207
Morris, D. B., 18
multiple landscapes, 62–63, 69–70
multiplicity
awakenings to, 56
of stories, 104–105
Muskwacicy, 61–63
mutual visibility, 116–117

N

narrative beginnings
attending to experience, 39–41
autobiographical inquiries as,
35–36
coming alongside youth, 41–42,
49–50, 54–55
importance of, 189–191

Janice, 47–50
Jean, 39–43
return to, 135
Sean, 43–47
Two-Stone Stories, 43–45
Vera, 50–55
writing as inquiry, 38
narrative inquirers
to attend as, 42–43, 45–47
definition, 13–14
drawing from previous experience,
60
narrative inquiry
autobiographical, 26
co-composing, 30–31
definition, 14–17, 25, 92, 186
from field to field texts to research
texts, 24–25
finding participants, 30–31
focus of, 20
impacts of, 210–213
negotiating entry, 83–84
ongoingness of, 57
ontological commitments of, 17–18
past experiences in, 66–68
personal justification, 29–30
practical justifications, 29–30
pragmatist groundings of, 176
quality markers of, 186
relational ethics in, 72
as relational methodology, 36–37
with scholarly literature, 28–29
shaping design considerations,
22–23
significance of, 178–179
terminology, 77–78
three-dimensional space of, 23–24
and understanding experience, 19
working alongside, 173
world travel as part of, 106–107
writing ourselves into, 25–26
narrative inquiry spaces, 187–188
narrative mode of thought, 12–13
negotiating entry
with Aboriginal children and
families, 86–87, 91–93
with early school dropouts, 93–95
to the field, 188–189
in narrative inquiry, 83–84
ongoing process of, 95–96
parental consent, 86

negotiating entry *(continued)*
  with participants, 86–87
  process of, 89–90
  at Ravine Elementary School,
    87–91
  in research relationship, 85
negotiation of relationships, 191
nested familial contexts
  intergenerational aspects within,
    114–116
  living alongside in, 110–113
  mutual visibility within, 116–117
  place in, 113–114
nestedness of children, 200
Neumann, Anna, 52–53
Nodding, N., 205
Nodding's ethic of care, 205–207

O

Okri, Ben, 189
one-on-one conversations, 124
ongoing experiences, narrative inquiry
    among, 92
ongoing wakefulness
  to listen for possibilities, 66–67
  need for, 99–103
  through narrative inquiry, 98–99
  world travel as part of narrative
    inquiry, 106–107
ongoingness of inquiries, 57

P

parental consent, 86
participants
  of Aboriginal heritage, 86–87
  challenge in locating, 85
  in communities, 79–80
  within institutional contexts, 78–82
  negotiating entry, 86–87
  ongoing participation of, 84
  parental consent, 86
  process of finding, 73–77
  research ethics boards and, 80
  school, 82
  story researchers into story,
    105–106
past experiences, 66–68, 133–136
personal justification, 29–30,
    195–196

place
  attending to, 182–183
  co-composing field texts and,
    121–123
  definition, 16
  identity, relationship with, 49
  narrative inquiry and, 24, 195
  within nested familial contexts,
    113–114
  woven into our becoming, 114
playfulness, 100–101
plotlines, 61
practical justifications, 29–30
Pratt, S., 36, 37
presence, example of, 40
Prochnik, G., 174

Q

quality markers of narrative inquiry,
    186

R

Ravine Elementary School, 86, 87–91,
    98–99
recursive reverberations, 57
reflexivity, methodological, 37
relational ethics. *see also* ethics
  definition, 199, 203
  description of, 33–34
  for engagement, 203–204
  tensions, 209–210
relational methodology, 36–37
relational response communities, 195
relational responsibilities, 201–203
relational spaces, 97, 109–110,
    188–192, 203–204, 209
relational tensions, 209–210
relationships, negotiation of, 191
re-presentation, 36
representation
  accurate, 180
  challenges in, 179–182
  introducing participants, 179–180
  public vs. private, 181–182
  shaping influences, 181
  shaping issues of, 172
  research ethics boards, 71–73, 80
research puzzles, 26–28, 136–137,
    177–178

research relationships, 64, 80–81, 84, 85, 93–94, 188
research self, 176
research texts, 24, 32–33, 133–136, 139, 175–177, 193–195
response communities, 31–32
retelling stories, 22–23
reverberations, 49–50, 57
Richardson, Laurel, 38
Rosiek, J., 12, 13, 16, 17–18, 36, 37

S

school dropouts, 169–172
School Landscapes in Transition: Negotiating Diverse Narratives of Experience project, 88–89
seeing narratively, Greene's way of, 28–29
self-facing, 37
sexual exploitation, 83
sideways teachings, 211–212
silences
    in living alongside, 173–175
    as stories, 56–57
situation, concept of, 15–16
slowing down, importance of, 55
Social Sciences and Humanities Council of Canada (SSHRC), 98–99
sociality, 15, 23–24, 195
Spirit of the People blanket, 163–165
Steeves, Pam, 202
stop and think, 171
storied lives, 12
stories
    defined, 11–12
    to live by, 104–105
    retelling, 22–23
    silences as, 56–57
story fragment, 14
stratified layers of landforms, 59–60
Swanson, Cindy, 177
Sweetland, W., 52

T

taking care of one's story, 170
temporal transition, 16
temporality
    definition, 23

Dewey's conception of experience and, 37
    importance of, 37
    of knowledge generation, 17–18
    sense of, 178
tensions, view of, 172–173
terminology in narrative inquiry, 77–78
the Field
    living alongside in, 110
    in narrative inquiry, 109
thinking, concept of, 18, 24
three-dimensional space of narrative inquiry
    field texts, 31
    place in, 16
    research puzzles, 27
    shaping design considerations, 23–24
    shaping familial contexts, 116–117
    to show experiences are always in the living, 182–183
to attend
    definition, 40
    as narrative inquirer, 42–43, 45–47
    slowing down, 55

U

university ethics boards, 73

V

valuing children, 200
Voices in the Park (Browne), 138
vulnerability
    concept of, 171
    concerns around, 169
    imagined, 171–172

W

wakefulness, 69–70, 75, 82–83, 207–209
Whiskeyjack, Francis, 76, 153–155
wide awakeness. *see* wakefulness
working alongside, 173
world travelling
    arrogant perception and, 99–100
    definition, 32
    example of, 158

world travelling *(continued)*
    learning to, 106
    the loving eye and, 175–176
    with loving perception, 101–102, 107
    narrative inquiry as part of, 106–107
    playfulness and, 100–101
    writing, as inquiry, 38, 57

Y

Young, Mary, 49–50, 115
youth who left school early, 129–131

About the Authors

D. Jean Clandinin is professor and founding director of the Centre for Research for Teacher Education and Development at the University of Alberta and one of the pioneers of narrative inquiry. A former teacher, counselor, and psychologist, she is author or coauthor of eighteen books and numerous articles. Clandinin received the 1993 AERA Early Career Award, the 1999 Canadian Education Association Whitworth Award for educational research, the 2001 Kaplan Research Achievement Award, and a 2004 Killam Scholar. She also won the 2008 Larry Beauchamp Award, the 2009 Killam Mentoring Award, and the 2010 Graduate Teaching Award at the University of Alberta. She was awarded the American Educational Research Association Division B Lifetime Achievement Award in 2002, the 2013 Division K Lifetime Achievement Award, and served as Division B vice president.

Vera Caine is an associate professor in the Faculty of Nursing at the University of Alberta and a Canadian Institute for Health New Investigator. Her research focuses on life-course perspectives in the area of health equity and social justice, particularly when it comes to advancing health equity for people whose lives are affected by HIV, poverty, social exclusion, and discrimination. Using a visual narrative inquiry approach, Vera worked in close relation with five urban aboriginal women, exploring their lives with HIV. Vera has also engaged in research alongside nurses, women at risk for or living with HIV during their early mothering experience, and, most recently, alongside children who are at risk for sexual exploitation. She is involved in sustaining and developing initiatives that reflect primary health care, value interdisciplinary work, and advocate health equity.

Sean Lessard is from Montreal Lake Cree Nation in Treaty 6 territory. He is a former teacher, counselor, and consultant, working within both urban and community settings. His research interests include indigenous youth, narrative inquiry, curriculum studies, and early school leaving. Sean is currently an associate professor in the Faculty of Education at the University of Alberta. His most recent research collaboration revolves around the intergenerational experiences of urban Aboriginal youth in an after-school program.

Janice Huber is associate professor and director for the Centre for Research for Teacher Education and Development at the University of

Alberta. Since 2001 Janice has been engaged in graduate and undergraduate teacher education. She is coauthor of three earlier books, *Composing Diverse Identities: Narrative Inquiries into the Interwoven Lives of Children and Teachers* (Routledge, 2006), *Places of Curriculum Making: Narrative Inquiries into Children's Lives in Motion* (Emerald, 2011), and *Warrior Women: Remaking Postsecondary Places Through Relational Narrative Inquiry* (Emerald, 2012), as well as chapters and journal articles. Janice has engaged in narrative inquiries with children, youth, families, teachers, principals, and Elders. Prior to completing her PhD Janice was a primary and elementary teacher in rural northern Alberta, the Netherlands, and with Edmonton Public Schools.